Bible Plants, Fruits & Products

Christian Year Publications
Bristol

Bible Plants, Fruits & Products

'A SPIRITUAL DIMENSION'

**Covering every common named plant and plant
product listed in the Bible.**

Tom H Ratcliffe

Former head of Seed Research, Analysis and Quality Control
for Suttons Seeds.

Printed and bound by the Bath Press, UK

Published by Christian Year Publications
The Glebe House
Stanton Drew
Bristol BS39 4EH
UK

First published 2002

ISBN 1 872734 26 X

ACKNOWLEDGEMENTS

I am grateful to John Allen Weston of Greenwich, London, for encouraging me to proceed with this work. For many years, John lived and worked in Israel and is blessed with an extensive and valuable knowledge of the land. I joined John on one of his recent annual tours of Israel for the sole purpose of photographing some of the Bible plants growing in their natural habitat. I offer my sincere thanks to Jack Simpson and family of Poole, Dorset, for their help and encouragement in the work.

My special thanks to Professor Michael Avishai, Scientific Director, University Botanical Gardens, Jerusalem, for his support and advice. The help of the Royal Horticultural Society – Lindley Library, and botanists at the Society's Gardens, Wisley, is gratefully acknowledged. I deeply appreciate the valued assistance of Bob Jarman; Head of Agricultural Crops, National Institute of Agricultural Botany for the supply of six-row barley ears; also, for the help of the Official Seed Testing Station of the same Institute, Cambridge, for providing samples of seed.

Finally, my heartfelt thanks to Muriel, my wife, who has with longsuffering patience accompanied me on all my journeys over the past three years to obtain data, plants and photographs. Her unstinting support and active encouragement for the project has contributed substantially to the achievement of a lifetime objective.

Contents

FOREWORD

It is with great pleasure I write this Foreword to a very remarkable book. Tom Ratcliffe, a seedsman of international repute has achieved this *magnum opus* through painstaking research both at home and abroad, but particularly in the Holy Land. Tom is well qualified to undertake such a work as this. It is the outcome of a lifetime involvement in the world of plants and seeds, and reveals a dedicated love for his subject.

The book is authoritative, delightful and informative; and will appeal to a wide readership throughout the world. Its comprehensiveness makes it an invaluable work of reference; and the way the book is presented makes it a pleasure just to browse through.

The extensive text; the exhaustive table of Bible references to Plants, Fruits and Plant Products together with the beautiful photographs and water colours make it an essential companion for Bible study. It is a definitive work in that it covers every named plant, fruit and plant product in the Bible.

However, what makes this book unique is the spiritual dimension attaching to each subject. If one were to comb the libraries of the world, it is doubtful one would discover any publication to match such a work of scholarship. The book is one of meticulous detail with a devotional exegesis; such a combination will bring joy to the prayerful reader. All who take up this book will acquire a deeper understanding of the spiritual significance for the inclusion of named plants, fruits and plant products in the Bible.

Truly, the book highlights the greatness and wisdom of our God – the God of creation. I heartily commend **Bible Plants, Fruits & Products** to a world readership.

John Allen Weston, 2001

INTRODUCTION

There are many tens of thousands of plants comprising the world flora, "…from the Cedar tree that is in Lebanon, even unto the Hyssop that springeth out of the wall" (1 Kings 4:33). However, the number of species referred to in the Bible is fewer than 110. The inclusion of named plants, fruits and plant products in the Bible occurred under the guidance of the Holy Spirit of God through the faithful writers.

The common names of the plants listed in the Bible are translations from the original Aramaic and Hebrew Semitic languages together with the non-Semitic languages of Greek and Latin. The plant names are those that have been used down through the centuries to the present day. Up to the middle of the 18th century, confusion reigned among botanists throughout the world regarding the nomenclature of plants in general. Taxonomists claimed that the practice of identifying plants simply by using the common native language of the country in which they are indigenous, was unscientific, imprecise, confusing and frequently inaccurate. For very many years, biblical scholars have wrestled with the problem of correctly identifying – in botanical terms – some of the plants referred to in the Scriptures. Notwithstanding the thoroughness of research undertaken to complete this book, no claim is made or implied that the book resolves every botanical anomaly.

The scientific classification of plants in general, was the inspired work of a Swedish botanist, Carolus Linnaeus, professor of Botany at the Uppsala University, Sweden, in the eighteenth century. Linnaeus published 'Philosophia Botanica' in 1751, a treatise that greatly influenced the thinking and direction of botanists and taxonomists throughout the world. However, Linnaeus's most renowned work was 'Species Plantarum', published in 1753, a book that, in his day became the bible of plant nomenclature. Linnaeus was a God-fearing man, the son of a minister of the Swedish Church. We now know that Linnaeus based his system of plant classification: '…on the construction of God's original and immutable creation of all plant species'. At the time Linnaeus began his work, Latin was the universal language for medicine and other scientific disciplines; he therefore decided that the language for the botanical nomenclature of plants should be Latin.

The first task undertaken by Linnaeus and his colleagues was the classification of plants by family; i.e. Natural Order. In his work, 'Species Plantarum', Linnaeus introduced his binomial nomenclature for the specific naming of plants. The first category was 'genus' and the second 'species'. Taxonomists worked hard to produce the new international nomenclature, classifying all plants primarily within three categories: i.e. Families, Genera and Species. An example is the lowly salad 'lettuce', the common English name for the salad plant we know so well. The Family of the Lettuce, is *compositae*, the Genus is *lactuca* and the Species, *sativa.* Different forms that existed, or have since been developed within a given species, have a varietal name.

While the common name might differ from country to country, the botanical name would be the same throughout the world. Linnaeus admitted his system had its shortcomings; a consequence of which is that International Taxonomists continue to meet at regular intervals to update plant nomenclature. Nevertheless, the great achievement of Linnaeus remains; botanists and taxonomists throughout the world are now able to communicate and work in harmony across international language barriers.

Some of the Aramaic, Greek and Hebrew plant names may be homonymous, i.e. the same common name given to more than one species, e.g 'Chatsiyr' for grass and leek; in a few cases, even polyonymous, i.e. one species having several common names, e.g. 'Corn wheat'. It is very likely that local (Middle Eastern) dialects impinged upon the identity of many plants, giving us a range of either Aramaic, Greek or Hebrew nouns that refer to the same subject. In pursuit of my objective, I have referred to the common names as they occur in the King James Authorised Version of the Bible. Only in those instances where the translation of the plant name is patently incorrect have I made a change to the more accurate rendering. Take for example 'Chesnut' (Chestnut) in Genesis 30:37 & Ezekiel 31:8; the Hebrew noun 'Armon should have been translated 'Plane tree'. Again, the 'Hazel' in Genesis 30:37, has the Hebrew noun Luz which is the White Almond tree, to mention just two. A valuable help to any Bible student is an understanding of the context in which the plant name occurs. The conclusions I have reached on the botanical identity of certain biblical plants, is the outcome of much prayerful waiting on the Lord.

Several of the plant names in the Scriptures are also the names of places and individuals. Take for example the reference to the deciduous oak in Genesis 35:8 with the Hebrew noun 'Allon. In Joshua 19:33, 'Allon was part of the inheritance given to the tribe of Naphtali; and in 1 Chronicles 4:37, 'Allon was a name given to a son of Jedaiah.

Many plant names listed in the Bible appear as a figure of speech, as in the case of Jehovah's reference to His people Israel. In Isaiah 5:1-7 He called the nation of Israel His 'vineyard' and the tribe of Judah His 'choicest vine', His 'pleasant plant'. He looked that His vine might bring forth good grapes – to minister joy to His heart; – but the vine brought forth wild grapes. As far as Jehovah was concerned, the nation was likened unto a corrupt vineyard and the men of Judah a false vine that brought forth wild grapes. In the New Testament, the Lord Jesus speaks of Himself as the 'True Vine' and His Father as the husbandman. In the figure, Christian believers are the branches in the True Vine. The Lord Jesus said, "herein is my Father glorified that ye bear much fruit" (John 15:1-14).

There are many scholarly, interesting and well-illustrated books on the Flora of Israel and the Middle East in general. However, as far as I am able to ascertain, none deals with the spiritual significance of the plants referred to in the Bible. A number of biblical scholars have commented on the spiritual importance of the more familiar Bible plants such as the Cedar, Fig, Hyssop, Olive, Vine, etc. but very little has been written about the majority of the less familiar plants.

The plants, fruits and plant products covered in the book appear in alphabetical order of the common names used in the Bible. The first biblical reference to the plant or product is given at the introduction of each subject, together with the number of additional references to the subject in the Bible. The list of Scriptural references at the end of the book includes the common names of Plants, Fruits and Plant Products as they are found in the King James Authorised Version of the Bible. The Hebrew and Greek spellings are from 'Strong's Exhaustive Hebrew, Greek Concordance. Bible translations referred to in the book are abbreviated as follows: King James Authorised Version – KJAV. New International Version – NIV. John Nelson Darby Translation – JND. Where no specific translation is indicated after a text, the quotation is from the KJAV.

The following plants are illustrated as botanical paintings by the author. Algum/Almug – Pterocarpus santolinus; Almond fruits – Prunus communis; Aloes – Aquilaria agallocha; Balm – Commiphora gileadensis; Calamus – Cymbopogon martinii; Camphire – Lawsonia inermis; Cassia – Cinnamomum cassia; Cinnamon – Cinnamomum verum; Cumin – Cuminum cyminum; Desire – Capparis spinosa; Ebony – Diospyros ebenum; Frankincense – Boswellia sacra; Gall – Papaver somniferum; Gourd (wild) – Citrullus colocynthis; Hyssop – Origanum syriacum; Juniper – Retama raetam; Mandrake – Mandragora officinarum; Oak (Terebinth) – Pistacia terebinthus; Branch of Oak (Terebinth) – Pistacia terebinthus; Nut (Pistachio) Pistacia vera; Olive fruits – Olea europaea; Pomegranate – Punica granatum; Spikenard – Nardostachys jatamansii; Stacte – Styrax officinalis; Sycamore – Ficus sycomorus.

The resin Onycha (Exodus 30:34) was obtained from a plant now extinct and cannot therefore be illustrated. The Hebrew word 'ezrach' translated Bay in (Psalm 37:35) in the KJAV is a figure of speech and simply means a foreign and wicked subject flourishing as if naturally indigenous (see reference in JND). The Cockle plant (Job 31:40) does not relate to a specific plant, but rather to any plant that is unpleasant, offensive and loathsome. Bay and Cockle are not illustrated. In cases where a specific species is unobtainable, the nearest in type is illustrated with no specific name, e.g. Quercus sp,

No attempt is made to define 'Bitter herbs' as referred to in Exodus 12:8 and Numbers 9:11. However, some biblical botanists believe such herbs included: dwarf chicory, dandelion, wild lettuce, reichardia, sheep's sorrel, watercress et al. Whatever the plants, their significance in the Passover was to impart an element of solemnity in the feast. The Israelites would recognise, with subdued spirits, that the blood of an innocent victim was shed to secure their redemption from the bondage of Egypt. So with Christian believers today, there is a daily need for self-judgment (the eating of bitter herbs) to sustain us in sweet and holy communion with our Lord.

While the book is not a botanical treatise, every attempt has been made to ensure that plant definitions are botanically correct. The primary object and exercise of the writer was to highlight the spiritual meaning and importance of all the plants, fruits and plant products listed in the Scriptures. No claim is implied that the thoughts expressed represent an exhaustive spiritual analysis of Bible plants and products. However, with God's help, the writer has recorded those impressions the Spirit of God has brought before him and made good to his own soul.

May all who take up this book for prayerful reference and study, be richly blessed by the Lord.

Algum / Almug Trees

Pterocarpus santalinus

Hebrew: 'Algummiym = Costly Sandalwood, Red Saunders.
1 Kings 10:11 & 12. 2 Chronicles 2:8; 9:10 &11.

Sandalwood is a tree found growing wild throughout India and Ceylon, reaching a height of 6 – 8 m. The tree belongs to the pea/bean family with trifoliate leaves and axillary spikes of yellow flowers. The tree produces a very hard, fine grained, fragrant red wood, having a beautiful garnet-colour finish when polished. It is a valuable wood for internal house fixtures such as stairs, staircases and terraces; also for making high-class cabinet furniture and a range of musical instruments. Although the references in 2 Chronicles 2 & 9 give the common name as algum, the subject is clearly the same as the almug in 1 Kings 10. To remove any lingering doubt one might have about the two references, it is helpful to know that the transposition of letters in Hebrew common names was a common practice in biblical days. The majority of biblical scholars now accept that the common names 'almug' and 'algum' refer to the same tree known as sandalwood or red saunders.

2 cm

The Hebrew word Mis'ad in 1 Kings 10:12, which means 'pillar' or 'balustrade' occurs nowhere else in the Scriptures. Mis'ad derives from a primitive root Sa'ad, meaning, to support, comfort, establish, hold up, strengthen, refresh and help. From the references in 1 Kings 10:12, and 2 Chronicles 9:11; it would appear the trees had been specially preserved by God for use in the construction of the Temple. The texts read, "there came no such almug trees, nor were seen unto this day". Botanists say it would be a rare occurrence to come across a red saunders tree today of the size Solomon required, which confirms that God had prepared and preserved the trees for His special work.

Solomon was most specific about the kind of wood he wanted to use for the different parts of the Temple structure. Almost without exception, the trees and woods of Scripture speak of the humanity of man. As we proceed in our study of biblical plants, we shall see that in most cases the nature and character of the different woods speak of the unique attributes attaching to the person of the Lord Jesus Christ as man. The characteristics of sandalwood reflect something of the perfect manhood of the Lord Jesus. The wood has a fine, uniform grain consistent with the disposition of the Lord Jesus in whom nothing was uneven. The wood is very hard and resistant to disease and pests; just like our blessed Lord who continued firm and resolute in His pursuit to do the will of His Father; unmoved by Satan's subtle wiles (Matthew 4:1-11). The fact that the wood has a reddish tint would remind us of His manhood. The lovely, distilling fragrance of the wood speaks of the effect generated by His presence wherever He went. When the wood is prepared ready for use, it reveals an intrinsic beauty. When our Lord commenced His ministry for the Kingdom of God, He revealed a beauty and perfection that distinguished Him as peerless. The unregenerate nation (Israel) saw no beauty in Him that they should desire Him (Isaiah 53:2).

The balustrades in the Temple gave support to those serving and moving within its precincts. The message of the algum/almug wood is this; as we move about in the service of God, we should ever be conscious of our need for support and strength from above. We learn to lean on the One who alone is our strength and stay. Jacob's physical strength lay in the staff on which he leant; when he came to the end of himself, he knew in his heart and soul that his spiritual strength was to be found, not in himself, but in Jehovah. Solomon said to the sons of Israel, "trust in the Lord with all thine heart, and lean not unto thine own understanding" (Proverbs 3:5). The apostle Paul said that he would lean on and trust in the strength of the Lord to bear with the 'thorn in the flesh' the Lord had given him. He bowed to the words of the Lord Jesus, "my strength is made perfect in weakness" (2 Corinthians 12:9). Paul assured the Christian believers at Philippi with the words, "I can do all things through Christ which strengtheneth me" (Philippians 4:13).

When the musicians played the different instruments made from the sandalwood, they were in perfect harmony, making one sound in praising and thanking the Lord (2 Chronicles 5:13). A glorious, harmonious song filled the courts of heaven when God's delight and good pleasure was for the first time found in a Man, the Man Christ Jesus

(Luke 2:13 –14). Furthermore, our Lord's life, His walk, ways, words, acts and thoughts all combined to yield a beautiful orchestral sound in perfect harmony with the chorus of heaven. We too will hear something of that wonderful musical symphony when we do what the Father's voice out of the cloud directs, "this is my beloved Son, hear Him" (Luke 9:35). May we continue to lean on Him, rest in Him, listen to His voice and go wherever He leads.

We lean on Thee, our strength and stay; and long to please Thee still;
To be in tune Lord, give thee praise; delight to do Thy will.

T H Ratcliffe

Almonds

Amygdalus communis

Hebrew: Shaqed = Life out of death, resurrection, awakening, to be alert, watching.
White Almond trees.
Hebrew: Luz = White Almond nut tree.
Genesis 43:11 + eight other references.

The almond tree referred to in the Scriptures can be found growing wild in uncultivated and rocky places throughout Israel and the Middle East in general. However, the tree is quite different in type to the new and cultivated varieties of almond trees we know today. The native almond of the Middle East is a shrubby tree of between 5 & 8 m high. The most distinctive feature of the almond is that it is the first of all trees to burst into flower after the long, hard winter. The pure white, five-petal flowers that appear before the foliage, are borne in great profusion to transform a barren landscape into a scene of hope, awakening and glory. In Genesis 30:37, we read that Jacob took hazel rods to set before his flocks in the water troughs. The Hebrew noun for hazel is Luz. Without exception, biblical scholars and botanists believe the tree, given as hazel in the KJAV, was the white almond tree.

The common Hebrew name for the almond is 'Shaqed'

which means: life out of death, resurrection, awake, to be alert, watching. There are many examples in the Scriptures to confirm the meaning of the Hebrew word 'Shaqed'. We have in Exodus 25:31-37, the making of the candlestick/lampstand. Each of its branches carried fashioned forms of bursting almond fruits. The lampstand stood over against the table of shewbread to cast light upon it and watch over it, illustrating what Jehovah said when Jeremiah answered His question, "what seest thou"? Jeremiah said, "I see a rod of an Almond tree". Jehovah replied, "thou hast well seen, for I am watchful over my word to perform it" (Jeremiah 1:11-12).

Then, in Numbers 17:8 we have the account of Aaron's rod that budded; a narrative that embraces all the definitions of the Hebrew word for almond. All twelve rods appeared as dead branches, but only one inherently possessed life. Within one day, Aaron's rod was full of swelling buds, flowers and fruits, and all this at the same time, whereas the other eleven branches remained dead. Never in nature would you get swelling buds, flowers and fruit together; but then, the miracle of life, resurrection life, is in God's hand. Aaron's rod was a type of Christ, "In Him was life, and the life was the light of men" (John1:4). The living rod was also evidence that the office of our blessed Lord is one of a continuing priesthood after the order of Melchisedec (Hebrews 5:6; 6:20; 7:17), "seeing He ever liveth to make intercession for us" (Hebrews 7:25). So today, our blessed Lord continues ever to watch over His own as we walk here in the power of resurrection life – His life.

How wonderful then to see the Spirit of God moving behind the scenes to influence the composition of Israel's gift to the 'man' in Egypt (Genesis 43:11). Israel, who for 22 years had believed his son to be dead, was going to share in the joy of a glorious, unexpected resurrection scene. He would again see alive the long lost 'son of his love', not as a shepherd boy or messenger, but as one exercising power and authority and surrounded with glory (Genesis 45:13). In a coming day, Israel "shall see the Son of man coming in the clouds of heaven with power and great glory" (Matthew 24:30). He will come, not as a lowly Galilean or a despised Nazarene, but as the executor of justice, the King of Glory with healing in His wings (Malachi 4:2).

Bursting Almond fruits
Prunus communis

5

During Joseph's first 13 years in Egypt, he was faithful and true in his works before the Lord and with all men. Joseph suffered greatly for righteousness sake. Potipher's wife falsely accused Joseph of attempted immorality, so Potipher had him committed to prison. Notwithstanding his darkest hours and protracted sufferings in prison, Joseph's living faith was a confirmation to him there would be a bright resurrection morn. In the beginning of the fourteenth year of his separation from his father and brothers, Jehovah crowned him with power and glory, making him 'Ruler of all Egypt' (Genesis 41:40-44). Pharaoh was the instrument Jehovah used to fulfil His purposes.

In so many ways, Joseph was a lovely figure of our Lord Jesus Christ. Our Lord was the perfect witness of the love of God to man, His moral glory revealed that man was in moral darkness and therefore under the sentence of death. Zechariah prophesied 350 + years earlier, that the Messiah would suffer at the hands of His own, and be wounded in the house of His friends (Zechariah 13:6-7). Our Lord was indeed rejected and cast out by His own people (John 1:11). However, from God's side, "Christ also hath once suffered for sins, the just for the unjust, that He might bring us to God, being put to death in the flesh, but quickened by the Spirit" (1 Peter 3:18). Now He is the "One out of death" and the One who alone is the source of all that is vital to life – eternal life. He is exalted and enveloped in glory, with power, might and majesty; having a name that is above every name, and before whom every knee, one day shall bow (Philippians 2:9-11). Meanwhile, just as Joseph watched over his family once they had settled in the land of Goshan; so our Lord watches over us while we journey here as "strangers and pilgrims" in a foreign land (1 Peter 2:11).

During this dark and dreary night, Christian believers should rejoice in the prospect of an imminent, bright and glorious translation into the likeness of our Saviour (1 Corinthians 15:52 & Philippians 3:20-21). In line with the meaning of Shaqed, we too should be awake, watching and alert, expecting the rapture of the saints to occur at any moment (1 John 3:2-3).

> *We are waiting for the morning of that promised, bright, new day:*
> *When the Saviour's voice and glory, will transport us all away.*
>
> T H Ratcliffe

Aloes

Aquillaria agallochum

Hebrew: 'Ahaliym = Sticks charged with fragrant resin. Ling aloes, Aloe-wood, Eaglewood.
Numbers 24:6 + four other references.

The ling aloes/eaglewood tree is native to North India and Middle Eastern countries, particularly Arabia and East Africa, and belongs to the same family of plants as the well known fragrant Daphnes. The tree is evergreen, and if left long enough to grow, will reach a height of between 25 & 35 m. Clearly all four references to aloes in the Old Testament, i.e. Psalm 45:8; Proverbs 7:17 & Song of Solomon 4:14, relate to the

product of the tree, aquillaria agallochum. The Hebrew name of the biblical aloe is 'ahalim or ahaloth – the 'Ling aloes'. Dr. Forbes Royle, in his book; 'Royle's Himalayan Mountains' is in no doubt that the aloes of the Order Liliaceae are nowhere mentioned in the Scriptures. However, the reference in John 19:39 has presented a difficulty with some biblical scholars. It has been suggested that the origin of the aloes brought by Nicodemus to embalm the body of our Lord, was from another and distinct genus of plants; viz. aloe vera. With the Lord's help, I hope to show that in all probability the source of the aloes brought by Nicodemus was the tree aquillaria agallochum, the lignum aloes or aloes wood of commerce. All scriptural references to the ling aloe highlight the value of its fragrance and the way in which the perfumed oil was both obtained and used.

We read in Numbers 24 that Balaam beheld and pronounce upon the beauty of Israel through the eyes of Jehovah. Balaam saw in his vision, the nation of Israel peaceful and resting in an idyllic environment of cultivated gardens beside rivers of water. Today, our blessed Lord would have His redeemed daily refreshed, at peace and restful in His love. Balaam says that all Israel are like 'aloe trees' (ling aloes) which Jehovah has planted. Through God's sovereign mercy, Christian believers have been planted in Christ; as we grow in grace and mature in divine things, we shall be like the ling aloe tree with our branches of service replete with the fragrance of Christ. We have a similar thought in Song of Solomon 4:14.

The fragrance of the resin (oil) from the aloe tree, aquillaria agallochum was so powerful and lingering that it was, and still is used to perfume clothes. In Psalm 45:8 we have the thought of our Lord in resurrection with His garments fragrant with the excellencies of the anointing glories of God. If we walk with Him day by day in humble obedience, moving in the sweet current of His will, we too will take on something of the fragrant nature of Christ. However, we must beware lest being void of divine understanding we fall into the snare of the devil. The young man's movements as recorded in Proverbs 7, were in the night of moral darkness. The youth was blind, and being overwhelmed with the deceptive influences of the devil, rushed into disaster. The narrative in Proverbs 7 is an exposé of what can happen if we move outside the influence of the light into which, through sovereign grace we have been brought. As children of the light, let us walk according to the light (1 John 1:7).

In John 19:38-42 we have the record of two relatively unknown yet faithful disciples of the Lord Jesus, Joseph of Arimathaea and Nicodemus. The action of the two disciples, having secured the body of the Lord Jesus, displayed their profound respect and affection for their Lord. The fragrant embalming material was a mixture of myrrh and aloes, strong antiseptic agents. However, they were quite unnecessary for preserving the body of the Lord Jesus from decomposition. Joseph of Arimathaea and Nicodemus would have known about the normal processes of degeneration and corruption that speedily affect the bodies of mortal man after death, hence their anxious endeavour to preserve and bury the Lord's body. We can understand they would not have known the truth, that notwithstanding the severity of the injuries inflicted on the body of the Lord Jesus, no degenerating influences could possibly affect the untainted body of that blessed person. The Psalmist said, "Thou wilt not leave my soul in hell (Sheol); neither wilt Thou suffer Thine Holy One to see corruption" (Psalm 16:10).

Myrrh speaks to our hearts about the fragrance that ascends to God from the righteous sufferings of the saints on earth. The fragrance of aloes on the other hand would relate to what is eternally for God springing from the death and resurrection of Christ. There is little doubt that the aloes referred to in John 19:39, which Nicodemus brought along to anoint the body of the Lord Jesus was obtained from the tree aquillaria agallochum. In parts of the tree, the wood becomes charged with fragrant resin (oil). Growers who produce the aloe resin are able to ascertain if a particular bough is worth processing to extract the resin. They throw the cut off boughs into water, the boughs are good if they sink, but if they float, they are discarded as being void of any precious resin and therefore of no value. You get the highest quality aloe product by burying resin-saturated boughs in the ground and leaving them there until all the woody fibre has decayed. The product of aloes tells us that we need to apply to our own lives, the death, burial and resurrection of Christ on a daily basis (Philippians 3:8-11). Otherwise, the fibres of our 'old nature' will retain a firm hold on us, and the outflow from our lives of the fragrant nature of Christ inhibited. The product of the ling aloe tree carries a wonderful message today. It is the unique sweetness of all the divine attributes springing from the life, death and resurrection of Christ for the glory of God. We might ask ourselves: Do our lives generate a sweet savour of Christ unto God? (2 Corinthians 2:15).

O keep us, Love divine, near Thee, that we our nothingness may know;
And ever to Thy glory be, walking in faith while here below.

J N Darby

Anise Dill

Anethum graveolens

Greek: Anethon. Matthew 23:23.

Cumin

Cuminum cyminum

Hebrew: Kammon = to store up, to preserve. Isaiah 28:25 & 27.
Greek: Kiminon = To store up, to preserve. Matthew 23:23.

Mint

Mentha longifolia

Greek: Heduosmon = Sweet-scented plant, giving pleasure.
Matthew 23:23. Luke 11:42.

Rue

Ruta graveolens

Hebrew: Peganon = With thick, fleshy leaves.
Luke 11:42.

The Lord Jesus referred to these herbs in the fifth woe He pronounced upon the Pharisees. According to the best authorities, anise, as given in the KJAV of the Bible, should have been translated 'dill'. Dill is an annual or biennial herb of the parsley family, having stems of between 0.5 and 0.75 m high with finely feathered/dissected blue-green leaves and hollow stems. The plant bears small yellow flowers and flat, oval-shaped dark brown seeds/fruits. Wild dill is cultivated for use as a condiment and for medical purposes. As a medicine, it is used to relieve flatulence. The oil from the leaves, stems and seeds is used as an effective emollient when rubbed on to joints to relieve pain. The oil also gives relief when applied to sensitive areas affected with neuralgia.

Anise (Dill)
Anethum graveolens

Cumin, which is an annual herb, also belongs to the parsley family of plants. It has deeply incised fennel-like leaves. The erect stems grow to about 0.6 m high, and like the common hedge parsley, head up with umbels of minute white or pink flowers, followed with twin-carpel, aromatic, highly flavoured fruits.

Mint belongs to the Labiatae family of plants. It is a perennial with a rooting system of underground rhizomes, vigorous and invasive. The biblical mint differs from mentha spicata, which is the common species we grow in our gardens today. Mentha longifolia has 0.5 to 1 m erect, densely hairy stems with lanceolate, sharp toothed, hairy leaves and cylindrical, dense spikes of purple flowers. Mint is a condiment for seasoning meats and for making tea. It was and still is used as a medicinal carminative, stimulant and analgesic.

Reference to the rue plant occurs just once in the Bible; the occasion being when the Lord Jesus censured the Pharisees for their hypocrisy. The wild rue of the Palestine hills is ruta chalepensis, and similar to the European species ruta graveolens. Rue is a heavy-smelling, shrubby plant, reaching a height of between 0.6 and 1.2 m. It has aromatic, blue-green, bi-pinnate leaves and bears heavily scented, yellow, 4 – 5 petal flowers. Rue has been cultivated for its medicinal properties since biblical times. The essential oils distilled from the leaves and stems of the plant and taken medicinally, are a stimulant and antispasmodic; and taken as a medicine to treat hysteria and flatulent colic.

Dill and Cumin occur in the parable given in Isaiah 28:23-29. Jehovah was speaking through the prophet Isaiah, reminding Israel that the faithful husbandman will always apply himself to the business of his calling, completing his work to the end. The ploughman ploughs all day in hope; in the way the servant of the Lord daily perseveres in his/her testimony of light to stir man's conscience toward conviction of sin and the need of salvation. The ploughman thoroughly prepares the ground as a seedbed in hope, just as the Spirit of God prepares the heart of man to receive the sown seed. The ploughman conscientiously sows his seed in hope. The faithful and prayer-supported preaching – the sowing of the Seed, the Word of God – will continue throughout this day of God's grace to bring forth fruit to His praise and glory (Luke 8:8). So God in His mercy is sowing the seed in the ground He has prepared. At the harvest, God will employ what is best suited to maximise in both quality and quantity, the increase he alone has produced (1 Corinthians 3:6-8).

Cumin
Cuminum cyminum

Turning now to the Lord's words to the Pharisees in Matthew 23:23. It is significant that the fifth woe related to the endeavour of the Pharisees to make something of themselves in the eyes of men. The number 5 in Scripture speaks of the completeness of man as God made him, with five senses and five digits on each hand and foot. The great tragedy is that no man, save our blessed Saviour, has ever used his/her senses and faculties perfectly for the glory of God. However, the Pharisees were always proud of their vain boast, believing themselves better than any other man or woman (Luke 18:11-12). They made much of their tithing of the lowly, cheap herbs of the field, which probably cost them very little or nothing at all, while they neglected the weightier matters of the law, such as justice, charity and faith. The tithing of herbs was right in itself if they were traded in commerce or cropped for one's personal use; however, the overt, false sanctity of the Pharisees was openly condemned by the Lord. The Lord Jesus said that the Pharisees were as whited sepulchres, full of dead men's bones (Matthew 23:27). They subtly disguised the corrupting influences they were having on the people by giving the appearance of being paragons of virtue. The Lord said they were like graves that had been grassed-over to conceal the risk of polluting those who unwittingly walked over them (Numbers 9:6).

While all the above herbs still have therapeutic benefits for the people in general, the Pharisees misused them for their own gain and self-indulgence. Sadly, – much like the Pharisees – there are those today who misuse God's Word to force through their own misguided interpretations, and this, to the hurt and spiritual damage of fellow believers. The four Gospels of the Word of God provide four perspectives of the same message concerning the Lord Jesus Christ and the kingdom of God. By the power of the Spirit of God, the Lord would have us develop a balanced understanding of the precious truths of Holy Scripture (2 Timothy 2:15). Furthermore, it would be our earnest prayer that our gracious Lord will daily help us display the love God has shed abroad in our hearts by His Holy Spirit (Romans 5:5).

Let us ask ourselves: What are the weightier things God is looking for from our hearts? The Old Testament Scriptures are

Mint
Mentha longifolia

Rue
Ruta graveolens

as relevant for us today as they were in the days before Christ. Micah 6:8 says, "what doth the Lord require of thee, but to do justly, and to love mercy, and to walk humbly with thy God". This is the obedience that is better than sacrifice or tithe (1 Samuel 15:22). Mercy is preferred before sacrifice (Hosea 6:6). As in the days of Malachi, the Pharisees stood charged with having robbed God. God said, "ye have robbed Me" (Malachi 3:8). If we allow our petty scruples to hinder the saints of God coming together for praise and worship, we are no better than the Phasrisees (Matthew 23:13). By our action, we would clearly be robbing God of what is due to Him from the hearts of the redeemed who want to praise Him (Hebrews 13:15).

May our gracious Lord preserve us from wanting to make something of ourselves by latching on to and expanding unscriptural expressions that are of no importance nor relevant to the Christian testimony in this day of God's grace. We seek His help to give time and prominence to the major Christian issues of today (Proverbs 23:23). May we daily ask the Lord to help us apply the truth given in Philippians 2:3-5.

> *In lowliness and gentleness; Lord we would follow Thee;*
> *Lose sight of self, have Thee in view, for soon Thy face we'll see.*

T H Ratcliffe

Apple
Malus sylvestris

Hebrew: *Tappuach* = Fragrance.
Proverbs 25:11 + five other references.

The apple tree develops into a spreading, shade-giving canopy. Solomon said, "I sat down under his shadow with great delight" (Song of Solomon 2:3). Some doubt remains to this day regarding the identity of the fruit 'apple' as mentioned in the Scriptures. However, the majority of biblical scholars' favour the identity of the fruit as

we know it today, notwithstanding it would have been somewhat smaller than the conventional apple. The hot, dry climatic conditions under which the apple trees grew in Lebanon and northern Israel, is reason enough why the fruits would have been small, sweet-smelling, bright golden and flushed with red. In some Middle Eastern countries, when a person feels sick or faint, they get an apple to hold, because the scent of the apple is said to be therapeutic.

"A word fitly spoken" Proverbs 25:11. The Hebrew word for 'fitly' is *'ophen*, which means: to revolve, to continue turning. A revolving that was not forced, but rolling smoothly as by the influence of the Spirit of God. Our beloved Lord and Saviour was gifted with the tongue of the learned, that He might know how to speak the word in season (Isaiah 50:4). How

15

wonderful is the thought that the Word of God in any faithful ministry given by His servants should continue to go round and round in our heads and move to our hearts never to be lost. Is it not true that when something makes a deep impression on us, we say, 'it keeps going round and around in my head'. That is exactly the effect God's Word should have on us until we allow the message to sink into our hearts from where its truth will be worked out in our lives through testimony. Then, like the apples, the faithful word will produce a lingering fragrance for the refreshment of others.

The apples were in silver filigree baskets. Silver speaks to our hearts about the work of redemption accomplished by the Lord Jesus Christ at Calvary's cross. We get the thought of silver as a figure of redemption from Exodus 30 and the numbering of the children of Israel. That the half shekel of the sanctuary was silver is confirmed later in

Exodus 38:25. The filigree baskets have a lovely thought in that those who have been redeemed back to God by the precious blood of His Son, should be visible for all to see; what a challenge to our hearts! So like the apples, God's message of love and grace is to be seen and heard all around; nothing hidden or mysterious.

Of all the trees of the forest, Solomon found that the apple tree gave him the greatest pleasure. The tree delighted his soul as He rested in the coolness of its shade, enjoying the fruit that was pleasing to his taste. So the apple tree here is a figure of Christ with his bride enraptured with His provisions and care, filled with happy and peaceful thoughts (Song of Solomon 2:3-5).

In Song of Solomon 7:8 we again have the fragrance of the apple tree as expressive of all that emanates from the heart of the Saviour. In chapter 8:5, we have another figure; telling us that it is only in Christ that we have life through God's infinite grace. In God's sovereign mercy and in His time, He woke us from our sleep and made us aware of our need of salvation through repentance before God and faith in our Lord Jesus Christ. We put our trust in a living Saviour and are eternally secure in Christ. Now we rest under His shadow with great delight.

The reference to apples in Joel 1:12 reveals a very sad situation. The narrative speaks about the Day of Judgment by Jehovah, shortly to come on the nation of Israel because of disobedience and idolatry. Everything required to sustain life will disappear. The gnawing, swarming, licking and consuming locust will ravage the land so that all the essentials for life will be gone. The Lord in His mercy will shorten His Day of Judgment on the nation; lest "there should no flesh be saved: but for the elect's sake those days shall be shortened" (Matthew 24:22).

> *We rest beneath Thy shadow Lord, and listen to Thy precious Word;*
> *The fragrance of Thy fruitful love, is therapy from Thee above.*
>
> T H Ratcliffe

Ash

Fraxinus syriaca or Fraxinus Ornus

Hebrew: 'Oren = Strength and toughness.
Isaiah 44:14.

As with quite a number of common plant names in the Bible, ash is one where there remains a substantial divergence of opinion on the interpretation of the Hebrew word 'oren. The noun 'oren means strength and toughness, a definition most aptly suited to the character of the ash tree. Furthermore, the word interpreted as ash in Isaiah 44:14

KJAV occurs nowhere else in the Scriptures. My own conviction is that careful consideration of the context in which the common name appears, helps us understand why Isaiah, under the influence of the Holy Spirit, was led to mention this particular tree.

We readily accept that all the common names such as box, cedar, cypress, fig, fir, myrtle, oak, olive, pine, shittah, vine and willow, referred to by Isaiah in his prophecy, are the correct translations of the Hebrew nouns. Why then should the singular mention of the ash as the translation of 'oren, be called into question? After all, the species fraxinus syriaca and ornus are indigenous varieties of ash to the Middle Eastern regions. The chapter highlights the tragedy of the nation of Israel, in that it had again turned to idolatry. Jehovah reminded the nation that He is the Lord,

the King of Israel, their Redeemer and the Lord of Hosts. He said to them, "I am the first, and I am the last; and beside Me there is no God" (Isaiah 44:6). Nevertheless, the nation made idols of iron, wood and possibly clay, which could in no way profit them, help them nor communicate with them. Rather, the idols testified to their own nakedness and shame before their God.

The ash grows into a tall, gaunt, erect forest tree, reaching a height of between 20 & 30 m. Ash wood is very hard with straight grain, making it a suitable timber for carving all manner of objects and furniture. Furthermore, the wood is one the hottest burning timbers of all the forest hard woods and therefore excellent for burning in cooking ovens and for keeping oneself warm. A poem that speaks of the virtues of forest timbers refers to the burning of Ash on the home fire. The words in the poem are; 'ash burnt wet or ash burnt dry, is suitable for a queen, to warm her slippers by'. Isaiah 44:15-16 confirms the virtue of the ash as a wood suitable both for warming and for cooking, also for making things. Due to its straightness in length and its uniform grain, ash timber is excellent as a building material, for making furniture and all kinds of industrial tools, wheels etc. Sadly, man misused this rich provision of God and made idols of the wood. May our gracious Lord help us to ensure that the good things our Creator God has put at our disposal are employed in His service for the glory of His Name, and for the blessing and comfort of others.

> *The trees of Thy creation, give glory to Thy Name,*
> *We value all from Thy good hand; and grateful praise proclaim.*
>
> T H Ratcliffe

Balm

Commiphora gileadensis / C. opobalsamum

Hebrew: Tsoriy = To crack as by pressure, to leak, distillation.
Genesis 37:25 + five other references.

The Middle Eastern plant that yielded the 'balm' of Scripture is an evergreen, thorny tree, belonging to the family burseraceae and reaching a height of 4-5 m. It bears clusters of white, multi-petalled flowers, followed with small, ovoid fruits. The entire plant abounds with a resinous fluid. The noun 'balm' is a contracted form for 'balsam'. The shrub spontaneously exudes its precious resin from the bark. To produce the resin in large quantities for the commercial market, growers incised the trunk of the tree to allow the resin to flow out freely. In biblical days, balm was the principal healing emollient for a wide range of wounds; it was also an effective antidote for snakebites. The evergreen balm speaks of the on-going healing power of the Lord Jesus to all who will avail themselves of God's rich provision of love, mercy and grace through Christ (Luke 4:18-19).

Jeremiah the prophet spoke of the Lord's intention to judge the people of Judah for their idolatry. Among other things, venomous snakes and cockatrices would bite them so that many would suffer and die. When the judgment occurred, the gravity of the situation prompted the prophet to cry, "is there no Balm in Gilead; is there no

physician there" (Jeremiah 8:22)? The prophet knew that the most effective antidote to relieve and heal the people was balm. Today, when the Lord's people suffer because of departure from the path of discipleship, there is only one remedy, confession and repentance before God in the sanctuary. Most of us, if not all, will have experienced at some time in our Christian life the healing and curative power of the love, mercy and grace of God (James 5:16 & 1 John 1:9). On the other hand, the severity of the judgement of Egypt as recorded in Jeremiah 46, was such that no balm or medicine could cure them (Jeremiah 46:11; see also: 1 Corinthians 11:30).

For Jacob's family to be harmoniously reunited in love, there would have to be a healing of the grievous wounds the brothers had inflicted on both their father and Joseph. Herein lies the significance of the balm in Jacob's gift to the ruler of all Egypt. At the time, Jacob did not know he was sending the gift to his son Joseph, the one who would exercise a healing influence over the family. During all his years in Egypt, Joseph had never forgotten his father and brothers, he ever yearned for the day when he would be reunited with his family in love. He knew that day would eventually come, as confirmed by his own words in Genesis 45:7. Joseph's initial behaviour toward his brothers when they stood before him in Egypt was not in the spirit of bitterness, nor was it the pursuit of a vendetta. Rather, it was a disposition to awaken a sense of guilt in their consciences. The beginning of a healing process can sometimes be very painful, as Joseph's brothers experienced following their first visit to Egypt (Genesis 42:21). We may rightly conclude that following Joseph's revelation of himself to his brothers, they repented of their heinous crime and told their father the truth about Joseph's disappearance 22 years earlier (Genesis 50:17). That was when the healing balm took effect. Similarly, Israel as a nation will, in due time repent of their apostasy; they will be healed and made fit to enjoy their inheritance (Isaiah 9:7).

Looking at the life of our Lord, we see that He occasioned a continuous outpouring of 'healing balm'. Luke put it very succinctly, "concerning all things which Jesus began both to do and to teach, until the day in which He was taken up" (Acts 1:1-2). Peter also has given us a beautiful summary of our Lord's life in Acts 10:38. Having triumphed over the devil in the wilderness, our Lord entered the synagogue in Nazareth and read from the first two verses of Isaiah 61. "The Spirit of the Lord is upon me, because he has anointed me to preach the gospel to the poor. He hath sent me to heal the broken hearted, to preach deliverance to the captives, the recovery of sight to the blind, to set at liberty them that are bruised, to preach the acceptable year of the Lord" (Luke 4:18-19). How wonderful to see that our Lord's first act of healing was to free a man possessed of an evil spirit (Mark 1:23-26). Our Lord's final act of healing was the restoration of the High Priest's servant's ear (Luke 22:50-51), and between these two events, our Lord healed thousands of people.

None today can deny the great need for the healing balm of the Lord Jesus. Lost souls who remain under the control of Satan need it, but also the saints of God. Sadly, many of God's children are wounded by fellow believers and remain injured and isolated because of the absence of shepherd care. The Lord Himself said, "by this shall all know that ye are my disciples if ye have love one to another" (John 13:35). The apostle Paul, writing to the saints at Corinth, said, "there should be no schism in the body, but that the members should have the same care one for another" (1 Corinthians 12:25). Writing to the Ephesians, the apostle expresses what to his heart is the balm of the Lord Jesus, "be ye kind one to another, tender-hearted, forgiving one another, even as God for Christ's sake hath forgiven you" (Ephesians 4:32). When the 'bond of peace' is broken, restoration will occur only when there is an open admission of responsibility for the failure. This is exactly what happened among Joseph's brothers. When there is repentance before God in the sanctuary; there will be no difficulty putting matters right with offended parties. The grievous wounds will heal through His loving application of the 'Balm of Gilead' (1 Thessalonians 5:23).

> *Inscribed upon the cross we see, in shining letters, God is Love;*
> *The Lamb, who died upon the tree, has brought us mercy from above.*
> *The Balm of life, the cure of woe, the measure and the pledge of love,*
> *The sinner's refuge here below, the theme of praise in heaven above.*
>
> T Kelly

Barley

Hordeum sp.

Hebrew: Se'orah = Having a sense and touch of roughness, coarse, hairy.
Greek: Krithinos = Made of barley. Krithe = pointed, piercing seed.
Exodus 9:31 + thirty four other references.

In biblical days, the type of barley grown was what we call the 'six-row' barley. When the grain was ground, it produced a cheap meal that was the staple food of the poor. Most of the barley varieties grown today are 'two-row' that is, there are just two rows of grain in the ear. Ground barley produces coarse flour compared to the fine flour of ground wheat. Unlike wheat, barley is not a naked grain, the actual seed is tightly enveloped in the original structures of the flower. Barley sets forth Christ in manhood, in all the lowliness and outward weakness in which He was here on earth. As man, He had no resources of His own; every thought, word and action came into expression at the behest of His Father. Made in the likeness of men, He was here in fashion as a man. Barley speaks so powerfully and eloquently of the One who came into poverty as the dependent One (Luke 9:58). The apostle Paul said, "ye know the grace of our Lord Jesus Christ, that though He was rich, yet for your sakes He became poor, that ye

through His poverty might be rich" (2 Corinthians 8:9). We are told in Hebrews 2:7 that He was made a little lower (somewhat inferior) to angels. Despised and rejected by the rich in this world, He was happy to be insignificant in their eyes. The world did not esteem Him (Isaiah 53:3).

Barley is also a figure of the littleness of man, as seen in the narrative of the man who told his dream in Judges 7:13-14. The interpretation of the dream confirmed to Gideon the truth of his own littleness (Judges 6:15). The barley cake tumbling into and smiting a tent of the host of Midian, showed that the battle against the Midianites was not Gideon's, but the Lord's. Today, in defence of the Truth against the enemies of the Lord, we may well say, "the battle is the Lord's, He will fight for us". Although we can do nothing of ourselves, we can with conviction rehearse the words of the apostle Paul, "I can do all things through Christ which strengtheneth me" (Philippians 4:13).

Hordeum vulgare

The only place in Scripture where we have the expression 'barley meal' is in Numbers 5:15. There it relates to the divine order for offering the oblation of jealousy, a memorial oblation bringing iniquity to remembrance. The use of the barley meal spoke of Christ in manhood, having come under all the consequences of His people's failure and unfaithfulness. The dust taken from the floor of the tabernacle and mixed with the sanctified, bitter water, spoke of Christ as man having gone into death to answer to God

24

Barley
Hordeum vulgare

for the sins of the people. Our Lord charged Himself with the responsibility for man's unfaithfulness to God and the failure of His people. He died for the world. In the ordinance laid down in Numbers 5, Jehovah was the faithful husband jealous for the undivided affections of His wife. Israel was the unfaithful wife. If we are to get the gain of this typical teaching, we need to daily apply the death of Christ to our own souls (Philippians 3:10).

In Leviticus 23:10-11 we have the offering of the wave sheaf. The day following the Sabbath, a sheaf of barley, being the first-fruit of their harvest was 'waved' before the Lord. Barley is the first cereal harvested, so the 'wave sheaf' would always have been a sheaf of barley. There seems little doubt that the reason Jehovah ordered the barley sheaf to be 'waved' was twofold. First, it spoke of the cause for the death of Christ on Calvary's cross. Secondly, the waving of the sheaf spoke of the resurrection of that same man on the first day of the week. He was the first-fruit to God (1 Corinthians 15:20 & 23; Colossians 1:15).

Following His resurrection, the Lord Jesus demonstrated to His disciples in many ways that He was the same man, their Lord and Master whom they had seen crucified and buried. He appeared in their midst through closed doors and showed them His wounded hands and side (John 20:19-20). He appeared with them on the shore of Galilee and ate broiled fish and a little honeycomb with them (Luke 24:42-43). The Lord in resurrection life did not have a need to eat, but He was anxious to confirm to the disciples that He truly was the same man with whom they had kept company for 3.5 years. As Lord of all creation, there was nothing outside the range of His omnipotent power. Dining with them in this way, the Lord would have left an indelible impression upon their souls, confirming His words to Martha, "I am the resurrection and the life" (John 11:25). Typically, the waving of the barley sheaf tells us that we now have a Man enveloped in glory at the right hand of the greatness on high (Hebrews 1:3). The Lord Jesus is the first and only Man God has glorified and to whom He has given a Name that is above every Name. In a coming day, all created intelligences will bow the knee and do homage before that Man, the Man of God's counsels (Philippians 2:9-11).

Ruth, the Moabitess was very happy to glean from the beginning of the barley harvest through to the wheat harvest. The faithfulness of Ruth carried her through to the wheat harvest, which today speaks to our hearts of a new relationship. Boaz was a type of Christ and Obed a worshipper. May our gracious Lord encourage our hearts to persevere day by day, learning of the ways of God through Christ and be ready to identify with the One who was despised and rejected of men. Only then shall we get the benefits from the wheat harvest – worshippers in a new relationship within the Father's house?

The record in John 6 of the Lord feeding the five thousand souls, has a message for us today. In the miracle, the Lord took up five barley loaves and two small fishes. The barley loaves spoke of the lowly, humble, dependent and obedient Man, the Saviour of the world. In faith, that Blessed Person was wholly at the disposal of God His Father, to do His will. No matter how little the provisions appeared to be, the Lord knew there would be enough to go round, with a surplus of twelve full baskets of fragments gathered up by His disciples. The original barley loaves were the product of man's preparation, but the fishes represented that which God provides in His sovereign grace. Clearly the fragments would not have been wasted, but set aside for subsequent need. The narrative looked on to the Millennial age, when that same Man whom the nation of Israel rejected, and the world crucified, will be Sovereign and Lord over all. His coming again will not be in weakness and dependence (barley), but, "with power and great glory" (Matthew 24:30). Furthermore, His appearing the second time will be without sin unto salvation (Hebrew 9:28). Our Lord will appear without the need to say anything about sin, for He settled the question of sin and its judgment in perpetuity at the end of His first coming.

> *Christ is risen, Hallelujah; where, O death, thy victory?*
> *He is risen and ascended, far above all mortal eye.*
> *He is risen, glorious Firstfruits, first-begotten from the dead;*
> *Thus to be to His assembly, over all things now as head.*
>
> L Sandell

Bay

Hebrew: Ezrach = A green tree flourishing as if native in the land.
Psalm 37:35.

Although the Septuagint translates the 'green bay tree' as the 'cedar of Lebanon', there is very little support for such an interpretation. It is unfortunate that the KJAV has attempted to identify the 'green tree' as a bay tree. The JND translation of the Bible gives the most accurate definition of the Hebrew word, Ezrach, i.e. 'spreading like a green tree in its native soil'. What the Spirit of God was saying through the Psalmist is this; that wherever the wicked go in the world, they may appear to prosper for a time, but God will have His way in the end (Psalm 2:4-5).

The Psalmist in Psalm 73, was greatly disturbed by the apparent prosperity of the wicked, until, as he says, "I went into the sanctuary of God; then understood I their end" (verse 17). There is much in the world today to disturb Christian believers. Wherever we look, we see wolves in sheep's clothing going about wreaking havoc in the Assembly of God's people. May the Lord give us the spiritual perception to identify those who masquerade as Christian believers. To act speedily and spiritually with any who give the impression of spiritual prosperity, yet are void of love, commitment and truth (Jude 12 & 13).

Keep us Lord, O keep us cleaving, to Thyself and still believing;
Till the hour of our receiving promised joys with Thee.

T Kelly

Beans

Vicia faba

Hebrew: Pol = A plump bean.
2 Samuel 17:28 & Ezekiel 4:9.

Vicia faba is the tick bean, grown today for cattle food and was in all probability the bean of Scripture. The broad bean we grow in our vegetable garden today has the same botanical name. Beans formed an important carbohydrate and protein ingredient in the diet for David's army. It was essential for the soldiers to be healthy, strong and well nourished. David was anxious his army should have a balanced diet to ensure they

would survive a long time in the battlefield. Ezekiel was told to lay up food, including beans, to eat by measure during the siege of Jerusalem which was to last a total of 430 days (Ezekiel 4:9).

Christian believers also need to take in a balanced diet of the Truth in God's Word. If we concentrate on just one or two basic Truths of Scripture at the expense of the whole Truth, we shall very soon find ourselves spiritually unwell due to an imbalance of spiritual understanding. In that condition, we would be of little help to anyone. Let us nourish our souls with every spiritual gem of Scripture we can comprehend. We shall then reflect in our lives and testimony, a little of the radiant glories of Christ, (2 Corinthians 3:18). The Lord help us to be balanced Christians.

Guide us, O Thou gracious Saviour, pilgrims through this barren land;
We are weak, but Thou art mighty; hold us with Thy powerful hand.
Bread of heaven, bread of heaven; feed us now and evermore.

W Williams

𝓑𝓸𝔁

Abies cilicica

Hebrew: Te'ashshur = To be straight, towering and erect.
Isaiah 41:19 & 60:13.

The Hebrew word Te'ashshur is closely related to another Hebrew word – Ashar, which means: to be upright, straight, to behave correctly, to go forward, to be honest, to prosper, guide and relieve. Both references to the box tree are along side other trees

such as the fir and pine, so clearly all three trees are distinct types of conifer. Botanists remain unclear about the exact type of conifer is applicable to the box tree as given in the Scriptures. However, because of the meaning of Te'ashshur, I suggest it could very well be abies cilicica. Of all the conifers indigenous to Lebanon and the Middle-East in general, the abies is a towering tree reaching a height of 30 m or more. Whatever the botanical nomenclature today, one thing is clear, each tree referred to in the above text, reflects an aspect of the majesty and greatness of the Lord of Glory.

Both references in Isaiah relate to the time when Israel will fully occupy the Land of promise. The behaviour and testimony of the nation will for the very first time correspond with the meaning of the Hebrew noun

Te'ashshur. The nation will be upright, behave correctly, be honest, flourish and go forward to great prosperity. The time will be the glorious millennial age when the nation will enter her Sabbath of rest. It will be a time when the Lord will plant every tree of beauty, stature and renown, so that the land epitomises the glory and dignity of the Sovereign of the universe. Repentant Israel will gladly acknowledge that their recovery is the work of the Lord alone, the One who was the long promised Messiah whom they once rejected, cast out and crucified. "They will see, and know, and consider, and understand together, that the hand of the Lord hath done it, and that the Holy One of Israel hath created it" (Isaiah 41:20). Furthermore, "the desert shall rejoice and blossom as a rose" (Isaiah 35:1-2).

Meanwhile, we should conduct ourselves in a way that parallels the habit of the box tree, ever towering upward. The Psalmist speaks a great deal about the upright in heart; whose heart and manner of life is upright before God, heeding God's word and seeking to minister pleasure to God. David says that it is the praise of the upright that is alone acceptable to God (Psalm 33:1-4); their inheritance shall last for ever (Psalm 37:18), for they shall dwell in the presence of the Lord (Psalm 140:13). The apostle Paul said to the Christian believers at Colosse, "if ye then be risen with Christ, seek those things which are above, where Christ sitteth on the right hand of God" (Colossians 3:1). May we ever be among those of whom God has said, "no good thing will He withhold from them that walk uprightly" (Psalm 84:11).

> *Praise is comely from the upright, pure and holy in their heart.*
> *As the trees reach up to heaven, so their lives with Him have part.*
>
> T H Ratcliffe

Bramble; Briar; Nettle; Thistle & Thorn

Hebrew: 'Atad = Bramble/Thorn branches, to hold one fast.
Genesis 3:18 + 77 other references, including Hebrew nouns: Barqan = Bramble branch used as a threshing tool. Charul = Nettle, a thorny sub-shrub. Chedeq = Briar, a prickly plant that stings. Mesukah = A thorn hedge. Na'atsuts = Thicket of thorn bushes. Qimmashon = Stinging nettle, prickly plant. Qimmosh = A stinging, prickly plant. Qots = Thorny, prickly plants. Sarab = Stinging briar, thistle. Seneh = Bramble bush. Shamiyr = Hard, firm point like a diamond. Shayith = Wild thorn scrub. Sillown = Stout, pendulous thorn. Siyr = Rapid growing thorn, fish hook. Tsen = Thorn hedge. Tsaniyn = Thorns piercing one's flesh.
Greek nouns: Akantha = A thorny plant. Akanthinos = Made of thorns.
Batos = Thorn bush. Tribolos = Triple pointed thistle.

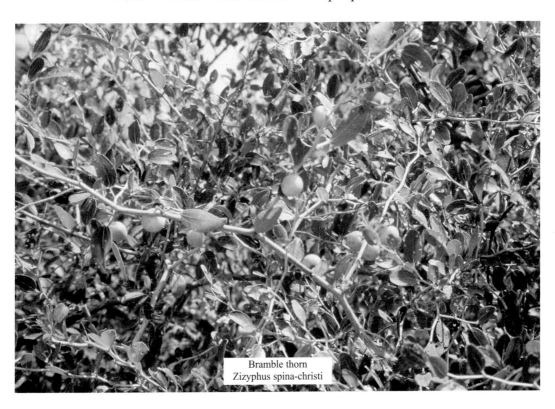

Bramble thorn
Zizyphus spina-christi

It has been stated many times that no other country on earth can boast of having so many species, types and varieties (over seventy) of brambles, briars, nettles, thistles and thorns as the land of Israel (Canaan). What is more, no other group of plants carries so many different common names. It is therefore understandable, that biblical scholars

31

up to the present time remain hesitant about being too specific on the botanical identity of the different plants, particularly in the bramble to thorn group. Putting it very simply, because of the curse God put on the earth; all thorns, briars, thistles etc. are a hindrance to man; in one way or another they hurt, damage and entangle. With the Lord's help, I shall consider this group of plants under the above composite heading, majoring on the cruelest of all thorns, the Zizyphus spina-christi, the christ-thorn.

God referred to the land (Canaan) in His covenant with Abram (Genesis 13:14-18). Jehovah told Moses He would bring His people, "unto a good land and large, a land flowing with milk and honey" (Exodus 3:8). It was 40 years later that Joshua led the children of Israel into the land, having crossed the Jordan (Joshua 3:17). The great

Rubus fruiticosus

tragedy was that Israel never took complete possession of the Land. Due to the nation's disobedience and idolatry, they suffered greatly from the curse God had pronounced on the earth (Genesis 3:18).

Botanists and biblical scholars are agreed it is impossible to say with any degree of certainty, which of all the thorn plants was used to make the crown of thorns placed on the head of the Lord Jesus (John 19:2). However, because of the character and nature of the plant, the majority believe the crown of thorns was made from the evergreen

32

bush/tree zizyphus spina-christi called 'the christ thorn'. A point in favour of the 'the christ thorn' is that it is one of the very few thorns plants that is evergreen. It grows like a bushy tree with long, twisting, pliable, cord-like, straggling, thorny stems. When you see the tree, it is easy to understand how such growths can be fashioned to make a cruel crown of thorns. The Greek word for 'thorn' in John 19:2 & 5 and many references in the New Testament, is akantha or akanthinos, which means, a thorn plant or made with thorns. A botanical name for this plant could well have been acanthus syriacus or spinosus, a plant related to acanthus mollis frequently found in English gardens. However, most scholars have translated akantha as zizyphus.

Roman Emperors wore crowns made of evergreen laurel leaves as a symbol of immortality and honour. While no Emperor was immortal, the only One who had the

Bear's breech
Acanthus spinosus

right to wear such a symbol, being Himself immortal, was made to wear a cruel crown of thorns. Even those who triumphed at the Roman games received a crown made of laurel leaves in honour of their achievement. However, when it came to crowning the Lord Jesus, the Messiah of the nation, they used an evergreen thorn plant. The thrusting of such a crown upon the head of that Blessed Person was an act of mockery, insult and indignity; designed to generate agonising pain.

God has now crowned the Man of His counsels, with glory and honour (Hebrews 2:9). The next time the world sees the Lord Jesus Christ, they will behold Him crowned with majesty, dignity and honour. He will be enveloped with glory, surrounded by the millions of the redeemed, and exercising power, might and authority as, King of Kings and Lord of Lords. What a contrast it will be to the dependent Man who was here on earth 2000 years ago. The lowly Galilean, the despised Nazarene, the carpenter's son, and of Whom they said, "we will not have this man to reign over us" (Luke 19:14). The nation compounded its sin of rejection by crowning Him with a crown of thorns and nailing Him to a shameful cross.

As we already have seen, brambles, briars, nettles, thistles and thorns speak of the consequences of the sin that came in by the first man, Adam. Such plants are of no value to man, who by the sweat of his brow spends his time trying to get rid of them. I have no doubt that such plants will remain in the earth until the incoming of the Millennial age. Meanwhile, rather than comment on every reference in the Scriptures to the brambles and their like, I will share some thoughts on the bramble referred to in Jotham's parable.

The bramble in Judges 9:14-15 has the Hebrew noun 'Atad, which occurs in one other place in the Old Testament, Psalm 58:9. Psalm 58 speaks of the conditions prevailing when David felt assailed by his enemies on every side, it also details God's intervention on behalf of the godly remnant. Verse 9 of the Psalm would indicate the rapidity of the fiery judgment before the pots feel the heat of the burning thorns. The Psalm confirms that the sole use of the bramble with its 25 mm long thorns is to generate pain, snare and hold fast. Abimelech's objective was to subdue (pierce) the children of Israel; to hold them in chains (make fast) and to dominate them for his own gain (secure). What is clearly for our instruction and help in Jotham's parable is that the character and growth of the bramble is typical of the unregenerate nature of man.

Nettle
Urtica dioica

Spear thistle
Carduus lanceolatus

We should always carefully consider our disposition toward our brothers and sisters in Christ; and like the olive, fig and vine, be more ready to serve than to rule. The Lord Jesus said, "I have given you an example that ye should do as I have done. Verily, verily I say unto you, the servant is not greater than his lord, neither he that is sent, greater than he that sent him" (John 13:15-16). "A new commandment I give unto you, that ye love one another as I have loved you, that ye also love one another. By this shall all know that ye are my disciples, if ye have love one to another" (John 13:34-35). Paul said, "be ye kind one to another, tender-hearted, forgiving one another, even as God for Christ's sake hath forgiven you" (Ephesians 4:32). Every Christian believer is a new creation with a divine nature, but due to the weaknesses of the flesh, features of the old nature occasionally express themselves against other Christian believers.

If one were foolish enough to shelter beneath the bramble, its long, waving, thorn-studded outgrowths would quickly tear one's clothes to shreds and inflict personal injury. The natural growth habit of the bramble parallels the objective of Abimelech; i.e. to ensnare, hold captive and control; that is why he said, "come and put your trust in my shadow" (Judges 9:15). Christian believers displaying such failings must be approached with extreme caution, for they are uncomfortable to be with, painful to handle, and like the bramble, to shelter beneath their shadow would be to court disaster. In times of stress and trial, such brethren afford no relief, comfort or protection. Rather than building up the saints, they just hold them down.

Milk thistle
Silybum marianum

The normal leaves of plants are miniature processing factories. By a process known as photosynthesis, leaves convert the nutrients they draw up from the earth via the roots and stems, into plant tissue, fruit and seeds. The energy leaves require to perform their vital function is exclusively drawn from the light of the sun. So it is with Christian believers, the life-giving energy for their spiritual growth, their fruit bearing and the exercise of the gifts given to the Church, is derived from the Son in heaven, by the power of the Spirit of God. On the other hand, the thorns of plants are, in the main, modified stipular leaves with no processing function whatsoever, they derive no energy from the sun and are therefore of no use to man. The objectives of the bramble and similar thorn-bearing plants, are resistance, self-promotion and domination to the hurt of others. Let us ever esteem others better than ourselves, more ready to serve than to control; and to be, "kind to one another, tenderhearted, forgiving one another, even as God for Christ's sake has forgiven you (us)" (Ephesians 4:32). The poignant words of Bernard of Clairvaux are most appropriate to conclude these thoughts on the subject of thorns and briers etc.

> *O head once full of bruises, so full of pain and scorn;*
> *'Mid other sore abuses, mocked with a crown of thorn.*
> *O Head! e'en now surrounded, with brightest majesty;*
> *In death once bowed and wounded, on the accursed tree.*

Based on words by: Bernard of Clairvaux

Bulrush / Rush

Cyperus Papyrus syn. C. antiqurum

Hebrew: Gome' = To absorb, swallow, imbibe.
Exodus 2:3 + three other references.

The name bulrush as given in the KJAV, is not the bulrush plant frequently found in English garden ponds. The English bulrush, which is common throughout the North Temperate Region, is typha domingensis or typha latifolium.

Cyperus papyrus can grow to a height of 2 m or more. The reeds used for the ark in which Moses was placed, would have been carefully and tightly woven together. As the Hebrew name implies, the papyrus foliage and stems are absorbent, so once the ark was complete, it was daubed with a waterproofing resin on both the inside and outside and then covered with pitch. The Hebrew word for the papyrus ark, tebah, is the same as that used for Noah's ark. The spiritual significance attaching to Noah's ark, can therefore apply to the ark in which Moses was placed, albeit the basic material used was different. The papyrus reed spoke of the humanity of Christ. The waterproofing resin and pitch are typical of the fact that no defiling influence could possibly penetrate that blessed and perfect Person (Matthew 4:1-11; 2 Corinthians 5:21; 1 Peter 2:22; 1 John 3:5). Water in

this instance, spoke of death, that the ark was placed in the water would remind us that our precious Saviour went into death for us. Moses was safe in his ark, which was in the water amongst the flag reeds. For the Christian believer, we are now in Christ Who has been into death for us, and raised out from among the dead by the glory of the Father.

Amram and Jochebed, the parents of Moses, beheld the uniqueness, beauty and perfection of their son (Acts 7:20). Under the influence of the Holy Spirit of God, they were fearless in the exercise of their faith. They did everything possible to preserve the child from the sentence of death passed on all newborn Israeli boys (Hebrew 11:23). Everything of true moral beauty and excellence has no place in this world. The only man this world wants to accommodate and nurture is the man after the flesh. Accordingly, in the scene where Satan is in control, all that is pleasing to God must take the place of death (2 Corinthians 4:10).

The reference to the reed, gome' in Job 8:11; would remind us that our Lord Jesus Christ was a dependent Man here on earth, and that His life and death were essential to secure our Salvation. In Isaiah 35:7, the prophet was speaking of the glorious millennial scene when Israel will be gathered together, never again to be divided. The land will be productive and glorious. None of the forces of evil known today and represented by the dragons (wild dogs), lions and ravenous beasts, will be there. The grass, reeds and papyrus will flourish.

Meanwhile, as far as this world is concerned, we should be happy to say with the apostle Paul. "I am crucified with Christ; nevertheless I live, yet not I, but Christ liveth in me. The life which I now live in the flesh I live by the faith of the Son of God who loved me and gave Himself for me" (Galatians 2:20).

Unto Thy death baptiséd, we own with Thee we died;
With Thee, our life, we're risen, and shall be glorified.

J G Deck

Calamus

Cymbopogon martinii

Hebrew: Qaneh = Palmerosa oil grass – reed stalk.
Sweet calamus.
Exodus 30:23 + 4 other references.

The Hebrew word Qaneh occurs 38 times with definitions such as, measuring reed, bone, branch, balance, stalk and spearmen, but the common name 'calamus' occurs just 5 times. Sweet calamus is a herbaceous, erect reed reaching a height of between 2 & 3

m. The plant flourishes on the banks of all streams and lakes in the Jordan Valley. The reeds are cut down just before flowering and while the plants are still rich green in colour. The fragrant, sweet calamus oil is expressed from the pith of the reed, purified, then added to other components to produce a fragrant embalming ointment. Sweet calamus was a constituent of the Holy anointing oil (Exodus 30:23). Reeds left to mature *in situ* make excellent measuring rods of the kind frequently mentioned in the book of Ezekiel.

The components of the Holy anointing oil, when perfectly blended together after the art of the apothecary, represented a rich tapestry of the nature, grace and influence the Lord Jesus exercised as dependent Man in the will of God. The constituents were so skilfully mingled together that no one fragrance masked the others, but together produced a unique and lasting sweet aroma. Moses anointed every part of the Tabernacle, including the furnishings and utensils, in order to hallow them for the exclusive use of the priests in the service and worship of Jehovah. Aaron and his sons also were anointed and thereby hallowed as priests for the service of Jehovah. Everything that was hallowed, was never again anointed. The fragrance of the Holy anointing oil was so powerful that those anointed carried the bouquet of its sweetness with them wherever they went. Today, the Holy Spirit of God, who dwells in every believer in the Lord Jesus Christ, is the antitype of the Holy anointing oil. The Christian believer should leave in his wake a fragrant sweetness of the Lord Jesus Christ and thereby have a moral impact on the world.

Every believer in the Lord Jesus Christ was anointed with the Holy Spirit of God at the time of his or her conversion. John the apostle said, "Little children…ye have an unction (anointing) from the Holy One" (1 John 2:20). Just as the Tabernacle and the Aaronic priesthood were anointed (hallowed) once; it follows that Christian believers cannot receive a second anointing of the Holy Spirit. To ask for a fresh outpouring on oneself of the Holy Spirit of God is to deny that one was baptised with the Spirit when converted to Christ. The important truth is this; Christian believers must allow the Holy Spirit who indwells them to take complete control of their lives. This is what the apostle Paul implied when he said to the Ephesian Christians, "be not drunk with wine wherein is excess, but be filled with the Spirit" (Ephesians 5:18). If Christian believers feel that the Spirit of God is not controlling their lives, it will be for one or two reasons. First, the Spirit of God may be grieved (Ephesians 4:30). Paul said, "you have put off your former manner of life which is corrupt, etc. and put on the new man which, according to God, is created in righteousness and true holiness" (Ephesians 4:22 & 24). The apostle goes on to say that if they do not live the new life, they will, 'grieve the Holy Spirit of God whereby they have been sealed unto the day of redemption' v.30. Secondly, the Spirit of God may be quenched (1 Thessalonians 5:19). In other words, the evidence and fire of the new life is no longer able to manifest itself in the individual, the Spirit of God cannot work. The light of the testimony of eternal life has gone out. Although this is a very sad state to get into, a second anointing of the Holy Spirit of God cannot restore one. What is necessary is a fresh commitment in one's life to doing the will of God. Allowing His Spirit to take control on a daily basis; then and only then will the joy of one's salvation return to fill the heart and light up the soul (Psalm 37:4-6).

Each ingredient for the holy anointing oil was a measured quantity for a very special reason. In the case of sweet calamus, it was 250 shekels (approx. 3.9 kg), only half the quantity prescribed for the liquid myrrh and cassia. The oil that came from the pith of the plant was expressive of the innermost thoughts, feelings, compassion and affections of the Lord Jesus Christ. Man could not comprehend fully, the deep emotions and affections that motivated the Lord Jesus when here as dependant man for the glory of God. The deep feelings of love in the heart of God toward man came into expression in the life of Christ. In Psalms 111, 112 & 145, we read these words, "the Lord is gracious and full of compassion". Peter said, "be ye all of one mind, having compassion one for another, love as brethren, be pitiful, be courteous" (1 Peter 3:8). As those who are in-dwelt (have been anointed) by the Holy Spirit of God, may we be helped to exercise God-wrought, heart-felt compassion on all around. Let us manifest a deep feeling for souls in our preaching, as exemplified by our blessed Saviour (Matthew 9:36-37).

The Lord Jesus was moved with compassion to heal the leper in Mark 1, and to restore to the widow of Nain her son (Luke 7). In John 11, we see the Lord Jesus weeping at the tomb of Lazarus. Although the Lord greatly loved Lazarus and his sisters, His tears were the consequence of seeing what sin had brought in through the disobedience of the first man, Adam. The word 'wept' in verse 35 occurs nowhere else in the Scriptures, its use is unique to this one occasion. The Greek word 'dakruo' literally means 'to shed tears silently'. Yes, our blessed Lord really did shed tears; they welled up from His innermost being and were an eloquent statement of His deep compassion for man. No man had ever wept as the Lord Jesus wept at the grave of Lazarus. For no mortal man could measure the gulf that separates unregenerate man from a Holy God, or feel so deeply the consequences of the sin brought in by the first man, Adam; the Lord Jesus alone could, and did. On Calvary's cross, the Lord Jesus answered to God for the sin of the world; He made Himself responsible before God for our sins. God's judgment on those sins, burnt out in His holy soul; so there is now no more sacrifice for sins (Hebrews 10:26). The Lord Jesus, the Saviour of the world has therefore bridged the gulf that once separated man from God. Now, through repentance before God and faith in the work of the Lord Jesus Christ on the cross, mortal men can be brought into relationship with God to appear as sons before His face.

> *Lord, none could staunch the outflow of Thy tears,*
> *When Thou wast moved with heart-felt grief and pain.*
> *What sin had done, Thy flowing tears revealed*
> *The life, that Thine atoning blood has gained.*
>
> T H Ratcliffe

Camphire / Henna
Lawsonia inermis

Hebrew: Kopher = A cover, ransom, satisfaction.
Song of Solomon 1:14 & 4:13.

Henna is twice mentioned in the Scriptures as given above. According to the majority of biblical scholars, there can be no doubt that 'camphire' as given in the KJAV is an incorrect rendering of the Hebrew word *kopher,* which should be translated 'henna'. The henna plant is a medium size, deciduous tree/shrub reaching a height of between 2 and 4 m. The tree is heavily branched, and in the spring, bears masses of delicate panicles of lilac to white, extremely fragrant flowers. In Middle Eastern countries, henna is used for purposes other than that referred to in the Song of Solomon. Leaves are dried, crushed and soaked in water to form a paste. After a few days, an ochreous red dye is produced and used for painting finger and toe-nails and other parts of the body including the dyeing of one's hair.

Solomon speaks of an Oasis at Engedi, a city situated halfway between the north and south ends of the Dead Sea on the West Side. Engedi was probably a bountiful place of vineyards, olive groves, orchards and date palms, where the henna tree grew quite freely. Solomon would have been a regular visitor to the area. The Christian believer today is in a world surrounded by barren desert places. Like Engedi, there are unproductive mountainous regions to the North, West and South, with the undrinkable Dead Sea water to the East. Where then can a Christian believer find his oasis and spiritual sustenance today? The answer is in the spiritual Engedi, which is the sanctuary of the Lord. Later in the book, we shall see in figure how the Lord Jesus is the sole source of goodness for producing the different fruits in the orchard of the spiritual Engedi. We shall also see how the Lord's servants are used to nourish the saints through the ministry of the Word

Typically, the bride who is speaking in Song of Solomon 1:14, is the Church. To the bride, Christ is not only the 'well beloved', but the 'best beloved'. The bride longs to have in her heart some lasting impression of the bridegroom. She will lay a symbol of the sweet fragrance of Christ – a cluster of henna flowers – between her breasts and rest complacent in the deep affections that first drew her to Him. The action of the bride is a lovely statement of her affection for Him. The Church today is adorned with the unique features of Christ, there is no requirement for material display. In our worship through Him to the Father, we give expression to affections and cherished thoughts about the worth of the Son to the Father. Like the cluster of henna flowers, we become overwhelmed with the fragrance of Christ, being more occupied with what He is, rather than what He has done for us.

Thy fulness, Lord, is now for me, all my fresh springs are hid in Thee;
In Thee I live; while I confess, I nothing am, yet all possess.
O Saviour, teach me to abide close sheltered at Thy trusted side;
Each hour receiving grace on grace, until I see Thee face to face.

J G Deck

Cassia

Cinnamomum cassia

Hebrew: Qiddah or Qetsiyah = Shrivelled rolls of perfumed bark.
Exodus 30:24 + two other references.

Cassia belongs to the laurel family of evergreen trees and shrubs, and can reach a height of 15 m. Commercially, the trees are cultivated as coppices. Non-showy, amply branched panicles of yellowish white, scent-less flowers appear in the Spring from the leaf axis. The bark of the tree is smooth, thick and charged with the precious resin.

Rolled bark of the Cassia shrub

Three to five year old branches are coppiced, the outer bark is then carefully removed in long strips. The fragrant, volatile oil, consisting of cinnamic aldehyde mixed with resins is distilled from the bark after the art of the apothecary.

The word cassia means shrivelled, to contract or bend the body in deference, to peel and to strip off, to bow the head. We see in the Lord Jesus Christ as Son of man after God's heart, a divine character of moral excellence that shone out to eclipse beyond compare, everything that had gone before in mortal man. Throughout His manhood, the glory our Lord had with His Father before creation, was veiled. The glory that enveloped the Lord Jesus on the mount of Transfiguration (Matthew 17:1-8; Mark 9:1-8; Luke 9:27-35) was not the glory He had with the Father before the world was made.

44

The glory on the mount was the 'Shekinah' or 'Dwelling' glory in which the saints of God will be enveloped and manifested with Christ throughout His millennial reign. In addition, the Shekinah glory is the glory in which we shall dwell throughout the golden ages of eternity.

Returning to the subject of our Lord's manhood; His holy body experienced hunger, thirst and weariness. He allowed those who had arrested Him to strip Him of His unique robe – a robe without seam – that spoke so beautifully of the perfection and completeness of Himself as man. He voluntarily bowed His head on the cross to signal His total obedience to the will of God. These were all outward, visible signals that should have touched the hearts of mortal man. Hence, the amount of cassia oil used in the composition of the Holy ointment was 500 shekels (approx. 7.8 kg) after the shekel of the sanctuary.

Cassia oil was and possibly still is used as a therapy in the treatment of many illnesses. The oil produces a warming of the body; it is a stimulant and a carminative; it effects an antispasmodic influence and has antiseptic and antiviral powers. Christian believers today face many problems that the presence and divine influence of the Lord Jesus alone can resolve. Individuals, for whom man could do nothing, depended upon the mercy of God and the loving intervention of the Lord Jesus. There was the palsied man in Mark 2:1-12 whom the Lord restored to full health. The man with the withered hand in Mark 3:1-5, was healed of his incapacity to work. The woman loosed from her infirmity in Luke 13:10-17 was able to rejoice and glorify the God of her salvation. Bartimeaus immediately receives his sight, whereupon he instantly bursts forth in praise, glorifying God. What an example for us! The sweet Psalmist of Israel could say, "Bless the Lord, O my soul, and all that is within me, bless His holy Name. Who forgiveth all thine iniquities…Who healeth all thy diseases…Who crowneth thee with lovingkindness and tender mercies" (Psalm 103:1,3 & 4).

Lord, like Thee in faith, meekness, love, in every beauteous grace;
From glory into glory changed, till we behold Thy face.

J Stennett

Cedar

Cedrus Libani

Hebrew: 'Erez = Firmness, from the tenacity of its roots. 'Araz = Made of cedar.
'Arzah = Cedar work, used for wainscotting.
Leviticus 14:4 + sixty-eight other references.

As the lion is the king of beasts in the jungle, so the majestic cedar is the king of trees in the forest. The cedar tree symbolises dignity, grandeur and strength. The natural habitat of the cedar is the rocky mountainous region of Syria and Lebanon. The evergreen trees tower amongst snow-clad mountain peaks in a pollution free environment, flourishing from the heat of the summer sun and the cold of the winter snow. A distinctive feature of the cedar is the way its branches out-spread to provide a broad over-shadowing and protective canopy. Unlike most other trees of the forest, the cedar is very rarely if ever, felled by natural forces; this is a factor of its form and the tenacity of its roots.

The stability, durability, strength and dominance of the cedar above all other trees, its resistance to decay and pests, together with its natural dignity and beauty, symbolise

the glorious character of the Lord Jesus Christ. The wood is excellent for structural building and for cladding, which is why Solomon used it so extensively in the building of the Temple (1 Kings 6:9). The completed Temple mirrored the glory of the One who will in triumph, reign for a thousand years. That illustrious Person, the Lord Jesus Christ, will very soon be brought into such prominence, that every eye will see Him, every tongue will praise Him and every knee bow before Him (Philippians 2:10-11).

The kingly cedar is also a figure of the royal line established by covenant with David (2 Samuel 7:16-17). However, mention of cedar wood occurs earlier in the Scriptures where it has to do with the cleansing of the leper and the plague of leprosy in a house (see Leviticus 14). In both cases, if the leprosy had cleared, the priest would direct that two clean live birds, cedar wood, scarlet and hyssop were taken. The priest first killed one of the birds; he then dipped the surviving bird, together with the cedar wood, scarlet and hyssop, in the blood of the slain bird, before setting the live bird free. The birds as one are a type Christ; one went into death and the other being a figure of life out from among the dead. The cedar wood spoke of the dignity and Lordship of Christ; the scarlet of the true and pure moral glory of His manhood, while the hyssop eloquently spoke of His humility, meekness and dependence as man. The ordinance in Leviticus 14 brings before us in type, the fact that it was necessary for Christ to go into death and shed His precious blood before the sinner (leper) could ever be pronounced clean.

Returning now to the royal line that Jehovah established by covenant with David; we know that the cedar tree (the kingdom of Israel) flourished for a while. However, following the death of Solomon, the kingdom divided, resulting in two kingdoms; Israel (10 tribes) and Judah (2 tribes) both going their separate ways. Although the two kingdoms turned to idolatry, they continued to be looked upon together as a type of the cedar tree. From time to time, fierce and terrible storms lashed the cedar, marring its glory and dignity; but nothing could uproot it, for its anchorage was secure from the influence of satanic forces. The royal line and root of David was preserved.

Around four hundred and fifty years on from the planting of the noble cedar, the Lord allowed the tip of the tree (Judah & Benjamin), to be snatched away by a great, long-winged, multicoloured eagle. The eagle was a figure of Nebuchadnezzar, King of Babylon (Exekiel 17:1-4). Due to the rebellion of Zedekiah, King of Judah, the Lord opened the way for Nebuchadnezzar to take him and all his seed and princes – the tip of the cedar – into captivity where the remnant would remain for seventy years. Zedekiah, together with those that stood by him, went to commercial Babylon (land of traffic, verse 4). Babylon was a place of moral darkness and far removed from the pure environment of the city where the Lord had originally planted His cedar.

For seventy years, the cedar tree did not flourish or grow, neither did it die, but became a little tree of mean stature. Instead, a great Gentile tree arose in Babylon; it was strong and its height reached heaven. The leaves of the tree were fair, it bore much fruit and was meat for all. The beasts of the field sheltered under the tree and the birds of the air nestled in its branches. The tree was a figure of Nebuchadnezzar and his kingdom. However, in the fulfilment of his dream, Nebuchadnezzar lost all his glory, power and authority in the kingdom. He lived and ate as the beasts in the field for seven years (Daniel 4:19-26). Meanwhile, the little Cedar tree – the children of Israel in captivity – survived.

The cedar tree remained in captivity for a total of 70 years, after which, Jehovah removed it and cared for it throughout the next 520 + years. He then took the highest branch in the cedar and nurtured it – a faithful remnant. From its growth, Jehovah secured for Himself a tender shoot and planted it in a high and eminent mountain in Israel. The shoot flourished, produced branches, bore fruit and became a noble cedar (Ezekiel 17:22-24). The noble cedar here is a type of the Lord Jesus Christ. Although the figure refers to His Millennial reign of glory, we may rightly say that our blessed Lord, as man here on earth, was in every way morally, a figure of the prosperous, majestic and noble cedar tree. Let us ever be ready to acknowledge in praise and worship, the dignity of His Holy Person, the majesty of His being and the over-shadowing, protective canopy of His glory and love.

> *God's dignity and grandeur, Lord; Thy holy nature showed;*
> *His majesty and honour, just, on Thee alone bestowed.*
> *Now that protective canopy, o'er-spreads us here below,*
> *As on the Christian pathway seek, Thy holy will to know.*
>
> T H Ratcliffe

Chestnut / Plane
Platanus orientalis

Hebrew: 'Armon = Deal subtly, to be cunning, naked, bare – from the shedding of its bark.
Genesis 30:37 & Ezekiel 31:8.

The translation of the Hebrew noun 'Armon as 'chestnut' is unfortunate in the above two references from the KJAV. All other translations give 'plane', which is significant because the plane tree thrives in the wetter areas of northern Israel. The chestnut on the other hand, is not indigenous to the country, and furthermore, requires much drier conditions in ground that is more fertile than desert rock and sand. The noun 'Armon, means naked, bare; and was in all probability attached to the plane tree because of the way the outer layers of the bark peel off annually. The London plane, platanus acerifolia is known for the mosaic pattern on the trunk of the tree which is created by the annual shedding of its bark. Some mature plane trees have trunks measuring 1 m in diameter, and between 15 and 30 m high. The plane is a deciduous tree with deeply lobed, palmate leaves and spreading branches extending as wide as the tree is tall.

We learn from the Scriptures that the patriarchs, including Jacob, knew a great deal about the value and use of plant materials, fruits, juices, saps and resins in relation to

medicine. When Jacob told his uncle that he wished to return home to the land of his fathers; Laban appealed for him to stay, confessing he had been blessed of the Lord for Jacob's sake. Laban readily agreed to a deal, which he believed would keep his nephew poor and dependent on him (Genesis 30:35-36).

The terms of Jacob's contract with his uncle and the way it was set up, appeared to disadvantage Jacob; yet unbeknown to Laban, Jacob had determined to apply his own cunning with a view to outwitting his uncle. Accordingly, whenever the strong ewes of Jacob's flock were ready to conceive, he directed them to the water troughs into which he had placed pilled rods from white popular, almond and plane trees. Jacob believed that traces of the sap in the rods would leach into the water, and ewes drinking the water would produce ringstraked, speckled or spotted lambs, which of course they did. Every ringstraked, speckled and spotted kid or lamb of the flocks became Jacob's property.

Now, although Laban had frequently cheated his nephew (Genesis 31:7 & 41), there was no divine reason why Jacob should have employed subterfuge to engineer an advantage over his uncle. Jacob had been a faithful servant to his uncle, and totally dependent on him for fourteen years. However, throughout the following six years, Jacob used all the skills of his trade to advance his own interest; i.e. providing for his own very large family. We know that Jacob's ends did not justify the means employed to achieve his objective. Furthermore, had Jacob not used pilled rods to taint the water his flocks were led to drink, the Lord would still have abundantly blessed him, but his faith did not rise to that level of dependence. Nevertheless, the Lord had His eye on Jacob, and had determined to make him prosperous with flocks, cattle, menservants and maidservants. Jacob had not yet learnt to cast all his cares on Jehovah and to lean on Him, nor was he ready to surrender his will to the One who controls all creation (Genesis 32:24-31).

We have in the trunk of the plane tree what is spiritually typical of the external testimony of an internal condition. Jacob's character was very much like the bark of the plane tree; a patchy mosaic, constantly changing and neither one thing nor another, much like the appearance of the ringstraked, speckled and spotted flocks. The sap of a plant is its life, and this gives character to form, appearance and product. In the same way, the old nature of man is infected by sin, and therefore yields features that cannot please God (Romans 3:20). After his encounter with the Lord, as recorded in Genesis 32, Jacob was a changed man. He was no longer of uncertain character, but one who surely would have rehearsed words similar to the Psalmist, "teach me Thy way, O Lord, and lead me in the plain path" (Psalm 27:11). The new life within the Christian believer cannot be infected by sin because the life is 'Christ Himself' (1 John 3:9). However, we have a responsibility to walk in the light of the gospel of God's grace. "Having renounced the hidden things of dishonesty, not walking in craftiness, nor handling the word of God deceitfully; but by manifestation of the truth commending ourselves to every man's conscience in the sight of God" (2 Corinthians 4:2).

Reference to the plane tree in Ezekiel 31:8, along with the cedar and the fir, represent figures of responsibility in Israel. The word of Jehovah came to Ezekiel, telling him to warn Pharaoh, king of Egypt of pending judgment because of his pride and independence of God. Furthermore, no matter how much he inflated his self-importance and domination over the African continent, the king of Egypt could in no way compare with the might of the original Assyrian kingdom which God had destroyed. Sadly, the great Gentile power of Assyria had dwarfed the hierarchy in Israel; yet according to the word of the Lord, no nation on earth should have exceeded her in greatness (Deuteronomy 4:7-8). Alas, disobedience and idolatry reduced the nation to captives in a foreign land, servants of a Gentile king, and worshippers of idolatry instead of worshippers of Jehovah (Deuteronomy 4:27-28). The responsibility for Israel's humiliation lay with the princes of the nation. The cedar was a figure of the High Priest of Israel, representing the people before God. The fir portrayed the Levitical order, responsible in the main for leading the singing in the worship of Jehovah (2 Chronicles 5:12-13); both of which were symbols that towered over and upward among the people. The plane tree on the other hand has palmate leaves which speak of the labour and endeavour that should have been exercised by the leaders of the tribes of Israel, working together for the glory and testimony of God. Accordingly, the princes were responsible for maintaining the people in worshipful communion with Jehovah, but they failed.

The plane tree would direct our thoughts to the local companies of Christian believers and to those in particular who labour tirelessly to maintain the testimony of God's love and grace to the world. May our gracious Lord encourage us to maintain the position of faithful servants in whatever He has called us to do, and to be effective testimonies of His saving grace in a world of deepening moral darkness (Philippians 2:14-16).

We bow and own Thy sovereign will, which prompted first our hearts to yield;
The Spirit giv'n when born anew, by power divine, Thou Lord didst wield;
The source of life we have in Thee, now moves our souls responsively.

Anon

Cinnamon

Cinnamomum verum

Hebrew: Qinnamon. Greek: Kinamomom = Erect rolls of dried, inner bark from which the Sweet cinnamon oil was obtained.
Exodus 30:23 + three other references.

Cinnamomum verum belongs to the laurel family of evergreen plants. It grows to a height of between 6 and 10 m with tough, ovate to oblong, 10–15 cm long leaves, with three distinct vein marks radiating from the base. The shrub bears panicles of small, yellowish-white flowers that carry an unpleasant smell. The fruit is a small, elliptical nut. Oil from the nut generates a pleasing odour in the home when fired in lamps. However, the valuable, clear fragrant oil used as an ingredient of the Holy anointing oil, comes from the inner bark of 3 – 5 year-old branches of the cinnamon tree. The inner bark, separated from the core of the branch, is dried and made ready for processing. As the bark dries, it contracts into rolls, from which we get the Hebrew word 'Qinnamon'. The oil is distilled, or as the Scripture puts it, obtained 'after the art of the apothecary' (the work of the perfumer).

We note that 250 shekels (approx. 3.9 kg) after the shekel of the sanctuary, was the amount of cinnamon oil to be included with the other ingredients of the Holy Anointing Oil. Like the prescribed measure for calamus, the quantity for the cinnamon oil again reflected the fact that mortal man could not possibly

Dried inner bark

5 cm

comprehend or fathom all the depths of the Saviour's feelings toward His people. The powerful resources of the precious inner feelings of the Lord Jesus, together with an abundance of the divine assets of God's love and grace, were ever ready to be tapped by those whose hearts were right before Him.

In Matthew 9:20 – 22 (also in Mark 5 & Luke 8) we have the story of a sick woman who, over a period of twelve years had spent all her resources in the hope of being healed. All was in vain. Then, by the power of the Spirit of God, her faith reached out to tap the inexhaustible healing resources residing in the Saviour; immediately, she was healed. The nobleman in John 4:46-54, believed that the Lord had power to heal his son. The nobleman first pleaded with the Lord Jesus to come to his home, but Jesus just spoke the word, 'go thy way, thy son liveth' and the nobleman believed. This was a case where the latent, inherent power of the Lord Jesus proved to be instantly active in answer to faith. A similar incident occurred in Capernaum, as recorded in Matthew 8:5-13. The centurion was outside the family and nation of Israel, yet he had faith to believe there was an inner resource in the Lord Jesus on which he himself could draw for blessing. The centurion's faith was greater than that of the nobleman; in fact, Jesus said that He had not found so great faith, no, not in Israel. On behalf of his servant, the centurion said to the Lord Jesus, "speak the word only, and my servant shall be healed".

These miracles and many others, present a powerful lesson for our souls to lay hold of today. Our faith should reach out to benefit from all that our gracious Lord has put within the range of our faith. "Ask, (the Father) and it shall be given you; seek, and ye shall find; knock, and it shall be opened unto you" (Matthew 7:7). However, everything is on the basis of our faith in the One who already has established our standing in Christ, and, "blessed us with all spiritual blessing in the heavenlies in Christ" (Ephesians 1:3) J.N.D. There are many other lovely thoughts on the significance of cinnamon, but perhaps we should content ourselves with what has gone before and saturate our souls with the fragrance of, 'The Person of the Christ who enfolds every grace'.

> *The fulness of Thy grace inspires, our hearts to worship Thee,*
> *Cast every care on Thee our Lord; trust soon Thy face to see.*
>
> T H Ratcliffe

Cockle

Hebrew: Bo'shah = Noxious, noisome, pernicious weed.
Job 31:40

Cockle is one of several plants in Scripture that stand alone having no positive identity in botanical terms. The Hebrew plant name Bo'shah is nowhere else mentioned in the Scriptures; nevertheless, it is significant because of the context in which it occurs. Although the Septuagint identifies the plant as 'bramble', the NIV gives 'weeds' and the JND translation says it is 'tares', none of the definitions come very near to the full meaning of the word 'Bo'shah'. The meaning of 'Bo'shah', as given above, throws some light on the kind of plant Job had in mind when he said, 'Let thistles grow instead of wheat, and cockle (Bo'shah) instead of barley. One thing is perfectly clear, the plant to which Job referred was unpleasant in every way.

So why did Job wish for such a plant to invade his crops. At this time, Job was still full of his own righteousness. Job had implied that if any could prove he had not acted righteously toward his neighbours and/or the rightful owners of the land he had cultivated, he was prepared for his crops to become contaminated and polluted. Job had completely disregarded the words of Bildad the Shuhite who had given him a detailed analysis of the inner state of man's heart before God (Job 25:1-6). Job's self-righteous disposition meant that his declared willingness to suffer loss, was an empty gesture. Job was still some way off from confessing to be a humble, repentant sinner, "I abhor myself, and repent in dust and ashes" (Job 42:6). In time, Job would readily confess that all his righteousnesses were as filthy rags before God (Isaiah 64:6). Job would recognise his own righteousness as the cockle plant, a stinkweed that is unpleasant, loathsome and offensive

May my gracious God help me to daily rehearse the words of David. "Search me, O God, and know my heart; try me, and know my thoughts; and see if there is any wicked way in me, and lead me in the way everlasting" (Psalm 139:23-24). If we fail or delay to judge those areas in our lives that dishonour God and the testimony of our Lord Jesus Christ; we shall become like the weed 'Bo'shah. That is surely a very grievous prospect that no child of God could possibly contemplate.

Touch Thou my heart Lord; for I long to know
Thy mind and will, to please Thee here below.
Clear any hindrance, seen in all my ways,
That I may render to Thee, fragrant praise.

T H Ratcliffe

Coriander

Coriandrum sativum

Hebrew: Gad = A troop. Round, fragrant, ribbed as the furrowed seed.
Exodus 16: 32 & Numbers 11:7.

Coriander is an annual herb belonging to the parsley and carrot family of plants. It will grow to a height of 0.6 m. All parts of the plant are aromatic. The finely cut leaves are useful for flavouring in cooking, in soups and as a green salad. Umbels of small white flowers followed by small, globular, ribbed fruits are 2-3 mm across. The seeds of the plant are ground and used as a condiment. According to Exodus 16:14 & 31, the manna was likened to the individual, round and ribbed coriander seeds. The mention of coriander in the Scriptures is only by way of similarity with the manna Jehovah provided for the children of Israel throughout their wilderness journey. Indeed, the plant coriander is not mentioned at all in Scripture, only the seed. Now, although the literal and spiritual teaching on the manna would be both helpful and interesting, it is clearly outside the scope of this book to develop the subject here.

Coriander seed
Coriandrum sativum

However, it would be somewhat remiss not to say something about the quantity of manna gathered each day. If we take account of the smallness of the individual, spherical seeds, 3-4 mm in diameter; gathering the manna would have been painstaking, time consuming and tiring. An 'omer' which was the amount to be gathered for each member of the household, is approximately 3 litres or 5.169 pints (after George Morrish, London 1899). To gather the equivalent of 3 litres of manna for each member of a household every morning and twice the amount on the sixth day would have been no mean undertaking. It would have required commitment and industry to gather enough before what remained began to melt under the heat of the sun.

The gathering of the manna is parallel to our taking up the Word of God day by day. We should take in the Word early each day to ensure its truth will influence the way we conduct our lives in this world of moral darkness. However, giving the Lord Jesus the pre-eminence in our lives will make demands on our time, just as the gathering in of the manna made demands on the children of Israel early each morning. When we take up God's Word in the right spirit, we shall always find it, "Sweet to our taste; a lamp unto our feet and a light unto our path" (Psalm 119:103 &105). Sadly, the children of Israel very soon lost the taste and the desire for the food that God provided for them. We are told in Numbers 11:6 that they first despised the manna and then they misused it, verse 8. Next, they loathed God's bountiful provision (Numbers 21:5). May our gracious Lord preserve us from ever despising, misusing and loathing what God in His mercy has freely given, even His Word in the Lord Jesus Christ.

Jesus, the Bread of life is given to be our daily food;
Within us dwells that spring from heaven, the Spirit of our God.

J Newton

56

Corn (Bearded Wheat)
Triticum sp.

Hebrew: Bar. Greek: Sitos. = Wheat and Corn grain.
Gen. 41:35 + one hundred & fifty nine other references, including Hebrew nouns:
Abur = Old, stored corn of the land. 'Arem = corn sheaf or heap of grain. Beliyl =
Mixed corn produce. Chinta' = Wheat grain. Chittah = Wheat. Dagan = Wheat &
Corn generally. Gadiysh = Shocks, stacks and sheaves. Geres = Green grain beaten
out. Karmel = Full green ears of grain. Qamah = Standing corn. Qaliy = Parched or
roasted ears of corn. Riyphah = Ground wheat, grits. Sheber = Grain in general.
Shibbol = an ear of grain.
Greek nouns: Kokkos = Kernel, seed grain. Sitos = Sifted wheat or corn. Stachus =
An ear of corn.

Biblical wheat was quite different to the wheat grown commercially throughout the
world today. The ear was thicker and similar in appearance to six-row barley, with long
awns and the grain being held more tightly within the glumes (dried parts of the
flower). Threshing the wheat required considerable effort, using flails that were the
threshing tools of the day, but oxen also were used to tread out the corn (Deuteronomy

Bearded Wheat
Triticum sativum

25:4). The richer families in Israel would have had their wheat ground by 'mill stone' turned either by slaves or by oxen; see Judges 16:21. On the other hand, the poorer families in the land would have used 'mortar and pestle' for grinding all their seed-based foods. In fact, such basic tools as the 'mortar and pestle' remain essential household utensils in Third World countries to this day. The principle cereal crops in Old and New Testament times were barley and wheat. Barley meal was relatively cheap and was the staple diet of the poor, whereas wheaten flour was considerably more expensive and the daily fare of 'well to do' families.

When wheat grain is ground, it produces what Scripture calls, 'fine flour'. The Hebrew word for 'fine flour' is Soleth, which occurs 52 times in the Old Testament. Wherever the term 'fine flour' or simply 'flour' appears in Scripture, the reference is always to 'wheaten flour'. Unlike the barley grain, the wheat grain is a naked seed, which is why, when it is ground it produces 'fine flour'. Wheaten flour together with the oil and frankincense, speak typically of the actual life of the Lord Jesus, a life that brought glory to God and occasioned the sweet fragrance of a perfect 'meat offering' (Leviticus 2:1-13). Furthermore, the life of our Lord brought in a new order of things in respect of man's relationship with God; a thought we shall expand on presently. Like the fine flour, the divine features our blessed Lord manifested in testimony were homogenous, balanced and unruffled. All the glorious and moral attributes that came into expression, were in perfect harmony with the mind of heaven (Luke 3:22).

Again, like fine flour, the feel of the lovely nature of the Lord Jesus was delicate, even and gentle to the touch; and notwithstanding the hostile reception He frequently experienced, He was always serene, relaxed and approachable. He was rejected, hated and misunderstood by His own people for teaching the ways of God in love. "For my love, they are my adversaries…they have rewarded me evil for good, and hatred for my love" (Psalm 109:4-5). Just as every grain of flour in the 'meat offering' was covered with oil, so every detail of our Lord's life was influenced by the Holy Spirit of God. Furthermore, the portion taken for a 'memorial' and burnt on the altar, included all the frankincense, signifying that the Lord Jesus as a man on earth, alone brought pleasure and delight to the heart of God.

In John 12:24, the Lord Jesus likens Himself to a 'corn of wheat'. Mark you, not a corn of barley, but a 'corn of wheat'. The barley grain speaks of the Lord Jesus as Son of Man. The shrivelled flower structures of the barley tightly envelop the grain, which parallels the truth that the Lord was here on earth clothed with all the features of humility, lowliness, dependence, meekness and obedience. The wheat grain on the other hand, is a naked seed telling us that the Lord Jesus, Son of God on earth, concealed nothing of the mind, nature and purpose of God. The Lord Jesus fully exposed all the counsels of the Godhead, including the bringing in of an entirely new order of things, based on the 'man' the 'firstfruits' out from among the dead (1 Corinthians 15:20). The Lord Jesus went into death in order to fill the earth with fruit for God; not only the earth, but that the whole universe should be filled with fruit arising from His death and resurrection. The death, burial, resurrection and glorification on high of our blessed Saviour, and the subsequent descent of the Holy Spirit at Pentecost, heralded the beginning of the 'new order' Christianity. When the natural man dies, his mortal remains lie buried in a grave where they corrupt. At the rapture, all the redeemed in the graves will rise first and be changed into the likeness of our Lord's glorious body. Then, within the time span of a twinkling of the eye, we Christians believers who are alive, will likewise be caught up and changed, and together meet the Lord in the clouds (1 Corinthians 15:52-53). The important truth within the context of our subject, is that the bodies of all the redeemed, past and present will be changed at the first resurrection, like unto His glorious body (Philippians 3:21.

When one sows seed wheat in the ground, all the endosperm making up the bulk of the seed is converted into sugars to nourish the developing embryo. Eventually, the embryonic structure develops into a plant and becomes self-sufficient through its own root system. During the seedling growth stages, the remnants of the original seed shrivel and rot. However, when the Lord Jesus likened Himself to 'a corn of wheat' that must fall into the ground and die, He knew that something unique to this world would happen when He laid down His life in death. First, friends of the Lord Jesus took His body down from the cross, then carefully and lovingly embalmed and wrapped it around before placing it in a new tomb.

Wheat
Triticum sativum

Now, unlike the natural man and ordinary seed corn, at no time while in the grave did the body of the Lord Jesus show signs of change, breakdown and decay. He had committed His Spirit into the hands of His Father; His soul was in Paradise (Luke 23:43), but His body lay in the tomb. Remember, He did die (John 10:17) and remained dead in the grave for three days; yet no corrupting influence invaded that unique vessel, prepared of God (Luke 1:35) in which our blessed Lord tabernacled here among men. The same body that was buried three days earlier, was raised in the power of resurrection life (Luke 24:46), unchanged and perfect, apart from the marks of His passion, by the glory of the Father (Romans 6:4). The Lord Jesus, as the incorruptible wheat grain, became the parent of a new order of things in which the saints, through sovereign grace, have a precious part (John 17:24). We rejoice even now, that the new heavenly order will fill the universe with fruit for God's eternal pleasure.

Thou wast alone, till like the precious grain,
In death Thou layest, but didst rise again;
And in Thy risen life, a countless host,
Are 'all of one' with Thee, Thy joy and boast.

T Willey

Cucumber

Cucumis chate

Hebrew: Qishshu = Hard and difficult to digest.
Numbers 11:5.

Cucumbers

Cucumis melo

Hebrew: Miqshah = A garden of cucumbers or cucumber patch.
Isaiah 1:8.

Melon

Cucumis melo

Numbers 11:5.

Opinion appears equally divided on the botanical identity of the cucumber. If we consider the fruit as being one of the Egyptian dainties at meal times, then, in all

probability it was cucumis chate, the fruit the Israelites lusted after while in the dry Sinai desert. The Israelites would have remembered the plant and fruit that flourished well in the rich soils of the Nile delta. The Egyptian agricultural economy depended on the flooding of the Nile delta each year for the enrichment of the agricultural land.

The meaning of the Hebrew word 'Qishshu' is sufficient to tell us that the fruit of cucumis chata was a constant cause of indigestion and probably pain. Most of us have probably experienced the uncomfortable after-effects from eating cucumbers. Furthermore, as with the majority of kinds and varieties in the cucurbit family, there is very little nourishment in their fruits. So what

Melon
Cucumis melo

lesson can we gain from the record that the Israelites lusted after cucumbers?

The food of the world will always conflict with our spiritual lives. If we try to mix the philosophies of the world with the spiritual teachings in the Word of God, we will most certainly have difficulty digesting both. Of one thing I am persuaded, if we daily feed our souls on the Word of God while seeking the help of the Holy Spirit to lead us into all Truth, we shall never get spiritual indigestion (2 Timothy 2:15). The apostle Paul warned the Christians at Colosse about the dangers of the philosophies of men. The JND translation of the Scriptures, gives Paul's warning in these words, "see that there be no one who shall lead you away as a prey through philosophy and vain deceit, according to the elements of the world" (Colossians 2:8). Moreover, the wisdom of this world will never nourish the spiritual soul, and over occupation with the things of this world will reduce our appetite for the heavenly manna, which is Christ. If we daily feed on God's Word, we shall, "grow in grace and in the knowledge of our Lord Jesus Christ" (2 Peter 3:18).

> *Lord, kindle within us a holy desire,*
> *Like that which was found in Thy people of old,*
> *Who tasted Thy love, and whose hearts were on fire,*
> *While waiting, in patience, Thy face to behold.*
>
> T Kelly

Cypress

Cupressus sempervirens

Hebrew: Tirzah = Tall, slender, tapering conifer.
Isaiah 44:14.

Although there is just the one reference in Scripture to cypress, it is in all probability a variety of the species to which the gopher tree belongs (Genesis 6:14). Some botanists

have thought the cypress tree to be the same as the fir and pine. If this is so, why does Isaiah elsewhere refer to both the latter trees in addition to the cypress? This leads me to believe they are different kinds of conifer. Of course, one cannot be certain about the correct identity of each type in botanical terms. Nevertheless, with God's help, I shall pursue my study on the basis that the cypress and the gopher are varieties of the same species. I shall develop my thoughts on the gopher-wood according to the alphabetical sequence of the listed plants.

The cypress tree is a tall, columnar shaped conifer that grows naturally in the same geographic region as the box and the cedar. While not having the majestic bearing of the cedar, the cypress is a most striking and impressive tree reaching 20 m or more in height. However, mention of the cypress in Isaiah 44 relates to the idolatry of the priesthood, the princes who stood out from among the people. They were the leaders of the nation who had lifted themselves up with pride and arrogance, becoming independent of Jehovah. In the context of our Scripture, we should note it is not by accident that the full meaning of the Hebrew noun Tirzah conveys the thought of being famished, weak and lean. The nation had misused the God-given pillars of support; wisdom, light, power and guidance – the towering strength of the cypress – and made idols out of those things that should have been used for the glory of Jehovah. Instead of the nation towering morally above the heathen, they had sunk below the lowest of the low. They were no longer the picture of strength whom the nations should have feared, rather the image of a thin, starving, weak and empty people.

The lesson of the cypress is this. Like Israel, God has blessed us in so many ways beyond anything we could possibly ask or think. Some of the towering pillars of truth we should treasure, are these. "The hope which is laid up for you (us) in heaven" (Colossians 1:5), "which hope we have as an anchor of the soul, both sure and steadfast" (Hebrews 6:19). "The peace of God that passeth all understanding, shall keep your (our) hearts and minds through Christ Jesus" (Philippians 4:7). The Lord Jesus imparted His peace to the disciples – and to us. He said, "peace I leave with you, my peace I give unto you, not as the world giveth give I unto you" (John 14:27). Perhaps the greatest pillar we have for support while we journey as pilgrims and strangers in a hostile world is, "the Truth as it is in Jesus" (Ephesians 4:21). Jesus said, "I am the Way, the Truth and the Life" (John 14:6). The most serious threat that Christian believers face today, is the open denial in Christendom of the Truth and authority of God's Word. The biblical pillars of Truth are being set aside and we are witnessing the removal of the ancient landmarks and the erasure of the old paths of Christianity. May our gracious Lord preserve us from mishandling and misusing His Word. "To hold fast till He come" (Revelation 2:25).

> *O may the very God of peace, us wholly sanctify,*
> *And grant us such an increase, rich, of power from on high.*
> *That spirit, soul and body may, preservèd free from stain,*
> *Be blameless still, 'til Thy great day, Lord Jesus Christ, Amen.*
>
> Anon.

Desire

Capparis spinosa

Hebrew: 'Abiyonah = The caper berry. A stimulant, appetiser.
Ecclesiastes 12:5.

The common caper berry that grows to a height of 1 m is a straggly, intricately branched, spiny, deciduous sub-shrub that appears to survive in dry, rocky places. The four-petal white flowers which come out at night and wither away at sunrise, have a prominent boss of mauve-coloured anthers. It is during the long night of our Lord's absence that the saints throughout the world should blossom to lighten this scene of moral darkness! The fruit is an oval, many-seeded, fleshy berry. Flower buds and fruit are pickled and used in cooking to stimulate appetite.

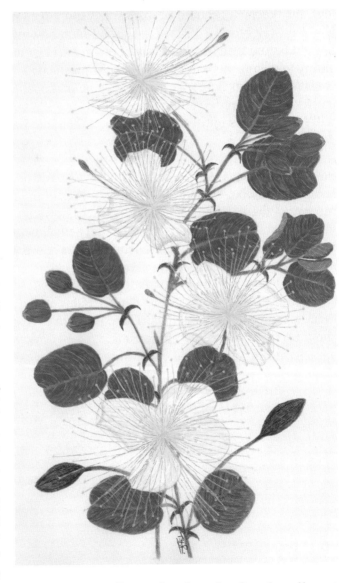

Ecclesiastes 12 is a comprehensive picture in words, of man in his old age. Consider for a moment the botanical definition of the plant; it is so much a picture of aged, unregenerate man. Sadly, many ageing and failing people become straggly; that is, they lose some of their personal dignity and orderly way of living. Some, like the shrub that is intricately branched, become mentally confused; and a few, happily not all, develop a prickly disposition. Finally, just as the shrub is deciduous, so aged people lose the evergreen image of eternal youth.

As an example of how Solomon graphically sketched the gradual demise of the human frame, let us look at verse 3 of chapter 12. We have the 'keepers' which are the hands and legs that tremble and wobble; the 'strong men bowing' relates to the bending of the spine; the 'grinders' are the teeth and the 'windows' refer to failing eyesight. When we come to the words in verse 5, 'and desire shall fail'; we see that the words clearly have reference to the advanced stages of decline when one loses all appetite for living or being stimulated. The way the Spirit of God led Solomon to write enables us to see and understand that all our physical faculties have their spiritual counterpart. Our hands and legs, the 'keepers', should be exclusively employed in doing God's will and walking in His ways (Hebrews 13:21). The 'strong men bowing' challenges our hearts to remain upright before God in all our ways (Psalm 84:11). Our teeth, the 'grinders' speak of our ability to take in the Word of God, chew, masticate and assimilate its full benefit for our souls (Colossians 3:16). The 'windows be darkened', would remind us that we should daily keep our eye fixed upon our blessed Lord; otherwise, the attractions of the world will blind our vision of the way along which our Lord would lead us (Psalm 139:23-24).

Solomon knew that to take account of one's Creator in the early years of one's life, by listening and obeying God's Word, would result in lasting blessing. Old age would not rob any of the blessings God bountifully bestows on all that fear Him. All our spiritual faculties would remain viable, strong and active, being daily stimulated by the Word of God and by time spent in the sanctuary of the Lord.

Spiritually, we should continue to be as Moses was at the end of his days (Deuteronomy 34:7). A serious danger today is the risk of Christian believers losing their appetite for divine things. There is much to learn and do, and much to which we should look forward to (Philippians 3:13-14). May the Spirit of God stimulate our appetite for the manna that came from heaven, even our Lord Jesus Christ.

> *Bread for our souls, whereon we feed, true manna from on high;*
> *Our guide and chart wherein we read, of realms beyond the sky.*
>
> B Barton

Dove's dung

Ornithogalum narbonense, subsp. Brachystachys

Hebrew: Dibyon = A cheap bulbous vegetable.
2 Kings 6:25.

Biblical scholars remain divided on the true translation of the Hebrew word dibyon. However, eminent botanists such as Carolus Linnaeus et al, believe dibyon refers to the plant genus, ornithogalum of the lily family. The context, in which the reference to

dove's dung occurs, would strongly suggest that Linnaeus was correct in his trans-lation. Ornithogalum has a bulbous root, narrow linear leaves with a flower spike no higher than 10 cm. The flowers have six white petals marked with a narrow green stripe. According to Nigel Hepper, ornithogalum grows freely on gravelly hillsides in Palestine, and from a distance the flowers appear like doves droppings, which is probably how origin-ally the plant got its common name.

In the days of Elisha the prophet, Ben-hadad king of Syria besieged Samaria to occasion a great famine in the city. The severity of the famine was such that the price for anything edible soared beyond the reach of most. The people resorted to cannibalism. So desperate were the people for food that, although ornithogalum bulbs have very little nutritional value, they dug them up to eat and to sell in the market. Israel greatly suffered under successive evil kings and neighbouring forces; often because of their idolatry and disobedience, but the Lord would not desert them. In spite of their waywardness, the nation remained the apple of His eye (Deuteronomy 32:9-10). Jehovah had determined punishment on the Syrians for their cruelty to His people. He would terrorise them with the noise of an approaching phantom army, knowing they would flee for their lives leaving behind all their possessions. The nightmare the Syrians experienced, brought to pass the words of the Lord, "on the morrow, a measure of fine flour would be sold for a shekel, and two measures of barley for a shekel in the gate of Samaria" (2 Kings 7:1). The famine ended.

Sometimes, the Lord's people suffer inexplicably and have to resort to the most meagre of resources to sustain any hope of recovery. Happily, it is a comfort to know something of the Lord's mercies in such circumstances; for we are not called upon to suffer beyond what we are able to bear (1 Corinthians 10:13). The secret is to get the spiritual gain of such experiences. "No chastening for the present, seemeth to be joyous, but grievous; nevertheless afterward it yieldeth the peaceable fruit of righteousness unto them which are exercised thereby" (Hebrews 12:11).

> *Though trials and affliction, may cast their shadows o'er us,*
> *Thy love doth throw a heavenly glow of light on all before us.*
> *That love has smiled from heaven, to cheer our path of sadness,*
> *And lead the way through earth's dark day, to realms of joy and gladness.*
>
> H Ware

Ebony

Diospyros ebenum

Hebrew: Hoben = Very hard, dark wood.
Ezekiel 27:15.

Diospyros ebenum is an evergreen, growing to a height of 20 m or more. The value of the wood is in the heart of the trunk. The wood in the outer sapwood layer of the trunk is white and of no value, while the core of the trunk is very hard, jet-black and of great worth. Unlike many trees, the ebony does not rot in the centre as it gets older; rather, the wood becomes harder as the tree ages. Mature trees can yield timbers up to 60 cm in diameter and 300 – 450 cm in length.

The lesson of the ebony tree is this. The natural man is of no value to God and nothing he does can give Him pleasure. The white sapwood of the tree parallels the life and works of the flesh in the natural man, and the centre core corresponds to man's immortal soul that is coloured by the evidence of a fallen nature. Although God has determined that no flesh (or works of the flesh) should glory in His presence (1 Corinthians 1:29), the power of His Spirit does bring about a change in the character of the soul (sinner) who repents.

The trunk of the ebony tree is a very good figure of the natural, unregenerate man; white and active on the outside, but black and dead on the inside. The outer layer of the trunk, called the sapwood, is the area of activity that continues unabated until the tree dies. The sapwood is a type of the natural man working independent of God's mind. All that is visible and active in the outer layers of the ebony trunk parallels the definition the Lord Jesus gave concerning the Pharisees. Whited sepulchres, appearing pure, beautiful and active on the outside, but within, full of dead men's bones and all uncleanness (Matthew 23:27-28). The works of man can never save a soul from the condemnation God has passed on all men, "for all have sinned and come short of the glory of God" (Romans 3:23). Furthermore, God has said, "by grace are ye saved through faith, and that not of yourselves, it is the gift of God. Not by works, lest any man should boast" (Ephesians 2:8-9).

Between the outer white wood and the inner black wood of the ebony tree, is an intermediate area where the wood is neither white nor black. This kind of wood is analogous to Christendom in general and is not that far removed from the judgment of the Lord on the Church at Laodicea when it was charged with being neither hot nor cold (Revelation 3:15-16). The world is full people who are professors, but not possessors of the eternal life that comes through repentance before God and faith in our Lord Jesus Christ (Acts 20:21). The lives and hopes of such individuals who bear the titular title of 'Christian', amount to a mixture of reliance on the works of the flesh and a nominal belief in the God of creation. Happily, the day of God's grace continues, giving all mankind the opportunity to take God at His Word; repent and believe according to the Scriptures. Paul's words to Timothy are both reassuring and a comfort. "Nevertheless, the foundation of God standeth sure, having this seal: the Lord knoweth them that are His; and let every one that nameth the Name of the Lord, depart from iniquity" (2 Timothy 2:19).

The spouse in Song of Solomon 1:5, speaking to those not in the enjoyment of intimacy with the Beloved, said, "I am black". The spouse, while acknowledging what she is by nature, goes on to confess what sovereign grace has accomplished, by adding, 'but comely'. According to the teaching of Romans 6:11-13, Christian believers are to reckon their old nature dead, but they themselves, as born anew, alive unto God through our Lord Jesus Christ. Living by the power of the Spirit of God will quench the activity of the flesh to allow the graces of our Lord Jesus Christ to radiate through our life and person. Furthermore, our light will shine the brighter if we daily and readily accept for ourselves the words of the apostle Paul, "for I know that in me (that is, in my flesh) dwelleth no good thing" (Romans 7:18).

So what is God able to do with the soul that believes yet remains black? Freshly felled ebony timber is dull, dead looking, rough and unattractive; very much like the condition of all believers in the Lord Jesus the moment before they were saved. Happily, ebony timber is not left or used in its raw, rough-cut state. The craftsman will plane, fashion, buff and polish it before putting it to use. We might say that the work of the craftsman on the natural wood parallels the work of the Holy Spirit on the newborn soul. The moment a sinner repents and believes in the Lord Jesus Christ, they are baptised with the Holy Spirit of God. The once dead, dark soul is now in-dwelt with the power and life of the Lord Jesus. God has said in His Word, "and this is the record, that God hath given us eternal life, and this life is in His Son. He that hath the Son hath life" (1 John 5:11-12).

The miracle of God's grace is this; His Holy Spirit is able to transform something, which to the natural eye is dull and lifeless, into an object radiating the moral excellencies of the Lord Jesus. When one looks upon a piece of highly polished ebony, the eye immediately focuses upon the brightness and radiance of the reflected light that appears to emanate from the very body of the object. It is the lustre of the polished ebony, not its colour that establishes the value of the wood (1 Corinthians 6:19-20). So it is with the Christian believer today, the value and power of the new life (divine nature) will always be evident if we heed the words of the Lord Jesus. "Let your light shine before men that they may see your good works, and glorify your Father, which is in heaven" (Matthew 5:16). We must ever remember that our old dead nature cannot possibly reflect anything that is of God or be for His delight. May the Lord help us to shine for Him every day as we seek to move in the current of His Will.

> *Let the beauty of Jesus be seen in me,*
> *His wondrous compassion and purity see;*
> *By His Spirit divine, my new nature shine,*
> *Let the beauty of Jesus be seen in me.*
>
> Anon

Fig

Ficus carica

Hebrew: Te'en; common fig tree. Pag = Young, green, hard and unripe figs. Greek: Olunthos = Out of season, unripe figs. Sukon = A fig fruit. Suke = common fig tree. Gen. 3:7 + fifty-five other references.

There are two species of fig referred to in the Scriptures, ficus carica, and ficus sycomorus. Ficus carica is first mentioned in Genesis 3:7, and is the fig with which we all are familiar. When Adam and Eve were convicted of their sin of disobedience, they took the leaves of the fig tree and made aprons to cover their nakedness. We shall consider the mulberry fig (ficus sycomorus) later under its common name, sycomore. Ficus carica grows into a moderate size, bushy tree reaching a height rarely above 5 m with a spread of 20 m or more. The tree is deciduous, and although lacking in symmetry, its sprawling branches provide excellent shade in the heat of the day.

The great majority of biblical scholars accept that the fig tree in Scripture speaks of Israel as a nation that, through divine culture under the law, failed to yield for God the sweet fruits of goodness and righteousness. God said, "I saw your fathers as the

Ficus carica

firstripe in the fig tree at her first time; but they went to Baalpeor (idolatry) and separated themselves unto that shame" (Hosea 9:10). It is not without significance that we have the fig referred to in Genesis 3:7. The fig tree in the first instance speaks of man and his potential in the world where God had placed him; in innocence, his life was to be lived by practical righteousness for the glory of God.

However, man's disobedience proved him incapable of living righteously (Romans 3:10-12). Before God had to cast man out from His paradise on earth, it was His plan that man should have dominion over all plants and animals. Furthermore, under the influence of God's goodness, man would multiply and be more fruitful than any other creature in creation. It is worthy of note that the ratio of the number of seeds to the volume of flesh in a single fig fruit, gives it a potential for the highest level of reproduction above all other fruit bearing trees. The fig tree speaks of the sweet 'fruit of righteousness' which Israel signally failed to produce for the glory of God. Paul prayed that the Church at Philippi might be filled with the fruit of righteousness (Philippians 1:11). We would do well to ask ourselves; what do we understand from the expression, fruit of righteousness? The phrase occurs four times in the Scriptures. In Amos 6:12, Amos says; 'Ye have turned judgment into gall and the fruit of righteousness into hemlock'. James says; 'The fruit of righteousness is sown in peace of them that make peace' (James 3:18); and Hebrews 12:11 says that the chastening hand of the Father; 'yieldeth the peaceable fruit of righteousness unto them that are exercised thereby'. Accordingly, we may safely say that the 'fruit of righteousness' relates to the divine qualities in the life of the Christian believer that reflect the moral attributes of our Lord Jesus Christ who indwells our mortal beings. Our lives are hid with Christ in God (Colossians 3:3)

In the Mediterranean region, the fig tree carries fruit all year round. The figs seen on leafless fig trees in the winter will mature and ripen to be the first fruits the following spring. So, no matter what time of the year one may go to the fig tree, there should always be fruit or the promise of fruit. One can therefore understand the great disappointment of the Lord Jesus who, being hungry and seeing a fig tree before Him, found nothing but leaves. The Lord pronounced a miraculous summary judgment on the tree (Matthew 21:18-20). The Lord's action on that occasion signalled God's coming judgment on Israel, the nation that had failed to yield the expected fruits of righteousness, sweetness and goodness. The Lord's reference to the faith of the disciples was, that if they had the faith, they could say to the mountain that was in view, 'be thou removed and be thou cast into the sea, and it shall be done'. In this figure, the mountain was Israel, the chosen of God who morally, should have stood out and above the nations around, but they were no different, perhaps even worse. The nation had failed to produce fruit for the pleasure of God. Nearly 40 years later under Titus the Emperor, son of Vespasian, Israel (the mountain) was cast down and scattered among the nations (the sea) of the world and thereby lost her distinctive identity.

Paul spoke of Israel as, "being ignorant of God's righteousness, and going about to establish their own righteousness, have not submitted themselves unto the righteousness of God" (Romans 10:3). Israel ignored the words of Isaiah who said, "all our righteousnesses are as filthy rags" (Isaiah 64:6). Sadly, in Christendom today there is a great show of leaves, with little or no fruit for God. As with the fig tree, the abundance of foliage conceals the absence of fruit. Let us beware of hyperactivity in the service of God. There are many Scriptures to confirm that the servant of the Lord should have a quiet and meek spirit (Colossians 3:12 – 16).

The best quality figs in any year are those of the first crop following the winter when the tree puts forth its new leaves. In the spiritual realm, we are always in that period when God is expecting the best fruit from our lives; i.e. the product of the profession of our faith. There should never be an occasion in our lives when we are not witnessing to the goodness and sweetness of God. Furthermore, we should ever have available some good and sweet sustaining food to nourish Christian believers.

The leaves of the fig tree are palmately veined and set forth the practical side of Christianity. James said, "faith without works is dead" (James 2:14-20). "Whatsoever our hand findeth to do (in the service of God) do it with thy might" (Ecclesiastes 9:10). The words of the Lord Jesus, are, "I must work the works of Him that sent me while it is day, the night cometh when no man can work" (John 9:4). The leaves of a plant absorb energy from the sun to enable them to draw up from the earth all the essential nutrients for conversion into growth, flowers and fruits. All the time we are wholly energised by the power of the Spirit, our endeavours will result in fruit for God.

Of all the flowering fruit trees in God's creation, the fig tree is the only one on which the flowers are not visible. Flowering shrubs and trees are primarily grown for the beauty of their flowers. The flowers of the fig on the other hand add nothing to the general appearance of the tree. The hundreds of star-shaped, translucent white flowers are borne on the inside of the receptacle (syconium) which develops into the fig we eat. The way in which the fig tree flowers tells us that in our service for God, nothing should be done with a view to courting the praise, respect and the admiration of mankind. We should not seek to enhance our image or heighten the esteem others may have of us. If you expose the flowers in a developing fig to the light of day, the fruit will wither. So with us, if in our service we seek the honour, praise and reward of men, there will be no glory, honour or fruit for God; neither will there be spiritual profit for the Christian believer. The hypocrites loved the praises of men; the Lord Jesus said of them, "...they have their reward" (Matthew 6:2,5,16).

Throughout our Saviour's life on earth, there shone forth from Him a unique moral beauty that was exclusive to the eye of God. Because of the moral excellencies of His beloved Son, God's Spirit reposed in Him with divine complacency, and God said of Him, "this is my beloved Son, in whom I am well pleased" (Matthew 3:17). Like the unseen flowers of the fig, our Lord's inner qualities as dependant man brought glory to God. His heart was set to do the will of Him that sent Him; His ear was open morning by morning to hear what the Lord His God would speak. These were the moral attributes that pleased His Father (John 8: 29). Paul said, "ye ought to walk to please God" (1 Thessalonians 4:1).

Hezekiah, King of Judah, on learning of the death of his archenemy Sennacherib, King of Assyria; was lifted up with pride as though he himself had achieved the victory (2 Chronicles 32:22-26). Because of Hezekiah's pride, God laid him low with a sickness unto death. God's purpose in dealing with Hezekiah in this way was to judge the flesh, bring it to nothing and show that any power opposing the people of God, can only be destroyed by God. Nothing can be achieved for the glory of God by the action of the flesh (1 Corinthians 1:29). The poultice of figs placed on Hezehiah's terminal boil, symbolised the curative power, goodness and righteousness of God's intervention (2 Kings 20:7).

The fig tree also speaks of security, prosperity and peace. It remains God's plan for His people, "that every one should sit under his vine and under his fig tree" (Micah 4:4; Zechariah 3:10}. A foretaste of God's purpose was Israel's experience in the days of Solomon, from Dan in the north to Beer-sheba in the south (1 Kings 4:25). In God's time, the nation will be prosperous, secure and at peace, experiencing the unparalleled goodness and sweetness of the nature of God in His righteousness toward them. In the

Song of Songs 2:13, Matthew 24:32, and other Scriptures, the fig tree is referred to in parabolic terms that, "when its buds begin to burst, it will denote that summer is near". In other words; the Millennial age of glory is imminent, when righteousness shall reign in the earth.

God's mercy, love and righteousness,
Were seen on earth in Christ, His Son,
Christ's goodness, sweetness, richness, strength,
Preserves His own with Him, as one.

T H Ratcliffe

Fir

Juniperus excelsa

Hebrew: Berosh or Beroth = A lance or musical instrument; wood that is pliable.
2 Samuel 6:5 + twenty other references.

With the exception of the cedar of Lebanon, the exact identity in botanical terms of each of the various conifers mentioned in the Scripture remains uncertain. However, with careful consideration to the context in which each of the conifer names appear, it is possible with the Lord's help, to settle for specific species as they are known today.

Juniperus excelsa, known also as the Grecian Juniper, is a pyramidal, evergreen tree reaching a height between 24 & 30 m. The tree flourishes in the same mountainous region as the box and cedar. Fir wood, although tough and resilient in its nature, is soft and sonorous in its responses; and it was for these qualities that David preferred fir wood for the construction of musical instruments. Throughout our consideration of the conifers mentioned in Scripture, we shall inevitably be guided in our thoughts to the time of which Isaiah spoke, "sing O heavens, and be joyful O earth, and break forth into singing O mountains. For the Lord hath comforted His people, and will have mercy upon His afflicted" (Isaiah 49:13). Isaiah was writing about the time when Israel will be healed, restored and settled in the land, to lead the praises on earth to the King and Sovereign of the universe. Psalm 149 takes up the theme of the praises on earth in that coming day, while Psalm 150 refers to the praises that will sound throughout the heavens among the redeemed. The chorus on earth and in the heavens will echo throughout the courts of the heaven of heavens as recorded in Revelation 5:12-14.

The heart of the Christian believer, like the fir wood, is soft and sonorous. Being indwelt by the Spirit of God, our heart has become a musical instrument in the hand of the Master Musician. Our Lord longs to pluck the cords of our heart to occasion the sound of praise. "Unto Him that loved us, and washed us from our sins in His own blood; and hath made us a kingdom of priests unto God and His Father. To Him be glory and dominion for ever and ever, Amen" (Revelation 1:5-6).

> *Of the vast universe of bliss, the Centre Thou and Sun;*
> *The eternal theme of praise is this, that God's beloved Son,*
> *Fills all that scene, where God alone in His own rest is fully known.*
>
> J. Conder (arr.)

Fitches

Nigella sativa

Hebrew: Qetsach = To incise, pungent.
Isaiah 28:25 & 27.

Nigella sativa is the familiar blue flowered 'love in the mist' that can be found growing in almost every country of the world. Nigella belongs to the buttercup family of plants, known also as fennel flower and black cummin. The plant is a hardy annual growing to a height of 45 cm with rich green, graceful and feathery foliage. Harvesting the jet-black seed is by very gentle beating of the plant haulm (Isaiah 28:27). Middle Eastern countries call the nigella seed, 'the seed of blessing', because an infusion of the ground seed is said to be an effective medicine for a wide range of diseases. On the other hand, the juices from the root, stem and leaves are extremely noxious. The black seeds are useful as a condiment, and bakers frequently sprinkle the top of their loaves with the seed before baking. Even the lowly plants in God's creation have a place in man's economy.

All parts of the nigella plant; the foliage, flowers and seed are quite delicate and easily

damaged. One can therefore understand why the prophet Isaiah was concerned about the kind of tools used to thrash out the seed. Every child of God is a delicate vessel, indwelt with the Spirit of God. Satan's purpose in this world is to damage and weaken the newborn vessel and thereby render it unsuitable for the service of God (Romans 12:1 & 3). Our ongoing service is to bear much fruit, and so glorify the Father. One might say that the Christian believer is like the delicate nigella plant, with foliage graceful and pretty, and flowers heavenly blue. However, 'appearance' is not fruit for

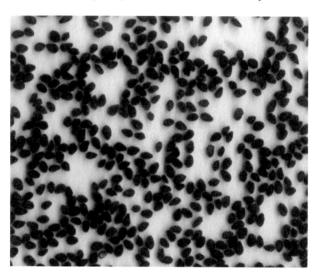

God. So what is it that God is looking for that will give Him pleasure? God is looking for fruit that is distinct in every detail to the form and natural makeup of the plant (vessel). In our analogy, the fruit is the seed that in appearance, size, colour and form bears no resemblance whatsoever to any part of the plant, yet the seed is the end product of the plant. God's gracious Spirit is working in and through His children to produce something that is of the Spirit and not of the flesh (Philippians 2:13).

We said earlier that every child of God is like a delicate plant. The Lord Jesus said as much when talking to His disciples. "Whosoever therefore shall humble himself as this little child, the same is greatest in the kingdom of heaven…, but whoso shall offend one of these little ones which believe in me, it were better for him that a millstone were hanged about his neck, and that he were drowned in the depth of the sea" (Matthew 18:4 & 6). Sadly, many of God's children suffer injury by the misuse of God's precious Word. Instead of being gentle with the application of the Scriptures, we use a flail (Isaiah 28:27) to beat the saints into submission, just like the cruel shepherds of Israel (Ezekiel 34:4 latter clause). If we misuse or damage the delicate plant (any child of God), it will be tantamount to robbing God of the fruit He has every right to expect from His children. May our gracious Lord touch our hearts to exercise a loving, caring and gentle disposition toward all, especially those of the household of faith (1 Thessalonians 2:7).

Help us O God, to handle well Thy Word,
Kind, gentle, truthful, like our blessed Lord;
The precious food, for lambs that are His own,
That, they may grow in grace, like Him alone.

T H Ratcliffe

Flag (1)

Cyperus esculentus

Hebrew: 'Achu = A marsh-loving reed, meadow.
Job 8:11.

The common name flag can be misleading because the plant is quite different to the lovely flag iris found growing in English gardens. Cyperus esculentus belongs to a family of plants known as cyperaceae; it flourishes in the mire of shallow water. It is a half-hardy perennial with long, tuber-bearing runners immersed in the watery mire. When the reed-like plant flowers, it produces a mass of long green stems drooping in umbrella-like fashion. If the marsh dries out, the plant withers and dies.

Bearing in mind Job's extremely adverse state of health, Bildad the Shuhite, a supposed friend and comforter of Job, is very unkind and misleading in some of his statements to him. Bildad's counsel was much like the proverbial Curate's egg, 'good in parts'. Job had lost everything including his children; and to add to his sufferings, painful boils covered his body from head to toe. Job needed to be encouraged to adopt the correct disposition toward God in his heart and soul; forgetting his own righteousness, and casting himself on the righteousness of God and His grace. In due course Job did adopt

the correct attitude before his God; he owned his nothingness and bowed before His creator in sackcloth and ashes (Job 42:6).

Meanwhile, Bildad continues with his questionable counselling using a similitude to enhance his message. "Can the flag grow without water? While it is yet in his greenness and not cut down, it withereth before any herb. So are the paths of all that forget God, and the hypocrite's hope shall perish" (Job 8:11-13). The flag plant is here likened unto a hypocrite; it may for a while look green, fresh, bright and healthy; but only for show; very soon and quite unexpectedly it withers and dies; so it is with the hypocrite. Like the flag, the hypocrite anchors himself in miry clay, an unstable foundation that spells certain death. The sweet Psalmist of Israel knew something about the hazards of miry clay (Psalm 40:2). The Lord Jesus also warns of the dangers of building up your faith on moving sands; those who ignore such a warning, face disaster (Matthew 7:24-27). It has always been God's plan to prosper the just and to root out the wicked, albeit, for a time the unjust may appear to flourish (Psalm 73:3).

Still sweet 'tis to discover, if clouds have dimmed my sight,
When passed, eternal Lover, toward's me, as e'er, Thou'rt bright.
O keep my soul, then, Jesus, abiding still with Thee,
And if I wander, teach me soon back to Thee to flee.

J N Darby

Flag (2)
Typha latifolium

Hebrew: Suph = A Red-sea water weed. Bulrush or Reed Mace.
Exodus 2:3 & 5 + two other references.

The Typha plant grows equally well in salt or fresh water. It was on the bank of a river leading into the Red Sea, among the moderately tall clumps of reed, that for security purposes, Moses' mother placed the ark holding her son. The typha plant develops stems up to 2 m high; terminating with the characteristic light-brown spike of closely packed flowers. As the specific Latin name 'latifolium' implies, the long leaves of the bulrush are broad when compared with the majority of other reed plants, making it an ideal water weed in which to conceal the little ark.

We have already considered the spiritual significance of the ark made of the reed plant, cyperus papyrus, and the placing of Moses in the ark. The ark was secure on a clump of reed mace to ensure stability and anchorage. I liken the clump of reed to the position of the Christian in this world. While the world is a place of death (the water), we who are in Christ should morally stand above the deathly influences that daily assail us from every side. The Lord has His eye on each one of us, just as Moses' sister kept a watchful eye on her baby brother. While Miriam would have been happy about the position and standing of Moses, which she deemed secure; she remained concerned for his state, hence her faithful vigilance. Our standing in Christ is secure and unchanging because of the efficacy of His precious blood shed at Calvary. However, the moral and spiritual state of many Christians is a matter of considerable concern. Perhaps we should challenge our hearts and ask, "how often am I cleansed (morally) by the washing of water by the word"? (Ephesians 5:26). May we experience a daily washing by His Word to maintain us in sweet communion with our Lord Jesus Christ, and with the Father through Him (John 13:8).

Thy Word, Thyself reflecting, doth sanctify by Truth,
Still leading on Thy loved ones, with gentle, heav'nly growth.
Thus still the work proceedeth, O Lord begun by Thee;
In each, made meet, through training; Saviour, with Thee to be.

S P Tregelles (arr)

Flax

Linum usitatissimum

Hebrew: Pishtah = Flax, wick, tow, white linen.
Exodus 9:31 + two other references.
Hebrew: Pishteh. Greek: Linon, = The finest thread. Carded and purified.
Leviticus 13:47 + fourteen other references.

There are five additional Hebrew nouns for 'linen' covering 65 references. The most significant of which is 'Sheshiy' = pure, white, fine twined linen. When Joseph was exalted by Pharaoh, he was arrayed in Sheshiy (Genesis 41:42). The next time we read about such high quality material is in Exodus 25:4 and in subsequent verses and chapters as Moses was receiving instruction from Jehovah in the Mount. From Exodus 35 we have the construction of the Tabernacle, including the making of the priests clothes from 'fine twined linen' after the pattern shown Moses in the Mount (Exodus 26:30). 'Sheshiy' in Exodus, refers to the material for the Tabernacle and the garments of glory and beauty for Aaron the High Priest. The noun also applies to the functional clothes Aaron and his sons had to wear when they served as priests. In the New Testament, we have five Greek nouns in 17 references, all referring to different

processes and qualities of linen. With the Lord's help, I purpose to centre my thoughts on the carded, pure, white, fine twined linen, while embracing all other references to linen.

The type of flax mentioned in the Scripture, now cultivated commercially for its fibre, is an annual, growing a little over 1m. high. The long stems head up with a delicate blue, five-petal flower. The plant also yields a modest amount of oil seed. Harvesting flax involves uprooting the whole plant. The long stems are carefully bundled together into sheaves, then set upright in stooks to dry, in much the same way farmers reaped their corn crops before the advent of the combine harvester. When the flax straw has dried, it undergoes a process know as 'retting'. The modern way of retting is to soak the straw in ponds, streams or specially constructed water tanks to promote the decomposition and removal of the fleshy part of the stem. The retting process takes about a week or two, depending on air temperatures. In biblical days, the straw lay on the ground or on flat roofs for weeks to expose it to cyclic wetting, drying, freezing and thawing; and although the retting process took very much longer, it was just as effective. The retted straw is then dried (Joshua 2:6) and crushed by rolling to facilitate the separation of the long fibre strands from the remaining fleshy part of the stem. The next process is called carding or hackling, the combing out of long straight threads ready for use in the manufacture of high quality linen; (a reference to hackling, the combing out of flax can be found in Isaiah 19:9). Broken pieces of fibre, called tow, are not wasted, but used for the production of cheaper materials the poor can afford to buy.

The preparation of flax fibres for spinning and weaving reminds one of the natural seed dispersal of the luffa plant, a member of the same family as the cucumber. The luffa grows wild in Middle Eastern Countries; its long, fleshy fruits remain lying on the ground long after the parent plant has shrivelled and disappeared. The cycle of rain and sunshine, cold and heat brings about a breakdown of the hard fruit. Eventually, the skin and flesh rot away, leaving a long, netted structure full of seed. The luffa, when free of all flesh, is driven by the wind across the desert ground. Through an orifice at one end of the netted structure, the luffa seed is scattered over a wide area. The examples of the flax and the luffa have a clear message for us all. We cannot be of service to the Lord in ministry and in spreading the Word of the Gospel, until the flesh – the old nature – has disappeared out of sight, dead and buried (Romans 6:4 & 11-13).

The expression, 'fine twined linen' implies that the individual strands of fibre were spun together to bind and strengthen the linen thread. The Lord would have His people working together to strengthen the local testimony. According to 2 Corinthians 6:4-10, the apostle Paul had been severely processed, and like the flax straw; it could truly be said of him, he was a pure fibre suited for service in the Lord's work. Yet Paul did not want to labour alone; identifying himself with the Corinthian Christians, he said, "we then as workers together with Him, beseech you also that ye receive not the grace of

God in vain" (2 Corinthians 6:1). The 'fine twined linen' speaks of the personal purity, moral glory and practical righteousness of the Lord Jesus Christ. We read, "He knew no sin" (2 Corinthians 5:21); "He did no sin" (1 Peter 2:22); "And in Him is no sin" (1John 3:5). In John 8:46 the Lord Jesus challenges the Pharisees, "can any of you prove me guilty of sin"?

Together with the instructions for making the Holy garments for Aaron and his sons; it is recorded six times in Exodus 39 that everything was to be made as, "the Lord commanded Moses". The women in the congregation of Israel played an important role in spinning, weaving and making the curtains and garments; at no time did they attempt to implant their own particular stamp in the divine design of the work. The silent industry of the women accorded with the will of Jehovah. There are many examples in the Scripture of women who quietly went about fulfilling their designated roles. Ruth was one such person; noted for her faithfulness, commitment, industry, modesty, affection and a willingness to sit and be still until she knew the mind of her master. Then we have Esther; her record in chapter two of the book bearing her name, is of a God fearing person going about her duties faithfully, with integrity and with a meek spirit. Because of Esther's godly disposition, God used her as a channel for blessing His own people. Mary, the sister of Martha and Lazarus, sets a lovely example for us all. In Luke 10:39-42, Mary was quietly sitting and listening to what the Lord Jesus was saying. Not a busybody, rushing around requesting that her voice be heard and her opinions taken into account; no, Jesus said to her sister Martha, "Mary hath chosen that good part, which shall not be taken away from her". In the book of the Acts, chapter 9 we read of Dorcas who was gifted in needlework and dress-making; she was also well known for her moral integrity. The Lord intervened in the life of Dorcas when she fell sick and later died. The apostle Peter revives Dorcas, and her testimony resulted in the salvation of many souls. While there are many other examples in the Scriptures; Peter in his first epistle, very succinctly summarises the godly disposition that should mark all Christian believers (1 Peter 3:4).

The Holy garments were not for sleeping in, nor were the priests to wear them in order to vainly vaunt themselves. The special clothes Aaron and his sons wore while they ministered as priests and daily served in the sanctuary, represented the holiness of Jehovah and His righteousness, and therefore stood for what was suitable in His presence. There may have been times when the priests were not wearing their priestly garments, in that event they could not partake in the service of the sanctuary. There are times when Christian believers are not morally suited to function as worshippers or engage in evangelical service; such occasions should generate deep exercise of soul and spirit. The apostle Paul said, "seeing ye have put off the old man with his deeds; and have put on the new man, which is renewed in knowledge after the image of him that created him" (Colossians 3:9-10). The apostle's words imply the need for a new moral apprehension of what is suitable to God. Today, through God's sovereign grace, Christian believers are clothed with His righteousness – they have none of their own

(Isaiah 64:6) – in order to serve and to worship the Father in Spirit and in Truth. Arrayed in His righteousness implies that the saints of God have their minds clothed and hearts filled with the divine worth and glory enveloping that blessed Person. The practical working out of this truth in our lives will include the clothing of our hearts and minds with holy thoughts about fellow believers (Philippians 4:8).

Matthew 12:15, records how the Lord Jesus withdrew Himself from the 'face to face' opposition of the Pharisees. Our Lord's action was in fulfilment of the prophecy in Isaiah 42:3. The Lord's presence humiliated and annoyed the Pharisees, for their pride and power base had been sorely bruised and fractured. Unlike the Lord Jesus, they could not do the miracles, perform the wonders nor interpret the prophetic signs. The Lord noted the wickedness of their hearts, but would not immediately and finally break the bruised reed, i.e. judge them as Sovereign Lord; rather, He would give them time to repent. Although the Pharisees were in figure like offensive smouldering flax, he would not quench the glimmer of light that was there, but for the time being bear with them, just as He did with Jerusalem. On the other hand, His own people were sorely battered and bruised.

Following the death of Solomon, the nation became two separate kingdoms, and the glory of Jehovah departed from them. Nebuchadnezzar had carried away to Babylon all the vessels of the House of the Lord, which would have included the, "Ark of the Covenant" (2 Chronicles 36:7). Nevertheless, Jehovah will not break the bruised reed, but restore it and make it a mighty cedar (Ezekiel 17:22-24). The light of the nation is just an ember at the present; the potential to light up is evident, but unbelief and disobedience keeps the flax smouldering. In a soon coming day, the Lord in His mercy will blow on the ember to light it up into a universal flame (Isaiah 42:1-7). A straw of flax being easily fractured, it is a symbol of weakness. The individual fibre strands are weaker still, but when skilfully twined together, produce a cord not easily broken (Ecclesiastes 4:12).

The last reference to 'fine linen' is in Revelation 19:8, "and to her (the Bride) it was granted that she should be arrayed in fine linen, clean and white, for the 'fine linen' is the righteousness of saints". The false church, the great Babylon and mother of harlots, had arrayed herself with earthly glory and held a cup full of abominations (Revelation 17:4-5). The true Church (the Bride) on the other hand, made no claim as to how she should be adorned, but acknowledged the sovereign mercy and grace of God who had made her fit for glory; see Colossians 1:12. It was therefore, given to her that she should be suitably adorned for the Bridegroom. The righteousnesses of Christian believers will exclusively comprise every recorded act on earth that was in alignment with divine thought. Before we can fully enter the joy of the 'marriage of the Lamb', our path of service must be reviewed before the judgment seat (Bema) of Christ (2 Corinthians 5:10). It will be before the Bema that everything in our service or otherwise on earth will be manifested between us personally and our blessed Redeemer.

Everything unrighteous we have committed in our Christian pathway will be set aside; we shall delight see it happen and then rejoice in the righteous judgment of the Lord. This is our Lord's objective in what He is now doing, "He loved the Church and gave Himself for it, that He might sanctify and cleanse it with the washing of water by the Word. That He might present it to Himself a glorious church, not having spot or wrinkle, or any such thing, but that it should be holy and without blemish" (Ephesians 5:25-27). We might rightly say, that the Christian believers are putting together their 'wedding garment' stitch by stitch as their righteous activities, in the power of the Spirit of God, are recorded in heaven. In that coming day, the church, arrayed in 'fine linen, clean and white' will be, "presented faultless before the presence of His glory with exceeding joy" (Jude 24).

With Thee in garments white, Lord Jesus we shall walk,
And spotless in that heavenly light, of all Thy sufferings talk.
Yet still we wait for Thee, to see Thee as Thou art;
Be with Thee, like Thee, Lord, and free, to love with all our heart.

J N Darby

Frankincense

Boswellia sacra

Hebrew: Lebonah. Greek: Libanos = Fragrant, pure white smoke, free burning.
Incense; something from the heart. Known also as Gum Olibanum.
Exodus 30:34 + twenty-two other references.

Boswellia is a shrubby, multi-branch evergreen tree, bearing spikes of white, five-petal flowers. The plant naturally exudes the fragrant resin through its leaves, twigs and papery bark. Incising the main branches of the boswellia plant greatly increases the flow of resin. The transparent to yellow coloured resin, quickly turns reddish pink on exposure to the air.

The Hebrew name for frankincense derives from the white, milk-like colour of the resin, and from the whiteness of the smoke the resin produces when fired. The fragrance of burning frankincense is recognised as the finest in the world. When Aaron

put the finely ground Sweet Incense on the burning embers in the censer, and carried it into the 'holiest of all', it was the frankincense in the mixture that occasioned the thick, pure white cloud. The cloud that spoke so beautifully of the inscrutable glory of the person of Christ filling the most holy place was so dense that it concealed the presence of Aaron as he served. Whenever we come together for worship, we too should have a spiritual awareness of the glorious Person of the Christ in our midst. His glory should fill out the holy place so that self is lost sight of, allowing the power of His presence to lead and direct our praise.

The natural exudation of the resin would speak to our hearts of the divine fragrance our blessed Lord left in His wake as He moved from place to place here on earth. When the people heard Him speak, they wondered at the gracious words that proceeded out of His mouth (Luke 4:22). The meaning of His words was clear; there was no shade of meaning; no murkiness or uncertainty; no ambiguity. Even when our Lord spoke sternly to the Pharisees and other reprobates, it was always with a yearning that they would repent. When they repented, they found they could rehearse from the heart the words of the Psalmist, "how sweet are thy words unto my taste! Yea, sweeter than honey to my mouth" (Psalm 119:103). When the chief officers of the Sanhedrim went to arrest the Lord Jesus, they could not do so. His words so convicted them, they were constrained to say, "never man spake like this man" (John 7:46). The words of the Lord Jesus were pure, transparent and perfectly translated in the way He graciously conducted Himself among the people.

Frankincense was an essential component of the 'firstfruits' sacrifice. The teaching of the 'firstfruits' sacrifice relates to all that was for God in the life of the Lord Jesus. There is no shedding of blood in the sacrifice, so sin and death are not the subject. The Spirit of God would focus our attention on the perfect life of the Lord Jesus, a life that was fully influenced and motivated by the power of God's Holy Spirit (Mark 1:11). Accordingly, oil olive – type of the Holy Spirit – covered the whole sacrifice, while the frankincense spoke of the fragrance that naturally flowed from the Person of the Lord Jesus. It is worthy of note, that although the priests were to eat their portion of the sacrifice, they were not to include with their portion any of the frankincense. The priest offered all the frankincense on the altar with the memorial part of the sacrifice. The message for the priests and for us today is that there is nothing in the natural man, the man after Adam that could possibly occasion a sweet savour to God (Romans 3:10-12 & Isaiah 64:6). The memorial was for God with all the frankincense, to be an eternal testimony to Him of the One, who as Man on earth, ministered unceasing delight and pleasure to His heart.

In Leviticus 24:5-9 we have the detail for the setting of the 'shewbread'. Twelve loaves were set in two rows on the table and pure frankincense put upon each row. The loaves typified Israel as a memorial before God in the light and glory of Jehovah, while the frankincense spoke of the fragrant nature of Christ enveloping His people. Our service to God, if carried out in the power of His Holy Spirit, will always occasion a sweet savour of Christ. Whatever the outcome of our prayerful service in the exercise of the gifts God has graciously bestowed on the Church, heaven will claim it, "a sweet savour of Christ to God" (2 Corinthians 2 15).

That natural, holy fragrance, Lord; its outflow was so free,
The frankincense, unique, divine, could only come from Thee.
It filled the 'holiest of all'; God's pleasure and delight
Was satisfied, by Thee alone; now Thou'rt in glory bright.

T H Ratcliffe

Galbanum

Ferula galbaniflua / F. gummosa

Hebrew: Chelbenah = an odorous gum. Giant Fennel.
Exodus 30:34.

Galbanum is a resin obtained from the giant fennel, a member of the parsley family. A hardy herbaceous plant with elegant, fern-like, deep green foliage, having a parsnip-like root and growing to a height of 2 m or more. The plant develops full umbels of small, yellow flowers. The Hebrew word 'galbanum' also means; the richest, finest, best, most choice, odorous, fatty essence from the root of the plant. When the giant fennel plant is cut down to ground level, about the time of full vegetative maturity, it produces a fragrant, distinctly green-tinged resin from the cut surface of the root. This is the galbanum spoken of in Exodus 30:34.

For past centuries, galbanum resin has been used for therapeutic purposes to bring about a calming effect on people who are agitated and disturbed; have inflamed gums; suffering with a fever or other physical complaints that cause distress. When our Lord met individuals who were distressed, His presence and His word immediately brought

a calming influence to bear upon their condition. Take the case of Peter's mother in law who was sick with a fever. The Lord came and took her by the hand and the fever left her (Mark 1:29-31). In Luke 8:43-48, we have the account of the woman who had haemorrhaged continuously for 12 years and was greatly distressed because no one could heal her; but then the calming and healing influence of the Lord Jesus intervened. There was the case of the impotent man who for 38 years had waited in the hope of one-day being the first to get into the water when it was disturbed by an angel of the Lord. Alas, the man's impotency was too great a handicap for him to achieve his objective, but then the Lord comes in; He not only calmed the man's fears and dispelled his doubts, but also removed his impotency (John 5:1-15). We also know that the Lord had control over the elements. In Mark 4:37-41; the Lord calms the storm; so too can that blessed One calm the storms that occasionally arise in our lives; He can remove our fears and the distresses that are beyond the therapies of man.

It is significant that galbanum resin is tinted green. Green is the most restful colour to man in creation; that is why all normal herbage is green. No matter what the mixture may be, the colours of flowers never clash because the colour green produces a calm and restful harmony. John's record of the feeding of the five thousand is significant because grass features in the narrative. It was near to the end of the day, and the disciples wanted the Lord to send the multitude away, but the Lord had compassion on the people for He saw them as sheep without a shepherd. He had healed many that had been sick, and knew they were now tired and hungry. The Lord told His disciples to, "make the men sit down. Now there was 'much grass' in the place" (John 6:10). The Lord knew that the place where the people were to sit and rest, would be a stress-relieving therapy because there was 'so much grass' there.

As we are considering a narrative in John's gospel, I wonder if you have ever noticed that his gospel is overflowing with abundance from chapter one through to the end. "The only begotten, full of grace and truth" (John 1:14). The water pots filled to the brim with new wine, (John 2:7). The abundance of God's love, (John 3:16). "A well of water springing up into everlasting life" (John 4:14). "A greater witness than that of John" (John 5:36) and so on. Getting back to our subject, how lovely to read the word of the sweet psalmist of Israel, "He maketh me to lie down in green pasture" (Psalm 23:2). Our Lord said, "come unto Me, all ye that labour and are heavy laden, and I will give you rest. Take My yoke upon you and learn of Me; for I am meek and lowly in heart, and ye shall find rest unto your souls" (Matt. 11:28-29). Everything points to the calming and restful influence the Lord Jesus Christ wants to have upon our lives.

Our Lord's death on the cross was the fulfilment of prophecy as given in Daniel 9:26. Like the giant fennel plant, the Lord Jesus was cut off from the earth (crucified). However, the Lord's resurrection and subsequent ascension into glory, occasioned the descent of the Holy Spirit 10 days later – Pentecost (Acts 2:1-4). Today, the presence of the Holy Spirit in the world and in Christian believers is the calming influence holding back the advent of a total breakdown of society. A breakdown that will occasion an unparalleled disturbance in every area of life (2 Thessalonians 2:7). May the Lord help us to experience the fragrant, calming influence His presence generates, "Lo, I am with you always, even unto the end of the world" (Matt. 28:20).

> *Blest Father, infinite in grace, source of eternal joy;*
> *Thou lead'st our hearts to that blest place, where rest's without alloy.*
> *There will Thy love find perfect rest, where all around is bliss,*
> *Where all in Thee supremely blest, Thy praise their service is.*
>
> J N Darby.

Gall

Papaver Somniferum

Hebrew: Ro'sh. Greek: Chole = Poison from plants, head, conspicuous head, a shaking of the head.
A poison or anodyne derived from the Opium Poppy, Papaver Somniferum.
Deuteronomy 29:18 + thirteen other references.

Opinions differ as to the source of Gall. However, if we carefully consider the meaning of the Hebrew word Ro'sh, there is a powerful argument for accepting that the biblical Gall in all probability originated from the opium poppy. Most will be familiar with the poppy, papaver somniferum, with its large, wrinkle edged, grey-green coloured leaves. The plant grows to a height of 1 m. It bears large, single, four petal flowers in various shades of colour, followed by prominent, semi-spherical seed pods (heads) that shake freely in the slightest breeze. While the seed pod is still green and developing, shallow, horizontal incisions are made around the pod to allow the white opium sap to ooze out. The sap hardens on exposure to the air. Collection is usually at two to three day intervals. Morphine and codeine are powerful anodynes obtained from opium. The 'gall' referred to in Job 16:13 relates to the natural bile within the gall-bladder in one's stomach.

Identification of the plant from which gall is obtained, is not as important as understanding the significance of the Bible references to the substance. References to gall in the Scriptures should be interpreted in one of two ways. In the first place, God has made clear in His Word that the evil intent of one's unregenerate heart is of such a character that it bears the symptoms of being infected with the bitterness of gall. The references to this condition are Deuteronomy 29:18; Lamentations 3:19; Amos 6:12 and Acts 8:23.

Jehovah, through Moses, warns of the consequences if an individual or even the nation turns it back on Jehovah to worship idols (Deuteronomy 29:18-19). When a soul gets away from the Lord, it becomes a source of bitterness and defilement that can rapidly spread like a cancer. The apostle Paul conveyed the same thought, not only to the Hebrew Christians, but also to Christian believers in general (Hebrews 12:15). Paul was concerned that the people of God should not only care for the weak, but also act to discipline any that desecrated the truth. Paul was counselling about those whose activities could produce a root of bitterness among Christian believers and thereby cause serious damage to souls.

In Acts 8:9-24, we have the record of Simon the sorcerer who was in the service of Satan. Simon had seen the apostles Peter and John laying their hands on Christian believers to communicate to them the power of the Holy Ghost. Simon, filled with envy, wanted to purchase the same power rather than experience a change of heart through repentance before God and faith in the Lord Jesus Christ. The apostles perceived a spirit of jealousy within Simon and it prompted Peter to say, "repent therefore of this thy wickedness, and pray God, if perhaps the thought of thine heart may be forgiven thee. For I perceive thou art in the gall of bitterness and in the bond of iniquity" (Acts 8:22-23). James, speaking about the tongue of the old nature, which is after Adam, said, "But the tongue no man can tame; it is an unruly evil, full of deadly poison". James goes on to say how the tongue expresses the feelings of our hearts. Christian believers should not glory if they have bitter envying and strife in their hearts toward their brethren, neither should they lie against the truth. "This wisdom" says James; "descendeth not from above, but is earthly, sensual, devilish. But the wisdom that is from above is first pure, then peaceable, gentle and easy to be intreated, full of mercy and good fruits, without partiality and without hypocrisy" (James 3:8, 14, 15 & 17). Should not the apostle John's word be indelibly registered on the fleshy tables of our hearts? "My little children, let us not love in word, neither in tongue, but in deed and in truth" (1 John 3:18).

Secondly, we should understand that the reference to gall also relates to a poison, sometimes used as an anodyne. The references under this definition are Deuteronomy 32:32-33; Job 20:16; Psalm 69:21; Jeremiah 8:14; 9:15 & 23:15; Hosea 10:4 & Matthew 27:34. In Psalm 69:21 we read, "they gave me also gall for my meat, and in my thirst they gave me vinegar to drink". This was a prophetic utterance against what actually happened just before they nailed our blessed Saviour to the cross. "They gave Him vinegar to drink mingled with gall, and when He had tasted, He would not drink" (Matthew 27:34). Our Lord would have nothing to do with an opiate designed to lessen His sense of physical pain and paralyse His mental faculties. He knew about the analgesic effect of the drink, and determined not to benefit from any relief it might give; for it was our redemption that He sought and not His ease. By refusing the opiate, the Lord and Controller of all creation, Who knew about the influence and efficacy of plant substances, would not allow men to think they could contribute relief to His physical sufferings. Although our Lord ever possessed the power (see Luke 22:50-51) to render any poison completely innocuous, nothing could turn Him aside from finishing the work His Father gave Him to do (John 4:34). Nevertheless, He would remain in complete control of a unique event, the greatest and most profound moment since before creation. For not only was He the offering for sin, He also was the Offerer of the sacrifice for the sin of the world (John 1:29). He refused the cup man offered Him, but drank up to the very last drop, the cup filled with divine wrath and judgment His Father had mixed and given Him to drink.

> *Death and the curse were in our cup, O Christ! 'twas full for Thee!*
> *But Thou hast drained the last dark drop, 'tis empty now for me;*
> *That bitter cup, love drank it up, left but the love, for me.*
>
> R A Cousin

Garlic

Allium sativum

Hebrew: Shum = To exhale because of its rank odour.
Numbers 11:5.

Leek

Allium porrum

Hebrew: Chatsiyr = The greenness of a courtyard, grass-like.
Numbers 11:5.

Onion

Allium cepa

Hebrew: Betsel = To peel.
Numbers 11:5.

Garlic
Allium sativum

The Israelites fed on garlic, leeks and onions, besides fish and cucumbers, during their time of bondage in Egypt. For their journey through the wilderness, God provided His people with angels' food – the bread of the mighty – in abundance so that none should go hungry (Psalm 78:25). The manna from God's good hand was perfect, sweet to the taste and sufficient to satisfy every physical and nutritional need for a company of over one million souls. Alas, Israel very soon dishonoured Jehovah by lightly esteeming the food God rained down from heaven; they hankered after the food of Egypt.

The food of Egypt is the food of the world that can never nourish the spiritual soul. For the Christian believer, our Lord Jesus Christ is the One upon whom we daily should feed. He is the bread of God that came down from heaven. The Lord Jesus said, "I am the bread of life, he that cometh to Me shall never hunger" (John 6:35). It is an easy matter to discern if one is or has been feeding on the leeks, garlic and onions of the world. The character of such foods is that they stamp their distinctive mark on the individuals who ingest them; and that is what the meaning of the Hebrew word 'Shum' implies. Likewise the "bread of life", if we daily take in God's Word as an essential part of our spiritual diet, we will reflect something of the features and moral attributes of Christ (2 Corinthians 3:18). For we shall, "grow in grace and in the knowledge of our Lord and Saviour Jesus Christ" (2 Peter 3:18). The apostle Paul

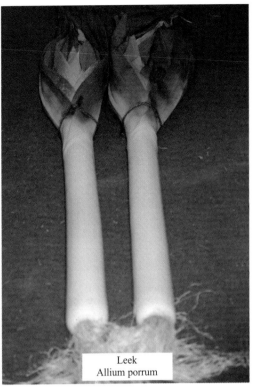

Leek
Allium porrum

Leek
Allium porrum

spoke lovingly and beautifully about the Christian believers at Philippi; yearning that they should be, "filled with the fruits of righteousness, which are by Jesus Christ unto the praise and glory of God" (Philippians 1:11). He then acknowledges the abundance of their practical love; saying, "I am full, having received of Epaphroditus the things which were sent from you, an odour of a sweet smell, a sacrifice acceptable, wellpleasing to God" (Philippians 4:18).

Christian believers whose daily lives are sustained on the garlic, leeks and onions (pleasures) of this world, manifest a tragic spirit of discontent for the rich, sustaining and formative spiritual food God has provided in the Person of His Son. A spirit of resentment in a Christian believer will generate all sorts of excuses

Onion
Allium cepa

for disregarding divine provisions, and simply serve to confirm that the active flesh has no appreciation of the preciousness of Christ, their Saviour. Those who love the Lord Jesus and yearn to be with Him and like Him will delight to nourish their souls on the heavenly food He supplies. The Church at Thessalonica relished every provision for their spiritual lives, to the extent that the apostle Paul gave thanks to God for their testimony. "We are bound to thank God always for you, brethren, as it is meet, because that your faith groweth exceedingly, and the charity of every one of you toward each other aboundeth" (2 Thessalonians 1:3).

The children of Israel were rebellious for the forty years of their wilderness journey, and became increasingly critical about the manna (angels' food) God had faithfully provided. Nevertheless, God in His mercy and love never for one day failed to provide all their needs. For, "He fed them according to the integrity of His heart, and guided them by the skilfulness of His hands" (Psalm 78:72). The apostle Paul, writing to the Philippian Church, was anxious to assure them about the only One able to meet all their daily needs. "But my God –said the apostle – shall supply all your need according to His riches in glory by Christ Jesus" (Philippians 4:19). May the Lord touch our hearts to awaken in them a conscious reality of His goodness; such as the sweet Psalmist of Israel said, "for He satisfieth the longing soul, and filleth the hungry soul with goodness" (Psalm 107:9).

And when He calls us home at length, to feast with Him above,
Through all eternity we'll sing, His never-changing love.

Anon

Gopher

Cupressus sempervirens pyramidalis

Hebrew: Gopher = To house in, abide.
Genesis 6:14.

In my earlier notes on the cypress tree, I suggested the tree belongs to the same species as the gopher, the wood of which, Noah used for building the ark. The gopher tree grows naturally in the same geographic, mountainous region as the box and cedar. One

might ask, how did Noah and those who helped him build the ark, produce the planks necessary for its construction. After all, they did not have anything mechanical to saw the wood into planks. The answer lies in the unique way one can split the wood of most conifers without the use of machinery. First, the branches on the long, straight trunk are removed; then wedges made from a harder wood such as oak, or flint-stone chisels are hammered in along the length of the trunk. The tree splits freely into planks of whatever thickness is required. Even today, the cedar wood shingles used for chalet houses and the like, are prepared in the same way as that probably employed by Noah and his helpers.

A distinctive feature of cupressus sempervirens pyramidalis is the impressive way mature trees reach an erect height of over 20 m. No other man has ever walked in this world with the uprightness that marked the Lord Jesus Christ. His walking here before His God was with unparalleled perfection (John 8:29). It says of Noah, "Noah was a just man and perfect (moral integrity and faithful) in (amongst) his generation, and Noah walked with God" (Genesis 6:9). We too, will bring pleasure to God if we keep our eye on the Saviour, daily seeking to do His will (Hebrews 13:21). God alone knew that gopher wood was the kind of timber that would survive the severity of the trial through which the vessel was to pass.

Although the wood of cupressus sempervirens pyramidalis is one of the most resinous of all conifers and therefore ideally suited for the purpose God had in mind, He commanded that the ark be pitched within and without with pitch. Initially, three valuable thoughts spring to mind regarding the ark. (1) The character of the wood was such that it was naturally resistant to the penetration of water. Our Lord Jesus, here in dependent manhood was totally resistant to the ingress of evil influences; nothing could possibly touch or infect that "Holy Thing" (Luke 1:35). (2) The ark itself speaks of Christ, within whom all the saints of God are forever secure. Furthermore, Christian believers know that all outside of Christ (the ark) are under judgment. (3) The pitch without speaks of 'a cover', 'a redemption price', 'a ransom', and the Hebrew word for 'without' means that those within are separated by an impermeable barrier, and protected from the judgment outside. The Hebrew word for the 'pitch' that was used within the ark, means 'to cover', 'to expiate', 'to cancel', 'to make atonement', 'to purge' and 'to reconcile'. The link word, 'within' carries the thought of being within the environment of a family home, the temple of our God.

The primary thought associated with the ark and the family within, is of a Jewish remnant experiencing and surviving the coming time of "Great Tribulation" (Matthew 24:21-22; & Revelation 7:13-15). Just as Noah experienced salvation from the world under judgment, so today, Christian believers should daily experience salvation from the corrupting influences of the world around (Philippians 2:12). The apostle Peter sums up perfectly the current position applying to all the redeemed on earth. "The longsuffering of God waited in the day of Noah, while the ark was a preparing, wherein few, that is eight souls were saved by water. The like figure whereunto even baptism doth now save us (not the putting away of the filth of the flesh, but the answer of a good conscience toward God) by the resurrection of Jesus Christ" (1 Peter 3:20-21). Our baptism was not an act to prepare us for heaven, but a testimony of how we should live for the remainder of our time on earth. Being baptised unto the death of the Lord Jesus Christ, was a confirmation that we had moved out of the sphere of this worlds activities and aspirations, "to walk in newness of life with Christ" (Romans 6:3-4). If we claim to abide in Christ (our ark), we ought also to walk, even as He walked (see 1 John 2:6)

Unto Thy death baptisèd, we own with Thee we died;
With Thee, our Life, we're risen, and shall be glorified.
From sin, the world, and Satan, we're ransomed by Thy blood,
And here would walk as strangers, alive with Thee to God.

J G Deck

Gourd

Ricinus communis

Hebrew: Qiyqayon = Nauseous, vomit, spue out. Castor Oil plant.
Jonah 4:6, 7, 9 & 10.

The vast majority of biblical scholars and botanists for the past 250 years have been in no doubt that the gourd referred to in Jonah 4 is the castor oil plant, ricinus communis. The plant is an annual and normally grows rapidly during the spring and summer months, reaching a height of approximately 4 m. The large, glossy leaves are palmate, as a hand with out-stretched fingers. The form of the leaves is probably why in some regions of the Middle East, the plant is known as 'palma christi'. The small, spiny fruits hold two or three black seeds that are full of oil, but the flesh of the seed, including the seed coat, contains the poisonous toxin, 'ricin' and may account for the Hebrew definition of the word.

The severity of Jonah's experience following his initial disobedience to the word of the Lord, gave him no option but to do as the Lord commanded him the second time. "Arise, go unto Nineveh, that great city, and preach unto it the preaching that I bid thee" (Jonah 3:2). Jonah preached a powerful message to the Ninevites; however, it is clear by his reaction he did not believe it possible for such an idolatrous people to repent in sackcloth and ashes, but they did. Furthermore, at the end of the forty days, Jonah expected the Lord to overthrow Nineveh in judgment in accordance with his preaching, but He did not. It would seem that Jonah never gave it a second thought that the Lord was ready to forgive the Ninevites for their idolatry. After all, the Assyrians were notorious for their savagery and empire building, and Jonah was conscious of the fact that they presented a serious threat to Israel and Palestine. It was not the message as such that so disturbed Jonah, but his prejudicial abhorrence and fear of the Assyrians. Why, thought Jonah, should the compassion and mercy of God reach out to the enemies of Israel? Herein lies the real reason why Jonah fled from the work of the Lord in the first place.

The hostile attitude of Jonah and the Jews against the nations continued up to and beyond the time our Lord was on earth. While the Jews rejected and disowned their long-promised Messiah, they certainly did not expect the Gentiles to benefit from the promised blessings as foretold in Genesis 22:17, The Jews always conveniently overlooked verse 18 of Genesis 22. Today, the message of the Glad Tidings is this, "God…now commandeth all men everywhere to repent" (Acts 17:30). "Testifying both to the Jew and also to the Greek, repentance toward God, and faith toward our Lord Jesus Christ" (Acts 20:21). Furthermore, that, "the righteousness of God, which is by faith of Jesus Christ, (is) unto all and upon all them that believe" (Romans 3:22). The work of the evangelist today is to, "go therefore and make disciples of all the nations, baptising them to the Name of the Father, and of the Son, and of the Holy Spirit" (Matthew 28:19).

We as Christian believers, represent the Lord in our service for Him. We do not question His wisdom and guidance, but carry God's message to all, announcing that He is full of compassion, slow to anger, plenteous in mercy and abounding with love, pity and forgiveness. Jonah had great difficulty coming to terms with the fact that God was gracious, merciful and slow to anger, of great loving kindness and ready to amend His intentions toward Nineveh if the city repented (Jonah 4:2). He had also conveniently overlooked the extent and application of God's mercy, "as the heaven is high above the earth, so great is His mercy toward them that fear Him" (Psalm 103:11).

If only Jonah had been more readily disposed to set aside his own will, and fulfil God's will, he would have rejoiced when the Ninevites repented of their sins. As it was, he became very angry and went out of the city, built a booth and sat under it to see out the forty days, obviously expecting to see the judgment of God fall on the city. He did not want to see the city spared. However, while Jonah sat under his booth with a spirit of discontent, God in His mercy prepared a gourd (castor oil plant) to grow up with extraordinary speed over the booth to protect him from the searing heat of the sun. Everything about the gourd carried a powerful message that should have spoken to Jonah about the way God deals with the repentant sinner. The large, palmate leaves of the plant should have been a message to Jonah that God's hand is over all that put their trust in Him, working to protect, care and provide, even for the repentant Ninevites (Psalm 95:7). The seeds, the fruit of the plant, are rich in oil, which all nations down through the centuries have used as a purifying purgative (Psalm 51:7).

Notwithstanding the grace, patience and mercy of God toward Jonah, we do not read of him thanking the Lord for His goodness (Psalm 107:8). On the contrary, Jonah retained a disgruntled spirit about the way God had shown mercy to and had pity on the Ninevites. God therefore arranged for an invasion of caterpillars to consume the gourd to remove the protective covering He had provided. Jonah was distressed about the gourd, and even felt a little pity for the plant the caterpillars had eaten. Jonah's pity for the plant is in striking contrast to his disposition toward the Ninevites for whom he had shown no pity. The word 'pity' in the Hebrew is 'Chus' meaning, to cover, to have compassion, regard, to spare. That is exactly the message God was putting over to Jonah. Just as He had protected (covered) him with the gourd, so with His mighty hand, He covered the Ninevites, He exercised compassion, regarded them and spared them because they repented. Unlike the book of Obadiah in which God is set forth as the 'God of judgment'; the book of Jonah presents God as the 'God of pity'. May our gracious Lord daily help us to remove any prejudices lingering in our souls that would inhibit our going forth into the world with the message of the Gospel. The apostle Paul said, "for I am not ashamed of the Gospel of Christ, for it is the power of God unto salvation to every one that believeth, to the Jew first, and also to the Greek" (Romans 1:16).

I'm not ashamed to own my Lord, or to defend His cause,
Maintain the honour of His Word, the glory of His cross.

I Watts

Gourd - Wild
Citrullus colocynthis

Hebrew: Paqqu'ah = Wild cucumber / melon, a splitting fruit.
2 Kings 4:39.

The plant referred to in the above text is an uncultivated perennial species belonging to the cucumber family. The plant, which is rough to the touch, trails along the ground in desert places, and with characteristic tendrils, climbs over low-growing shrubs. The greenish-yellow coloured fruits are 8-12 cm in size and melon-shaped. When ripe, the fruits split open to reveal a pulp that is drastically cathartic, containing highly poisonous seeds.

The narrative in 2 Kings 4:39-41 tells us thät Elisha came again to Gilgal. Approximately 550 years earlier, Gilgal was the place where, through circumcision, Jehovah "rolled away the reproach of Egypt from off the children of Israel" (Joshua 5:9). From that point onward, Israel should have been, in testimony, a distinct and

special people the Lord had chosen for Himself (Deuteronomy 7:6). Provided the people remained faithful to Jehovah, the land would not fail them (Deuteronomy 28:1-14). Alas, they quickly slipped back into the ways of Egypt, and therefore, frequently experienced famine and dearth in their souls. Elisha, as a faithful shepherd, returns to the Seminary for the sons of the prophets, and in view of the dearth in the land, was anxious to ascertain their well being and to offer further instruction in the ways of God.

It is very likely that following his stay in Shunem, Elisha had brought along provisions to share with the sons of the prophets. Having asked his servant to prepare some food, one of the young men went out into the field to gather herbs. Clearly the young man was not going to be content with the basic, yet nutritional fare Elisha had to offer; so he set his heart to 'spice up' the food. Ignorant of the life-threatening consequences his wild-cat enterprise would occasion, he gathers up a lap-full of coloured, eye-catching poisonous gourds; chops them up and casts them into the pot. It is most likely Elisha did not see the foolish act of the young, discontented prophet; so, when the pottage was ready to serve, all sat around to eat. Almost immediately, the young prophets perceived that the food was poisonous, and cried out in unison, "there is death in the pot". Elisha calls for some meal, which he casts into the pot to neutralise the toxin. The result was miraculous, for the food was no longer poisonous, but safe and sufficient to satisfy the hunger of the prophets.

The action of the young man was a repeat of the act of disobedience in the Garden of Eden. God had provided a generous sufficiency for Adam and Eve, but they were not content with the adequacy of divine provision, and at the behest of Satan took and ate what God strictly forbade. Their disobedience brought in death, and it required a 'handful of meal' – the Lord Jesus Christ – given from the hand of Almighty God to annul the power of death (1 John 3:8). Sadly, today there are many Christian believers who are very much like the young, discontented prophet, they are not satisfied with all that God has given us through His Word. They want to add something to the Scriptures, make them more appealing, more lively and exciting, while at the same time disregarding what God has said about His Word. In Proverbs 30:5-6 we read, "every Word of God is pure; He is a shield unto them that put their trust in Him. Add thou not unto His Words lest He reprove thee, and thou be found a liar". The adequacy of the divinely inspired Scriptures to reveal the full mind and Will of God and to sustain us in our pilgrim pathway, is confirmed in many of the Bible's sixty-six books.

Our sinful actions outside the assembly will undoubtedly result in damage to the testimony of God's love and grace to sinners and also affect the spiritual well being of the Christian believers with whom we meet. The spirit of envy and bitterness in our hearts toward fellow believers is a grievous poison; its affect on others is a very serious matter before God (Ephesians 4:30-31). Besmirching the integrity and name of other Christian believers; the determination that others shall not succeed where we have failed; the reluctance to esteem others better than ourselves are all features of the poisonous influence of the wild gourd (Philippians 2:1-3). The wild gourd is therefore typical of the flesh, and sadly, its product is all too evident among us today. The very nature of the plant, like the flesh, is such that it can never come under cultivation, nor yield anything for God's pleasure (1 Corinthians 1:29). Like the young prophet who caused his contemporaries such pain; Christian believers too, can be a source of trouble in the assembly of God's people. In that event, the spiritual element in the assembly would quickly perceive the risk of serious damage to souls, and take appropriate action (Galatians 6:1). As Elisha threw in the 'handful of meal', so the spiritual man would bring the Spirit of the Lord Jesus Christ to bear upon a given situation to effect healing and occasion praise to the glory of His grace.

> *Lord, since we sing as pilgrims, O give us pilgrim ways;*
> *Low thoughts of self, befitting, proclaimers of Thy praise.*
> *O make us each more holy, in spirit pure and meek,*
> *More like to heavenly citizens, as more of heaven we speak.*
>
> M Bowly

Grass

Gramineae sp.

Hebrew: Deshe' = Tender green grass.
Genesis 1:11 & 12 + one hundred other references including Hebrew nouns: 'Ash =
Herb grass. Chatsiyr = Grass, hay, fodder & herb. Dethe' = Tender grass. Dush =
Trodden down pasture. 'Eseb = Green, lush, edible herbage. 'Orah = Glistening, dew
covered green herbage. Yereq & Yaraq = Mixed, lush, edible vegetation.
Greek nouns: Botane = Herbage grass. Chortos = Fodder grass. Lachanon = Probably
root vegetables.

Some doubt remains among biblical scholars and botanists regarding the identity of the plant/s referred to with the Greek noun lachanon. For the purpose of our studies, it is probably just as well if we include the subject lachanon along with our consideration of grasses and herbs in general. Grass species together form the most populous group of plants throughout the world. There are perennial, biennial and annual species, from the very tall, like 'brome grass' (bromus sp.), to the very low-growing types such as the browntops (agrostis sp.). As we have noted from our thoughts on 'galbanum', green is the colour most restful to man. There are a few exceptions, but in the main, all ground plants, shrubs and trees have green foliage. The colour green effects a beautiful harmony among all the different flower colours. In nature, through the wisdom of God, colours never clash where the background is green.

On the third day of Creation, God by His Word brought forth grass and herd-yielding seed (cereals) and fruit trees. So grass was the first green plant to appear on the earth, to enable man (created on the sixth day) to live in harmony with all around and to rest in peace and tranquillity. In six days, God created a paradise for man; He saw that everything He had made was good according to His divine standard. Where there had been chaos there was order, permanent darkness replaced by daily light, disturbance calmed by peace, death gave way to life, barrenness transformed to fruitfulness, frustration to contentment and discord to harmony. Alas, man by disobedience soon lost his paradise; he was driven out into a world where everything was against him, and where he would have to strive for existence by the sweat of his brow (Genesis 3:18-19). However, through God's sovereign grace, there is for man a paradise in heaven (2 Corinthians 12:4), not material, but spiritual and heavenly, the destined place for all the redeemed (Luke 23:43). Meanwhile, the Lord has given us a spiritual environment wherein we can recline, be restful and content in rich green pastures (Psalm 23:2). Fellowship with the Christian believers and being sustained by the Truth of His Word equates with what the Psalmist had in mind and what the Lord has provided to help us through our wilderness journey (1 John 1:3-4).

God gave the grass of the field as food for animals (Psalm 104:14), and He gave the animals that feed on the grass to be meat for man (Leviticus 25:7). Tragically, in the pursuit of greed and economic gain, man has disobeyed God's law. The animals that are by God's ordering exclusively herbivorous, have been fed processed remains of diseased animals in order to increase protein intake and thereby speed up their development. In the case of cows, the objective in the food diet programme was to increase milk production. Today the world is greatly disturbed about the immediate and long-term health hazards arising from the consumption of beef infected with the virus 'Bovine spongiform encephalopathy', BSE for short, 'mad cow disease'. It is beyond all reasonable doubt, that this serious health problem is the consequence of mans' mismanagement in animal husbandry.

The natural man is looked upon in Scripture as grass, and his glory as the flower of grass (Psalm 103:15 and five other scriptures). The apostle Peter in his first epistle refers to the ephemeral nature of grass – figure of the natural man – together with the eternal excellencies of the Word of God, and finds there is no comparison (1 Peter 1:24-25). The grass is here today, but maybe gone tomorrow, just as James said, " whereas ye know not what shall be on the morrow, for what is your life? It is even as a vapour that appeareth for a little time and then vanishes away" (James 4:14). A blade of grass on its own is weak and must rely on other blades for support to hold it up, so it is with man, particularly with the saints of God. The world uses expressions like, 'unity is strength, division is weakness' and 'united we stand, divided we fall', how very true! Many Christian believers are keenly aware of how essential it is to have the support of other like-minded believers for their collective witness. The apostle Paul in speaking of the Gospel outreach said, "we are labourers together with God" (1 Corinthians 3:9).

However, for our individual and personal walk before the Lord in this world – wherein we see ourselves as a single blade of grass -, we greatly need the help of the Holy Spirit of God; see Act 8:26-40. Never for one moment should we think we are able to go alone and in our own strength. Paul said he was weak in himself, but that he found his strength made perfect in the acknowledgement and acceptance of his weakness (2 Corinthians 12:9).

Of all the flowering plants in God's creation, the flower of grass is the most insignificant. In the vast majority of plants, the colourful flower structures are called petals and sepals, the latter form the outer floral envelope protecting the flower bud and collectively called the calyx. We call the flower structures of grasses, glumes and palea. The colour of the glumes and palea is nearly always a similar green to the plant and therefore insignificant. God has said in His Word through the apostle Peter, "all the glory of – the natural – man is as the flower of grass. The grass withereth, and the flower thereof falleth away" (1 Peter 1:24). We conclude therefore, that man's glory is not only insignificant, but also transient.

> *Man's life is as the grass, or like the morning flower;*
> *If one sharp blast sweep o'er the field, it withers in an hour.*
>
> I Watts

Hemlock

Conium maculatum

Hebrew: Ro'sh = Conspicuous head, gall, venom of serpents, poison.
Hosea 10:4, & Amos 6:12.

Conium maculatum is a biennial herb belonging to the parsley family of plants. Growing to a height of 1 m it is very similar, albeit larger than our well-known hedge parsley. With fine feathery leaves, the much-branched inflorescence produces a mass of umbels comprising little white flowers. Juice from the stem is extremely poisonous. The Hebrew noun Ro'sh occurs 561 times in the Old Testament, KJV. The following definitions give some idea of the difficulty biblical botanists' encounter when attempting to identify plants and plant products. 'Ro'sh' means: bands, beginning, gall, captains, chapters, chief, companies, excellent, first, gall, head, high, highest, poison, principal, the sum of, tops and venom of serpents. Having already considered the Hebrew noun Ro'sh with the translation as 'Gall', an anxious enquirer might justifiably ask: 'how does one decide which definition of Ro'sh applies to a given Scripture'? The answer will always be, 'the context' in which the noun occurs.

The messages of Hosea and Amos are to Israel, a people who were the privileged

depositories of the 'oracles' of God (Romans 3:2). Both books detail the sin of the people and the wickedness of their way of life. The prophets not only announced the judgments that were going to fall on Israel, but also the details of the nation's recovery and blessing (Hosea 14:4-7). Meanwhile, the Lord says of Israel, "ye have ploughed wickedness, ye have reaped iniquity, ye have eaten the fruit of lies; because thou didst trust in thy way, in the multitude of thy mighty men" (Hosea 10:13). The furrows in the field of Hosea 10:4, are a figure of the path of idolatry that Israel had taken away from God. The outcome of Israel's wickedness was death and judgment – hemlock, the venom of serpents – rather than blessing and the good fruit of the land. The nation had ignored the words of David who said, "happy is he that hath the God of Jacob for his help, whose hope is in the Lord his God" (Psalm 146:5). A serious situation also occurs when Christian believers get so far away from the mind and will of God, they allow bitter and evil feelings to spring up in the furrows of their hearts, producing tragic and dishonouring results.

Israel had received much divine light, for no other nation had been privileged to experience such intimate relationship with God (Deuteronomy 7:6-9). Accordingly, Israel's measure of light and privilege became the measure of their responsibility Godward. Alas, just as idolatry abounded in the days of Hosea and Amos, so apostasy in Christendom abounds on every hand today with an ever-increasing move to idolatry and iconology, a consequence of departure from the Truth of God's Word. The divine responsibility of Christian believers is to, "earnestly contend for the faith once for all delivered unto the saints –Christian believers -" (Jude 3). Through sovereign grace, all such are associated with the dignity and honour God has bestowed upon His Blessed Son, and are depositories of the, "riches of God's grace" (Ephesians 1:3-11). So long as we are daily moving in the current of His will, we shall be happy satiating our souls with the fullness of His love and grace to the glory of God our Father and the Lord Jesus Christ. "Now the God of peace, …make you perfect in every good work to do His will, working in you that which is well-pleasing in His sight, through Jesus Christ; to Whom be glory for ever and ever, Amen" (Hebrews 13:20-21).

And though the wilderness we tread, a barren, thirsty ground,
With thorns and briars over-spread, where foes and snares abound.
Blest Saviour, keep our spirits stayed, hard following after Thee,
Till we, in robes of white arrayed, Thy face in glory see.

J G Deck

Hyssop
Origanum Syriacum

Hebrew: 'Esob. Greek: Hussopos. The Syrian hyssop, a variety of Marjorum.
Exodus 12:22 + eleven other references.

The Syrian hyssop belongs to the Marjoram family of plants; it is a sub-shrub with erect, wiry stems no longer than 0.7 m and bearing grey-green, hairy leaves. The pale, whitish and insignificant flowers develop in regularly spaced whorls around the stem. All the physical characteristics of the Syrian hyssop render it eminently suitable for producing a kind of brush with which to apply blood or water to persons, things and building structures (Exodus 12:22). Although there is nothing startling or attractive about the hyssop plant, the juices in its leaves give relief to sore throats.

Hyssop – Springing out of a wall
(1 Kings 4:33)

Hyssop speaks to our hearts of the spirit of meekness and lowliness that marked the disposition of the Lord Jesus as Son of man here on earth. The humility of our Lord was evident in all His miracles, signs and wonders. In every footstep of His lowly pathway, He left a fresh imprint of His love and grace. He never sought the acclaim and praise of men; neither would He have men promote Him because of His works (Matthew 8:4; 16:20). The use of the hyssop in Exodus 12 to sprinkle the blood on the

114

doorposts and lintel, was a figure of the lowly, obedience of the Lord Jesus Christ. He was the One Who delighted to do the will of God; Who in meekness, humility and submissiveness, shed His precious blood to atone for the sin of the world (John 1:29), and redeem to God all who believe. Just as the households of the Israelites who obeyed the word of Moses were covered and protected from the avenging angel; so today, the redeemed are covered, protected and secured by the shed blood of Christ (1 Peter 1:18-21). The apostle Paul said, He was the One "Who made Himself of no reputation, but took upon Him the form of a servant, and was made in the likeness of men. Being found in fashion as a man, He humbled Himself and became obedient unto death, even the death of the cross" (Philippians 2:7-8).

The hyssop in Leviticus 14:6-7 was used to sprinkle the blood of the slain bird seven times on the one cleansed of leprosy. The sprinkling of the blood seven times implied perfect and complete cleansing; and only then was the living bird – a figure of Christ's resurrection (Romans 6:4) – released into the open field. The cedar wood, scarlet and hyssop, used according to the law for both the cleansing of the leper and the cleansing of the leprous house, spoke of the uniqueness of our Lord's manhood. The cedar wood speaks of the unparalleled moral glory and stature of Christ, towering above all men, while the scarlet brings before us the very distinctive character and glory of His manhood. Hyssop on the other hand reminds us of His meekness, lowliness and submission to His Father's will (Psalm 40:8). He bore God's righteous judgment against the sin of the world. Thus, only hyssop – the lowliest of all plants – featured in the sacrifice on the cross of the One who was an innocent victim (John 19:29).

In Numbers 19, we have the teaching on the application of the 'ashes of the red heifer' and the 'water of separation'. In this ordinance of the law, the cedar wood, scarlet and hyssop do not speak of Christ, but of the transient glory of sinful man from the highest point of his vanity and achievement to the lowest. The teaching of Numbers 19 is not redemption, but the restoration of communion with divine Persons; communion that had been broken through contamination by the defiling influences of this world. The red heifer was a figure of Christ, perfect in every detail, unused and unaffected by the corrupting influences all around. That the heifer was red, spoke of the distinctive manhood glories that marked the Lord Jesus as a peerless man. The blood of the slain heifer sprinkled seven times before the tabernacle of the congregation, signified the full vindication of God's righteousness, and that the consequence of sin was perfectly and completely cancelled, as in the death of Christ. The casting of the cedar wood, scarlet and hyssop into the burning of the red heifer spoke of the end of the natural man. The Scriptures teach us, "that no flesh should glory in His presence" and that "by the works of the law shall no flesh be justified" (Galatians 2:16). The ashes of the heifer together with the cedar wood, scarlet and hyssop are a confirmation that God's fiery judgment against sin and sinful flesh is exhausted; there can be no further sacrifice for sin. This unimpeachable fact is confirmed by the Lord's own words on the cross, "it is finished" (John 19:30).

The 'water of separation' has reference to the word of God and the impact it should daily have upon us when applied to our souls. The Lord Jesus yearned for His own to be morally separated unto Himself. In His prayer to His Father, He cried, "sanctify them through Thy truth, Thy word is truth. For their sakes I sanctify Myself, that they also may be sanctified through the truth" (John 17:17 & 19). In verses 18–19 of Numbers 19, we have the ordinance for cleansing a person defiled by contact with unclean things. The ashes of the red heifer are put into a bowl of pure, running water. The ashes here carry the thought that it is the death of Christ and our death with Him that gives efficacy and power to the Word in our souls – water of separation. We ever need to have before us the words of the apostle Paul. "I am crucified with Christ, nevertheless I live, yet not I, but Christ liveth in me. And the life which I now live in the flesh, I live by the faith of the Son of God, who loved me and gave Himself for me" (Galatians 2:20). A clean person takes a bunch of hyssop, dips it into the 'water of separation' and sprinkles the contaminated home, vessels and persons. Here in type, we have a spiritual person in the spirit of humility and lowliness of mind applying the water of the Word of God to cleanse a defiled person. The hyssop on this occasion would surely speak of the lowly, gracious nature and disposition of Christ that should mark the brother or sister the Lord may use for the restoration of another. One will accomplish nothing in this service if a spirit of self-righteousness, bitterness, arrogance or aggression motivates the servant. The apostle Paul tells us who is suitable to undertake the task. "Brethren, if any be overtaken in a fault, ye that are spiritual, restore such an one in the spirit of meekness, considering thyself, less thou also be tempted" (Galatians 6:1).

Hyssop – growing in University Botanic
Garden, Jerusalem

David, in his plea for the mercy of God, asked that he might be purged with hyssop and so be clean. Following his encounter with Nathan the prophet, David became profoundly aware of how defiled he had become. It occasioned the ransacking of his heart and soul before his God, together with an acute awareness of his need for the application of the 'water of separation'. David's confession of his sin and his yearning to be clean was associated with a godly disposition from which we can learn a great deal. David came before his God, not as a mighty conqueror – the cedar – or as the King of Israel – scarlet -, but rather in the spirit of the lowly hyssop. He came as one in need of the mercy of God once he had confessed his sin. David knew his approach to God must be in accordance with, "the sacrifices of God are a broken spirit, a broken and a contrite heart, O God Thou wilt not despise" (Psalm 51:17).

According to Solomon, hyssop symbolised the lowliest of plants on earth. No man could or will go lower than the place our Saviour stooped to in order to cancel out the consequence of sin. We may safely say that on the cross the Lord Jesus reached the highest point of moral excellence as man on earth. However, it is also true that on that same cross our Lord plummeted to the lowest depths of humiliation and degradation. On the cross, "God made Him to be sin for us, who knew no sin, that we might be made the righteousness of God in Him" (2 Corinthians 5:21). He bore God's righteous wrath and exhausted His judgment on the sin of the world. Doubtless those standing around the cross were anxious to do what they could to alleviate the Lord's physical sufferings, and may well have had prepared a sponge soaked with vinegar tied with hyssop stems to a reed. They would have been familiar with the words in Psalm 22:15, "my strength is dried up like a potsherd, and my tongue cleaveth to my jaws". Also, the word in Psalm 69:21, "they gave me also gall for my meat, and in my thirst, they gave me vinegar to drink." Knowing that the juices in the leaves of the Syrian hyssop can bring considerable relief to sore, painful tongues and throats, it is possible this was another reason why hyssop stems were used to bind the sponge to the reed.

The Lord's physical sufferings persevered after the three hours of darkness; yet, notwithstanding the fact that His parched tongue was cleaving to His jaw; in patient grace He continued to be the lowly, subject one. Not until our Lord cried out, "I thirst" did they offer Him something to slake His thirst. The drink He received would have helped free up His tongue and enable Him to utter His last words on earth as a dependent man, "Father, into Thy hands I commend my spirit" (Luke 23:46). The hyssop gives us a powerful message on humility. May our Lord help each of us to be daily clothed with humility (1 Peter 5:5-6).

We wonder at Thy lowly mind, and fain would like Thee be;
And all our rest and pleasure find, in learning, Lord, of Thee.

J C Deck

Juniper/White Broom
Retama raetam / Lygos raetam

Hebrew: Rethem = Pole-like stems. White broom.
1 Kings 19:4-5; Job 30:4 & Psalm 120:4.

The Juniper bush, also known as Genista Raetam with the common name White Broom, belongs to the Pea (Leguminosae) family of plants and is a deciduous shrub throughout Sinai, Syria and Palestine, surviving in arid conditions. It develops 3 m long, slender, erect, and drooping stems, flowering on current year's wood. The dense groups of flowers along the stem are white, turning cream with age, and produce single seeded pods. By all accounts, the wood, including the root, is excellent for producing very hot burning charcoal.

The story we have in 1 Kings 18:30-40 is of a prophet whose faith was tested to the limit, yet a faith that triumphed, resulting in the death of 850 prophets of Baal (verse 19) at Mount Carmel. Elijah's faith and trust was in the God of Abraham, Isaac and Israel; without such faith, nothing so miraculous could have happened. Yet, in chapter 19 of 1 Kings, the prophet fears for his life, he receives a threat based on the whim of a wicked woman, queen Jezebel, who had determined to take his life within 24 hours. Elijah fled from Jezreel in fear; lacking faith in the power of the God of Abraham, Isaac and Israel to deliver him, not from 850 apostate

2 cm

Israelites, but from just one evil woman. Elijah arrived at Beer-sheba where he left his servants, and went a day's journey further south into the northern part of the Sinai Peninsula. Weary from his journeying, he became tired of life and rested under a juniper shrub from where he wished to rise no more. As with Elijah, the strongest and most faithful of the Lord's servants are subject to qualms of fear and doubt, and may suffer infirmity, more especially after a successful mission in the Lord's service. To be unchangeably sustained in the will, joy and service of the Lord is something we all desire, but recognise that such an objective is not possible on earth. Happily, it will come about when we are translated into the likeness of our blessed Redeemer (1 John 3:2). Meanwhile, Satan determines that such servants of the Lord should not continue their service for the Master's glory and honour, and therefore does everything possible to hinder (1 Thessalonians 2:18). Nevertheless, those who triumph over the testing of their faith, do not run away, they stand fast as the apostle Paul exhorted, "watch ye, stand fast in the faith, quit you like men, be strong" (1 Corinthians 16:13).

Toil and despair lulled Elijah into sleep under a juniper shrub. So what can the juniper shrub teach us about God's provision for his servant? Clearly, the shrub was there in the desert at God's behest. The juniper, although sparse in foliage would, in a remarkable way protect Elijah from the scorching heat of the noonday sun. How could this be? We have already noted that the shrub produces long, erect and drooping stems, very much like reeds that freely sway in the slightest breeze to create a movement of refreshing air. No matter how still the air, a shrub like the juniper will always generate a cooling breeze through the gentle movement of the lengthy stems, a breeze sufficient to cool and refresh the prophet. One might consider a gentle breeze the minimum of God's provisions, but as the prophet was greatly agitated, hot and bothered, any cooling winds stronger than a gentle breeze might have affected his physical well being. Jehovah knew exactly what conditions would best suit His servant to revive his state of body, mind and spirit. The juniper shrub speaks of the way God communicates and cares for His servants. God is able and ready to bring refreshing winds from out of His treasuries (Psalm 135:7). An angel of the Lord had twice fed Elijah, whereby he regained his strength both mentally and physically and was ready to come under the influence of the Spirit of God. The blowing of a cool breeze is similar to the movement of the Holy Spirit in this day of grace (John 3:8).

At Mount Horeb, Elijah learnt how God speaks to His servants. Not through the ferocity of winds or the violent upheaval from earthquakes, nor even from the vehemence of destructive fire, but via a "still small voice" (1 Kings 19:12). The descent of the Holy Spirit at Pentecost was a unique event and should not be confused with the gentle way God speaks to us today through His Spirit (John 10:27). On that remarkable day, as recorded in Acts 2:2; the impact on creation was such that it was likened unto, "a rushing mighty wind". Alas, a day is coming when a voice from heaven will have a devastating impact on all creation; its destructive force on the earth will exceed anything man has known since creation (Revelation 16:17-18).

Elijah in the Sinai Peninsula was far away from the commercial activities of the world. We too, in the spiritual realm of things, are in desert conditions where it is essential to follow the pattern the Lord Jesus set as dependant Man on earth. He opened His ear morning by morning to hear what the Lord His God would speak (Isaiah 50:4-5). May our gracious Lord daily help us to hear His still small voice, that says, "this is the way, walk ye in it" (Isaiah 30:21).

In the wilderness before thee, desert lands where drought abides;
Heavenly springs shall there restore thee, fresh from God's exhaustless tides.

J N Darby

Lentils

Lens culinaris

Hebrew: 'Adash = Lentil pea.
Genesis 25:34. 2 Samuel 17:28; 23:11. Exekiel 4:9.

The Lentil pea is a native plant of the Mediterranean and Middle Eastern region. The plant is an annual, developing several straggly, basal stems rarely exceeding a height of 45 cm and having pinnate leaves terminating in tendrils. The pea-like, pale blue flowers produce small pods containing one or two reddish-brown seeds. The seeds produce highly nutritious soups, and when mixed with barley flour, make bread for the poor. When David was hiding from Absalom, friends brought him and his supporters victuals that included lentils, because they knew something of the dietary value of lentils for hungry men (2 Samuel 17:28).

The book of Genesis, as the title implies, is full of the beginning of things both good and bad, all of which stand out plainly to the prayerful reader. The narrative of Esau and Jacob in chapter 25 is yet another genesis of events that falls into line with the counsels and promises of God, and highlights the fact that divine sovereignty

supersedes man's ingenuity. We know from verse 23 of the chapter before us, that God had told Rebekah about the two sons to be born to her, and how that, "the elder shall serve the younger". There seems little doubt that Rebekah would have told her husband the outcome of her enquiry of the Lord regarding the twins she was carrying. However, according to what is subsequently recorded about Isaac, it would appear he disregarded the Lord's message to his wife. Nevertheless, let us look at Esau.

Esau had returned from a day's activity in the field; he was weary, exhausted and famished to the point of total collapse. In desperation and for fear he might die of hunger, he appealed to his younger brother to share some of the red pottage (lentil soup) he had prepared. Without a second thought for what should have been his most cherished possession, Esau despised and devalued his birthright (inheritance) for the immediate and temporary satisfaction of the flesh. In Genesis 49:3, we read that the inheritance of the firstborn is, "the beginning of strength, the excellency of dignity and the excellency of power". Esau profaned his birthright by selling it, and Jacob did wrong in deviously securing something that in God's time would be his by right. How often do we hear it said? It is one thing to know God, but quite another to wait His time. David said, "wait on the Lord, and keep His way, and He shall exalt thee to inherit the land" (Psalm 37:34).

It was while Esau was at his lowest ebb physically, that he fell into the trap of making an irrevocable oath with his brother regarding the family inheritance (Genesis 25:33). Later, Jacob secures the assurance of entitlement to the inheritance by receiving the primary and final blessing of his father (Genesis 27:26-29). While the activities of Jacob are an integral part of the Esau saga, he is not the focus of our attention at this time. Nevertheless, we can say that Jacob seized upon an opportunity to secure, by devious means, what God had already determined should be his in due time (Genesis 25:23). May the Lord in His goodness, keep us from scheming and devising plans of our own whenever we have exercises about issues affecting our spiritual lives. Let us leave everything to Him Who knows the end from the beginning. David's 37th Psalm is reassuring. In verse 1 we have, "fret not thyself because of evil doers"; verse 3 "trust in the Lord"; verse 4 "delight thyself in the Lord"; verse 5 "commit thy way unto the Lord" and verse 7 "rest in the Lord" (Psalm 37:1-7).

Nothing in God's plan could excuse Esau from being personally responsible for the gravity of his action. Esau despised and sold his birthright for a mess of pottage, thus meriting the judgment of Almighty God, "Jacob have I loved, but Esau have I hated" (Romans 9:13). The highly nutritious lentil broth Jacob sold to Esau would have been both filling and satisfying, but its benefits would only have lasted for a day. Esau found the 'red pottage' very attractive, just as the world today wraps everything in glitter to deceive the eye and tempt the unwary. Red is the colour associated with the earth, and Esau was a man of the earth, after the flesh. Likewise, everything the world has to offer the Christian believer is of the earth. Nothing from the world is of an enduring or spiritual character; such provisions provide only temporary satisfaction to the carnal mind and body. Esau's occupation and the profaning of his birthright are typical of unregenerate man after the flesh; the natural heart of man attaches no value whatsoever to divine things.

John in his first epistle said, "for all that is in the world, the lust of the flesh, the lust of the eyes, and the pride of life, are not of the Father, but of the world" (1 John 2:16). In Christ, "we (Christian believers) have obtained an inheritance, being predestinated according to the purpose of Him (God) Who worketh all things after the counsel of His own will" (Ephesians 1:11). The inheritance of an estate naturally belongs to the 'firstborn'. According to Romans 8:29, Christ is the 'Firstborn' among many brethren (the redeemed). However, in sovereign grace, "the Spirit of God itself beareth witness with our spirit that we are the children of God. If children, then heirs, heirs of God, and joint heirs with Christ" (Romans 8:16-17). We have the earnest of our inheritance now, so may its value to our souls increase as we see the day approaching for the redemption of our bodies (Romans 8:23). This is a great matter, not to be lightly esteemed as Esau profaned his birthright. Through prayer, our gracious God will help us to comprehend more of the vast treasury of divine truth His Spirit would bring within the compass of our understanding.

> *His purposes will ripen fast, unfolding every hour,*
> *The bud may have a bitter taste, but sweet will be the flower.*
> *Blind unbelief is sure to err, and scan His work in vain;*
> *God is His own interpreter, and He will make it plain.*
>
> W Cowper

Lily

Lilium candidum

Hebrew: Shushan = From the whiteness of the flower, a straight trumpet, tubular shape. Madonna lily.
Shoshannim in the headings of Psalm 45:1, 69:1 & 80:1.
1 Kings 7:19, 22 & 26 + ten other references.

The Madonna lily grows freely throughout Galilee and even on Mount Carmel. A bulbous, herbaceous perennial plant, with stems up to 1 m high and terminating with clusters of large, pure white trumpet-like flowers held at right-angle to the stem. The lily flower speaks of the clarity, power and purity of our Lord's testimony on earth. The noun Shoshannim in the headings of Psalm 45, 69 & 80 indicates that the message in the said Psalms is to be heard and understood by all nations. Psalm 45 gives us the celebration of the Messiah the King and tells aloud of His majesty, glory and righteousness. Psalm 69 begins with the cry of the One who answered to God for our sins in His body on the tree, and ends with the glorious result of His atoning work. Psalm 80, written by Asaph, is a brief account of the consequences of God's wayward people – Israel. Asaph called on the Lord to restore Israel in the land, that they might again be a fruitful nation for the glory of God. The lily flower also conveys the thought that every Christian believer is an instrument for oral praise in the service of God and a messenger of the Gospel of God's grace to needy sinners.

Trumpets had an important role in the economy of Israel. In Leviticus 23:23-25 we have the Feast of the Blowing of Trumpets. Such a Feast looked on to a coming day when the faithful remnant of Israel will blow the trumpets as a reverential memorial of the Messiah they once rejected and crucified. The trumpet call will also signal the coming in of the glory and blessing that will reside on and in Israel for a thousand years. In that day, the resonance of the trumpet sound will reach the four quarters of the world; no nation will be unaffected by the coming in of the Millennial age. However, in Numbers 10:1-10, the significance of the trumpet blowing has a current application. The clear sounding of the silver trumpets by the priests was a signal for the nation (camp) to move forward in an orderly way. This trumpet blowing parallels the spiritual ministry of the Lord's servants today; a ministry that encourages Christian believers to move forward in their spiritual lives. The apostle Paul said, "I press toward the mark for the prize of the high calling of God in Christ Jesus" (Philippians 3:14). The trumpets would also sound whenever the people were to prepare for war. To venture a war without a sounding of the trumpets would expose the people to defeat by their enemies, because the Lord would not be with them. The warfare today in which the Christian gets involved is defined in Ephesians 6:12. Victory in such warfare is accomplished through prayer (Ephesians 6:18). We should never engage in a warfare of words, either with or against our brethren; to do so would be confirmation that the Lord is not with us, and we shall suffer loss (James 3:14-16). Finally, the trumpet sounded to announce a victory and the time for rejoicing. The apostle Paul exhorted the Philippian Christians to, "rejoice in the Lord always, and again I say, rejoice" (Philippians 4:4).

In Joshua 6:20, we read that the priests, after they had circumnavigated the city of Jericho seven times on the seventh day, gave a continuous blast on their trumpets. The children of Israel recognised the clear, unmistakable sound of the trumpets, and knew it was the signal to shout in unison. Accordingly, the entire company lifted its voice with a great shout of triumph. Whereupon, the mighty walls of Jericho disappeared from sight before their very eyes, opening the way for them to go in and take the city. If the children of Israel had not responded to the sounding of the trumpets, the consequences for them would have been disastrous. The message of the gospel through God's servants today, is the clarion call to the world that the Lord Jesus Christ has triumphed over sin, death and the grave. Through repentance before God and faith in our Lord Jesus Christ, individuals can now be saved from eternal loss and condemnation (John 5:24). Christian believers today have a responsibility to sound the trumpet call of the gospel, warning the people that very soon it may be too late. As watchmen, we can see the time fast approaching when God's day of grace will end; and end abruptly, within the twinkling of an eye. See Ezekiel 33:1-9 & 1 Corinthians 15:52.

Solomon had two large brazen pillars built to support the porch of the Temple, one he called Jacin, the other Boaz. At the top of each pillar he set a bowl-shaped chapiter 5 cubits (2.3 m) high, decorated with seven linked wreaths of chain-work fashioned as lilies and containing 200 brazen fruits in the design of pomegranates. I hope, in the will of the Lord, to discuss the significance of 'pomegranates' later in the book. The two pillars named Jacin, meaning 'I will establish' and Boaz, meaning 'strength' form an integral part of the typical teaching of the structure and magnificence of Solomon's Temple. The Temple itself spoke of the glory and splendour of the Millennial age, when the Prince of Peace will reign in Righteousness throughout the world with His Throne in Jerusalem. The two great pillars of truth, Jacin and Boaz will be evident throughout the 1000 years. However, heading the conspicuous and permanent great pillars, will be the continuous witness, testimony and praise of the redeemed, reigning with Christ; hence the significance of the lilies decorating the top of the pillars in the Temple. The foundation of the Church of Christ is well established and sustained with great strength. The Lord's response to Peter's confession, that He is, "the Christ, the Son of the living God", was, "upon this rock will I build my Church and the gates of Hades shall not prevail against it" (Matthew 16:16 & 18). The Lord's statement embraced the typical significance of the two pillars in the temple. Christ has established His Church on a firm foundation, and its strength is such that Hades gates will never prevail against it.

The design of lilies in the linked wreaths and their position at the top of the pillars would say something about the importance of ensuring that the testimony of God's grace will be heard throughout the world. It is generally known that whenever trumpeters are required to play fanfares on special occasions in castles or state buildings, they are always set in some elevated position to ensure the fanfare is heard throughout the building. While Christian believers have no desire to be set in high places by the world, they do have a responsibility to preach the 'Gospel of the grace of God' to every nation, people and tongue (Matthew 28:19-20).

We have a lovely thought in Song of Solomon 2:1 where the bride identifies herself as 'the lily of the valleys'. That is not a statement of pride or arrogance, but a humble recognition and declaration of one's spiritual apprehension of the divine dignity bestowed on her by the Bridegroom (Ephesians 5:25-27). Although the world cannot appreciate the bride's beauty, the Bridegroom was happy to say. "as the lily among thorns, so is my love among the daughters". Here, the title 'lily' is the Bridegroom's estimate of the bride. The bold flower of the lily stands over and above the ground-hugging thorns, the latter being a figure of the ungodly. Such a picture conveys a message to our souls that the Christian believer ought to be known and read of all men (2 Corinthians 3:2-3). In Song of Solomon 2:16 we have a touching millennial scene. In that coming day of glory, the Lord will delight to be refreshed as He moves among His own, the children of Israel who at long last will be resting and at peace in their own land. Meanwhile, our blessed Lord loves to be refreshed by His own – the bride of Christ – finding satisfaction and delight as He is exalted in their hearts. We have a similar thought in chapter 6:3 where it speaks of the Bridegroom feeding among the lilies. The Lord Jesus loves to presence Himself in the midst of His own where He leads the singing.

In S. of S. 5:10-16, we have a record of the bride's spiritual apprehension of her beloved. "His lips like lilies, dropping sweet smelling myrrh"; verse 13. What a lovely definition of the lily's reflexed petals. The open character of the lily beautifully illustrates the way in which the words of grace freely flowed from the Saviour's lips (Psalm 45:2; Luke 4:22). Lily petals gently moving in the breeze – His lips moved under the influence of the Spirit of God – everywhere spreading the fragrance of His gracious words and lovely disposition. "Never man spake like this man" (John 7:46). The Lord Jesus had the tongue of the learned, and therefore knew how to speak a word in season to him that was weary (Isaiah 50:4).

Hosea, like most of the minor prophets, highlighted the gravity of Israel's sin, the severity of God's judgment on the nation, and their future recovery and blessing. However, God has determined the nation will only be brought back into relationship with Him on the basis of repentance and acceptance of the One they cast out and crucified. God has said through Hosea, "I will heal their backsliding, I will love them freely; for mine anger is turned away from them" (Hosea 14:4). God has also said that the nation, "will blossom as the lily", verse 5 (JND). The thought here is that the nation of Israel will be prominent, standing above all other nations for glory, beauty and honour, and that her influence will spread throughout the world. May the Lord help us in our Christian witness, to stand firm with holy dignity, and to boldly sound out the Gospel of God's grace for the glory of Christ (2 Corinthians 4:3).

'Tis well when on the mount, we feast and joy in love;
And 'tis as well, in God's account, when we the furnace prove.
But above all, how well, when Jesus speaks the word;
And, at the trumpet's sounding swell, we rise to meet the Lord.

J Kent

Lily - Anemone

Anemone coronaria

Greek: Krinon = The Crown anemone.
Matthew 6:28; Luke12:27.

The 'lily of the field', to which the Lord Jesus referred in Matthew 6 and Luke 12, is anemone coronaria, the 'crown anemone' or 'wind flower'. This lovely flower, found in the majority of English gardens, covers the fields and mountains of Palestine every Spring. Colours include red, purple, pink, blue and white, with red being the most

common. The plant belongs to the buttercup family and is a perennial with a rhizome/ corm. Breaking out into growth after the winter snows, anemone flowers adorn the mountainous region of Palestine. The more severe the winter, the more abundant and brighter the flowers. Very much like Christian believers who are rightly exercised by the chastening hand of the Lord; they will always be found more pleasing, bright and refreshing (Heb. 12:11). The name 'wind flower' comes from the Latin meaning of 'anemone'. The ancients called the anemone, 'wind flower', because the plant prospers where it is exposed to the winds in open and elevated places such as mountain regions. Christian believers too, should be aware of their elevated place in Christ – out of this world – and daily coming under the influence of the Spirit of God (Romans 8:4, 14 & 16).

The anemone flower is unusual in that unlike most flowers, it does not have separate calyx and petals, instead, it has what we call 'sepals'. The calyx that envelops the flower bud in the vast majority of flowering plants, is typical of the flesh, for even when the flower is fully open, the calyx remains closely attached. The apostle Paul was conscious of the fact that the flesh was ever with him. Nevertheless he triumphed in the knowledge that it was the 'new man' that served God in the Spirit, and the 'old man' – the flesh – that served the law of sin (Romans 7:25). In the case of the Anemone, we observe only the developing bud – the new man – gradually changing to the final colour and open beauty of the flower. Christian believers are daily taking on the features of Christ, and as growing up in Him are reflecting His moral glories (2 Cor. 3:18). The range of flower colour fits in beautifully with the Lord's reference to the 'lilies of the field'. No two Christians are alike, for we reflect the Person of Christ in different ways and with different degrees of intensity; just as the four Gospels give us a fourfold impression of the glorious worth of our blessed Saviour. Our potential to show forth the praises of Him Who hath called us out of darkness into His marvellous light, was implanted within us the moment we believed and were in-dwelt (baptised) with the Holy Spirit of God (1 Peter 2:9).

The statement in Matthew 6:25, 31 & 34; & Luke 12:22 'take no thought', as given in the KJAV, is incorrect; the text should read 'be not anxious'. At no time did the Lord imply that His disciples should be mindless and indifferent about the things of life. Rather, He would have them prayerfully exercised about everything around them. The Lord knew that at times, those to whom He was speaking would be unduly anxious about material things. He therefore lovingly assures them that His Father already knows about the things they will need when they follow Him in the pathway of discipleship. The moral qualities of life are more important than tangible provisions. Material things are entrusted to our stewardship, but spiritual things are given for our retention, growth, enjoyment, service and blessing. If only we were as unconcerned about tomorrow as are the birds, we would sing as cheerfully as they do. It is our over concern about worldly and temporal needs that disturbs our peace, dampens our joy and silences our praise.

Solomon in all his glory pales to insignificance when set against the splendour of the crown anemone; to say nothing of the moral excellencies that clothed that blessed Person through Whom all the resplendent glories of the Godhead shone. Sadly, the Lord's own people for whom He had come, saw no beauty in Him (Isaiah 53:2-3). They mockingly stripped Him of the robe that marked Him out as One who was complete and perfect in every glorious, moral attribute of His manhood. The One they rejected, was He who first clothed man with raiment, the beasts with hide, the birds with feathers and the fishes with scales; He covered the land with trees, the fields with flowers and the heavens with stars. Yet, all His wondrous works of creation, together with those on earth as Messiah, were of no consequence to a rebellious nation. Nevertheless, no matter what sinful man did to that glorious Person, they could not diminish the unique, moral beauties that shone through the human veil.

The crown anemone is not an aggressive subject and does not compete with other plants; but is gentle, delicate and unassuming with its flower head appearing just above the grass of the field. The 'field' in Matthew 6:30 & Luke 12:28 is the world; while the 'grass' speaks of mankind generally. However, the 'Lilies of the field' are a figure of the redeemed who clothe the world with the moral comeliness of the 'new man' (Ephesians 4:24). Everything about the crown anemone tells us that the Christian believer should be a bright testimony in the world, clothed with the moral graces of the Lord Jesus Christ. Grace and knowledge are the perfection's of the saints. Peter said, "grow in grace and in the knowledge of our Lord Jesus Christ" (2 Peter 3:18). Our physical appearance and status before the eyes of men must always be secondary to our spiritual state before God. Material adornments will perish, but the adornment of Christ will endure throughout eternity. May we ever seek to be clothed with the divine beauty of humility (Galatians 3:27).

> *Thy beauties Lord, Thy holy precious worth,*
> *Surpassing far the deepest joys of earth;*
> *Attract our hearts, our joy Thy constant love,*
> *Thyself our object in those scenes above.*
>
> C A Coates

Lotus

Diospyrus lotus

Hebrew: Tse'el = To be slender, shady, lotus tree/shrub.
Job 40:21 – 22.

The N.I.V. and J.N.D. versions of the Bible suggest the 'shady trees' of Job 40:21-22 are 'lotus trees' which is in line with the translation for Tse'el, as given in Strong's Exhaustive Hebrew/Greek Concordance. However, such a logical interpretation appears to command very little support from other biblical scholars and botanists, who themselves offer no suggestions as to the kind of tree referred to by Jehovah. As far as I am able to ascertain, the only tree that comes near to the interpretation for Tse'el, is Diospyrus lotus. A deciduous, well spread, loosely branched tree, reaching a height between 6 & 8 m and providing excellent shade over the water's edge wherein the reeds grow and the Hippopotamus is able to hide and rest unseen.

Notwithstanding the severity of Job's trial, he remained self-righteous and proud of his inner strength that had enabled him to survive his ordeal to date. He persevered in his reluctance to acknowledge that, "we are all as an unclean thing, and all our

righteousnesses are as filthy rags" (Isaiah 64:6), and that, "there is none righteous, no not one" (Romans 3:10). Jehovah enlightened Job on the fact that his natural attributes as man, could do nothing when it came to getting right with God. Job appeared full of pride, arrogant about his survival through great trial, and boastful of his strength. Jehovah would have him recognise that in God's creation there are forces infinitely greater than the natural man, albeit the natural man tries to emulate such forces. As an example of the proud, indifferent spirit of the natural man, Jehovah refers to the Hippopotamus as a creature that excels in strength, fears nothing, cannot be tamed, and vainly living for itself. The characteristic traits of the Hippopotamus were in Job. If he was ever going to be of use to Jehovah, he must come to the end of himself. Happily, in due course that is exactly what Job did according to chapter 42:5-6.

The shady lotus trees are like companies of Christian believers who unwittingly afford shelter, comfort, and space to unregenerate persons, unaware of their destructive force. Jude spoke of, "certain men who crept in unawares, who were before of old ordained to condemnation, ungodly men" (Jude 4). There are many people today who are making use of Christianity as a cloak under which to hide their true, unregenerate state. Such individuals are lurking dangers, appearing passive yet ready to exercise force should the occasion arise. Like the Hippopotamus, they feed on the pastures – hospitality of the saints – with avaricious greed while remaining indifferent about their need of salvation. Jude said of such people, they are hazardous rocks to avoid at all costs; they walk after their own lust and have not the Spirit of God (Jude 12, 18 & 19). May our gracious God help us to be humble in His service, to be empty of self, dependent on Him, vigilant, defensive and protective about all matters touching the glory, dignity, worth and work of our Lord Jesus Christ.

Oh, keep us, Father, near to Thee, that we our nothingness may know;
And ever to Thy glory be, walking in faith while here below.

J N Darby

Mallows

Atriplex halimus

Hebrew: Malluach = Saltiness. Shrubby Orache; Sea Purslane.
Job 30:4.

The mallow plant that grows wild in the English and European countryside is a completely different plant to the mallows referred to in the KJAV of the Bible. The consensus is that the Bible translators, who gave us the Authorised Version, decided on mallow because the name of the plant is similar to the Hebrew noun, malluach. The Septuagint and NIV give 'salt herbs'; while JND gives 'salt wort' instead of mallow. The shrubby orache is an evergreen sub-shrub growing to a height between 1.5 – 2 m and is a common plant in the desert region around the Salt Sea. The silver-grey, hairy leaves were a source of nutrient rich food for the poor, and in times of drought, nomadic shepherds fed on the foliage and gave it to their sheep. The annual 'fat-hen' plant, chenopodium album, and the perennial 'good king henry' chenopodium bonus-henricus grow freely as a weed throughout Europe and belong to the same family of plants as the shrubby orache. The foliage of such plants is a useful food, either in salads or cooked and served as greens.

The young men who mocked Job were the outcasts of society; beggars, forced to live among the rocks and in holes in the ground. During the period of Job's prosperity, such people had respect for him and probably benefited from him, but now that he was destitute of all things and disfigured from the boils that covered his body, they despised him. One would not question the fact that it was very cruel of the young men to mock Job while he was in such a pathetic and grievous state of health. Nevertheless, Job's reaction to the insults of the young men was far removed from the gracious disposition of the Lord Jesus. "Who, when He was reviled, reviled not again; when He suffered, He threatened not, but committed Himself to Him that judgeth righteously" (1 Peter 2:23). The young men fled to the desert and found a meagre food supply in the small leaves of a shrubby orache.

I see in the provision of the orache leaves, the mercy of God toward the outcasts of society. While such continue alive in the day of God's grace, there remains the opportunity for repentance toward God and faith in the Lord Jesus Christ. The Lord Jesus confirmed this important truth in His assurance to the penitent thief on the cross (Luke 23:42-43). "The Lord is…longsuffering…not willing that any should perish, but that all should come to repentance" (2 Peter 3:9). The Lord Jesus cried from the cross, "Father, forgive them, for they know not what they do" (Luke 23:34). What we have in these words of the Lord, is a powerful lesson for all Christian believers. Whatever the reaction to our testimony of God's grace to man, we should never give up reaching out to souls, nor be discouraged by adverse reaction; rather, we should persevere in faith. Our primary mission while in the world, albeit not part of it, is to sow the seed of the Gospel, water it with our prayers and leave God to give the increase (1 Corinthians 3:7). May the Lord help us not to be disturbed by the world's estimate of us or by what it may do. Let us remember the reassuring words of the Lord Jesus, "in the world ye shall have tribulation, but be of good cheer, I have overcome the world" (John 16:33).

In the midst of opposition, let them trust, O Lord, in Thee;
When success attends their mission, let Thy servant humble be;
Never leave them, never leave them, till Thy face in heaven they see.

T Kelly

Mandrakes

Mandragora officinarum

Hebrew: Duday = An aphrodisiac, love apple, boiler, basket.
Genesis 30:14, 15 & 16. Song of Solomon 7:13.

The mandrake belongs to the potato, tomato and black nightshade family of plants. It is a stem-less perennial that develops a rosette of thick, glossy, wrinkle-edge leaves about 30 cm long and 12 cm wide at their broadest point, with prominent, thick set veins. The short-stem flowers are mauve to purple in colour and arise from the crown of the rosette, followed by fragrant, tomato-like yellow fruits. A belief reaching back to biblical times is that the mandrake fruits possess the properties of an aphrodisiac drug. While this may be perfectly true, it is also now recognised that the fruits will induce a voluptuous disposition if eaten. There remains a lot of superstition about the root of the mandrake plant having the appearance of a 'human being' if removed from the ground unbroken, but this is simply the interpretation of an imaginative mind working without inhibition. Notwithstanding the unusual bouquet of the mandrake fruits, they remain a pleasing and much sought after delicacy in Middle Eastern countries.

It is clear from the record we have in Genesis 29 & 30 that Jacob actually lived with Rachel whom he greatly loved above Leah. Leah was Rachel's elder sister whom Laban tricked Jacob into accepting as a wife. However, when the Lord saw that those near to Leah hated her (Genesis 29:31-32), He gave her four sons by Jacob, while her sister Rachel, remained childless. From a natural viewpoint, Rachel was understandably envious of her sister, and after the pattern of her scheming father Laban, was prepared to do anything to redress the situation. Rachel had already surrendered her handmaid Bilhah to Jacob on two occasions to be a surrogate mother for her. To Bilhah were born two sons, Dan and Naphtali, but still, Rachel did not have children of her own. Apart from Rachel's confession that God had judged her for what she had done (Genesis 30:6); she continued her tireless attempts to shortcut God's plan for her. One day during the wheat harvest, an excellent opportunity presented itself. Her young nephew Reuben found some mandrake fruits in the field, and being anxious to know if the attractively coloured fruits were safe to eat, brought them home to his mother Leah. Rachel, on seeing the mandrake fruits immediately appealed to Leah that she might have them. Leah demurs, but when Rachel barters her husband Jacob for the fruits, she obliges. Rachel believed that if she ate the fruits, she would more readily conceive and thereby achieve her great longing to have children of her own; but she had left the God of Abraham and Isaac out of her reckoning. Rachel was to see her sister bear two more sons and a daughter before she would have her first child.

The mandrake fruits represent the drugs of this world designed to excite the passions of the flesh; help short-cut natural, divinely designed and appointed procedures, and to overcome the disappointments in life. Rachel was not the first to attempt circumvention of God's timing of events. Abraham, albeit believing by faith all the promises God had made to him, nevertheless fell to the persuasion of his wife with disastrous results, Ishmael, the son of a bond-woman (Genesis 16:16). Jacob, 'the supplanter' on two occasions had attempted to shortcut God's timing to secure the 'birthright' God had already promised should be his. Rachel, as we already have seen, displayed much impatience with the timing of God's plan for her, and suffered the anguish of seeing her husband Jacob acquire10 sons while she remained childless. However, God did not forget Rachel; He heard her cry, and in His time blessed her with a son, Joseph. There are other examples in the Scriptures of individuals who, professedly God-fearing, displayed impatience about God's timing of events. Today, many of us behave in exactly the same way. We may have a genuine exercise about a divine issue, and pray earnestly for the Lord's help, guidance and intervention. However, all too frequently, instead of waiting on the Lord to show clearly the way ahead, we energetically seek our own solution to the problems we supposedly had left at the Throne of Grace (Hebrews 4:16). Impatience is like a spirit that craves for something to happen and to happen quickly; it is a spirit that disturbs our peace and contentment (1 Timothy 6:6). If we do not let patience have its perfect work in our souls, Satan will entice us to resort to the stimulants of the world to achieve our objectives, with disastrous results. James, in his epistle, said, "the trying of your faith worketh patience. But let patience have her perfect work, that ye may be perfect and entire, wanting nothing" (James 1:3-4).

> *To wait for that appointed day, when Christ His glories will display,*
> *Be this our one great care. In patience then we now would rest,*
> *Assured the Father's time is best; and all His word obey.*
>
> T Kelly

Millet or Sorghum

Panicum miliaceum or Sorghum vulgare

Hebrew: Dochan = Millet corn.
Ezekiel 4:9.

Biblical scholars accept that the Hebrew noun 'dochan' can apply equally well to both millet and sorghum. While the two plants are quite distinct and both indigenous to Middle Eastern countries, most translate 'dochan' as millet. Millet is more like grass, about 1 m high, with a loose panicle of insignificant flowers and yielding a reasonable

quantity of seed. Sorghum, on the other hand can reach a height of 3 m, heading up with densely branched panicles of flowers, producing five to six times as much seed as the millet plant. The seed of both plants was ground and used to make bread for the poor in the land. While millet is nowhere else recorded in the Scriptures, it is included in Ezekiel 4:9 because it made up the complete list of basic seed foods God provided for His people in the Promise Land.

God had determined that once His people had taken possession of the Promised Land, they would want for nothing in either food or drink. Sadly, the nation never realised the full potential of the land because they turned to idolatry and forsook the Lord that blessed them (Judges 2:12 -13). Now, in the time of Ezekiel, God's favoured nation was captive in a far off land, when it should have been enjoying the blessings of liberty and rest in the Land God gave them. The people had become servants of a heathen monarch instead of being worshippers of Jehovah. A nation that at one time was the envy and fear of nations around them, was now a despised remnant. Food and drink for the majority of the captive people was severely rationed, almost to starvation point, whereas in the Promised Land everything should have overflowed with the abundance God had promised, as 'milk and honey' for richness.

Ezekiel remained faithful to his God while a captive in Babylon, and was clearly repentant for all the sins of the people that occasioned their captivity under Nebuchadnezzar, King of Babylon. God required the faithful prophet to bear the iniquity of the children of Israel. First, the Lord told Ezekiel to portray Jerusalem and her fortifications on a brick tile, and then cover it with an iron plate on which he was to lay with one of his arms uncovered. The tile portraying Jerusalem was the city itself; while the iron plate set over the tile represented the iron force of the Chaldeans. Ezekiel laying on the plate with an uncovered arm was a figure of the arm of the Lord executing judgment. The Chaldeans would lay siege against Jerusalem and starve into submission the remaining Jews who had rebelled against God's plan for the whole nation to go into captivity. Ezekiel was to lay on his left side – the side of dishonour – for 390 days, and then on his right side – the side of favour – for a further 40 days. Throughout each of the 430 days, Ezekiel's food was a meagre portion (about 200 g) of very coarse bread made from a mixture of all the seed foods listed, and a very small amount of water (0.7 l). J. N. Darby calculates these two periods as follows. 'The 390 days would cover the 390 years since the death of Solomon to the destruction of the Temple, when the children of Israel were carried away captives. The 40 days would have had reference to the 40 years reign of Solomon.' The duration of the Solomon Kingdom determined the ruin and future judgment of Israel, including the most favoured tribe Judah, who, by turning away after other gods, misused the benefits yielded by so long and prosperous a reign.

God had provided all the seed foods necessary to ensure His people would be well nourished and sustained with a balanced diet in the Promised Land. Millet constituted an equally important element in the dietary requirement of the people. However, the manner in which the coarse bread was prepared and cooked for the prophet, was designed to reflect the unclean and idolatrous way Israel had polluted herself, the food and the Land. She had by her idolatry, also defiled the Name of Jehovah. Under normal conditions, the people would have used each seed item separately, for each had its own particular value and use in the economy of the nation. In captivity, the nation had no choice but to eat the polluted food of their Gentile captors.

We gladly render thanks to God, that in His mercy He has provided us with a rich, diverse yet divinely balanced spiritual menu for our sustenance and growth in the mind and things of God. We all are very much aware of the activities of Satan today, whose purpose is to confuse the saints of God by misinterpreting the Truth of Holy Scripture, and by mixing and misapplying types, figures, symbols and facts. The apostle Peter told us, "that no prophecy of Scripture is of any private interpretation" (2 Peter 1:20). In other words, no one Truth of Scripture can be fully understood in isolation from all that the Word gives elsewhere on the subject matter. May the Lord help us to, "study to show ourselves ('thyself' in the text) approved unto God, workmen (a workman) that needeth not to be ashamed, rightly dividing the Word of Truth" (2 Timothy 2:15). All Scripture, whether the profound truths of the Word (the Wheat and kernel) or the basic, fundamental teaching (the millet and rie), is essential and vital for our spiritual development in the school of God. "All Scripture is given by inspiration of God, and is profitable for doctrine, for reproof, for correction, for instruction in righteousness, that the man of God may be perfect, throughly furnished unto all good works" (2 Timothy 3:16-17).

> *When He makes bare His arm, who shall His work withstand;*
> *When He His people's cause defends, who then shall stay His hand?*
>
> Gerhardt

Mulberry

Populus tremula

Hebrew: Baka' = A weeping tree; gum distilling tree.
2 Samuel 5:23-24 & 1 Chronicles 14:14-15.

J N Darby's New Translation of the Bible, along with the KJAV, translates Baca' as mulberry. Most other expositors of the Word, believe the tree referred to in the above Scriptures is in fact an aspen, Populus tremula; while a few, because of the meaning of the Hebrew noun, think it is Populus balsamifera. According to some botanists, 'poplar tremula' was so named because the foliage is in a perpetual state of agitation, much like the population of the world. J C Loudon says that the aspen poplar tree was found planted along every street of traffic in ancient Rome and thereby gained the name 'arbor populi'. However, notwithstanding the forgoing, we know that the Mighty Creator of all things could have made any tree to rustle and sound like 'marching troops'. Matthew Henry has beautifully interpreted the incident recorded in 2 Samuel 5:23-35. 'Angels tread light, and He that can walk on the clouds can, when He pleases, walk on the top of trees.' While an accurate identity of the tree is helpful, it is nowhere near as important as the lesson the Spirit of God would have us gain from the narrative. The poplar mentioned above is deciduous and grows to a height of between 20 and 25

m; a forest of such trees would meet the criteria of the narrative as it appears in the Scriptures before us. Populus tremula suckers profusely to give adequate ground cover.

The record we have of David seeking the Lord's mind about meeting the Philistines (2 Samuel 5:23-25), shows him in the spirit of Proverbs 3:6, "in all thy ways acknowledge Him, and he shall direct thy paths". As a servant of the Lord, David was ready to let the Lord take the initiative, just as he did when he came face to face with Goliath. On that occasion he said to Goliath, "the battle is the Lord's, he will give you into our hands" (1 Samuel 17:47) and that is exactly what happened. Although David had great resources, he still owned his dependence upon the Lord. Our blessed Lord Himself, as dependent Man on earth, was ever the Mighty Creator with all the resources of the universe at His disposal; yet as Man, He daily sought to know and do His Father's will (John 8:29). So, here in 2 Samuel 5:19, David asked the Lord, "shall I go up against the Philistines"? The Lord answered no, but advises David to manoeuvre his forces to position them strategically behind the forest. A vital lesson for souls today is this. No matter how resourceful, good and strong we think we are, we shall achieve nothing for the glory of God in our service for Him if we are not unconditionally wholly dependant on the Lord. The apostle Paul readily acknowledged his weakness, and in so doing became conscious of his spiritual strength in the Lord (2 Corinthians 12:10). The many doxologies (over 1 dozen) of the apostle Paul are a confirmation of his readiness ever to give God the glory in every area of his service for Him. "Now unto the King eternal, immortal, invisible, the only wise God, be honour and glory for ever and ever, Amen" (1 Timothy 1:17).

God had told David He was going out before him to smite the Philistines and that his army must not move against the enemy until they hear the sound of 'marching troops' in the tops of the trees. So frightening would be the sound to the Philistines, they would be put to flight. David's army would then pursue the Philistines and smite them from Gibeon to Gazer. (Gibeon lies 10 km N.W. of Jerusalem, and Gazer is approx. 30 km West of Gibeon). The lesson we gain from the way God used the trees to signal the advance of David's army is both helpful and instructive. First, it is vitally important for every servant of the Lord to have a firm conviction they are where the Lord has sent and put them, and not necessarily, where they personally want to be (Acts 8:26-40). Secondly, the servant must have his/her ear open and ready every day to hear what the Lord their God would speak (Isaiah 50:5). Jehovah spoke from Mount Sinai with the sound of thunder and with great force that it occasioned an earthquake (Exodus 19:18-19). The Lord called Samuel in the middle of the night, and as soon as he realised the calls were from the Lord, he replied, "speak, for thy servant heareth" (1 Samuel 3:10). Jehovah spoke to Elijah in a still small voice; yet he clearly heard what the Lord said to him (1 Kings 19:12-13).

From the many records we have of God speaking to His people or to individuals, it is evident the modulation of His voice was appropriate to the occasion. Compare the voice of God at Mount Sinai with His voice to Elijah. We see this also in the way the Lord Jesus spoke in the Temple, to the crowds, the unregenerate Pharisees, His disciples and to individuals. So with us, if we are daily waiting to hear the voice of the Lord for help and guidance, it may be the 'still small voice'. However, if we are out of touch with the Lord in our lives and out of alignment with divine thought, His voice will be loud enough to arrest us in our tracks to make us stop and listen. Finally, when the Lord speaks to His servants, there should be an immediate response to follow His call to service. No debate, no second thoughts, no running away and no delay, but a total commitment and delight to do His will (John 12:26). Daily communion with the Lord will leave us in no doubt when we hear His 'still small voice', saying, "this is the way, walk ye in it" (Isaiah 30:21).

Send us forth at Thy direction, to the places of Thy choice,
Yielding in complete subjection, listening only to Thy voice.
Bless and use us; in Thy service to rejoice.

T Kelly (arr.)

Mustard

Sinapis arvensis

Hebrew: Sinapi = To sting, to hurt. A mustard plant. Charlock.
Matthew 13:31 + four other references.

The mustard plant is an annual herb belonging to the cabbage family, bearing irregular-shaped leaves covered in firm hairs that can sting and leave a nasty rash if the plant is handled roughly. The mustard plant grows to a height of about 1.5 m with the many branches heading up with the characteristic yellow, four-petal flowers.

Each of the parables given in Matthew 13 relates to the Lord's definition of a kingdom within the sphere of God's creation. Accordingly, a more accurate reading of the heading to the parables is 'the kingdom of the heavens' because 'the heavens', like 'the earth', were also created. It is neither possible nor conceivable that the redeemed of the Lord comprising His Kingdom, could include anything offensive or unregenerate. The Lord's parabolic ministry was highlighting the environment in, and from which, He was building and securing His Church; and will continue to do so until God's day of grace closes.

Some have promulgated that the mustard grain (seed) applies to a plant that naturally develops into a tree; but this interpretation disregards the significance of the Lord's ministry. Our Lord was describing something out of the ordinary, something abnormal, unnatural and substantially different to the original character of such a plant. When the Lord Jesus said that the plant, when grown, would be the greatest of all herbs, He was forecasting the growth of Christendom. Our Lord described through the telling of the 'mustard seed' parable, how the Church, that began with just twelve disciples, would develop into a system we know today as Christendom. Such a system would grow in respect of size and character into something out of all proportion to what accorded with God's will. Nowhere in Scripture will you find that it was in the mind of God for the Church (the company of Christian believers) to become a large, powerful and influential body in the world. Such an objective runs counter to the considerable and crystal clear ministry of the Lord Jesus, confirmed by the apostles in the New Testament epistles. While exhorting His disciples to exercise a spirit of humility, meekness and lowliness, the Lord Jesus also told them what the world's attitude would be toward them (Matthew 10:16-18; & John 15:18-19).

From the year A.D. 54 to A.D. 312, ten Emperors in succession, from Nero to Diocletian, exercised a tyrannical reign throughout the world. During those 258 years, the Church experienced horrendous persecution, for it was the time of her severest trial and suffering. Nevertheless, the Church, while remaining like the small mustard plant, despised and disregarded, never gave up its faith in the expectation of the Lord's immediate coming to call His redeemed home to glory. However, when Constantine cancelled the Diocletian edict that demanded the persecution and death of all Christians, he, as an unregenerate man, unwisely married the Church to the state. It was from this time, the beginning of the Pergamos period, that the Church fell asleep and lost its hope and faith in the immediate return of the Lord Jesus for His own; see Matthew 25:5. Happily, the Church was awoken to such a hope in the early 19th century, and still cherishes the expectation of the imminent call from the clouds by the Lord Jesus for His own (Matthew 25:6-7 & 1 Thessalonians 4:16-18). The early 4th century was also the time when the mustard plant began to grow out of all proportion to its natural habit; in other words; it was the beginning of Christendom as we know it today.

How then should we define Christendom? It includes national Churches such as the Church of England and Church of Scotland; the Roman Catholic Church; Greek and Russian Orthodox Churches; Lutheran Church, Baptists; Methodists, Non-Conformist, and Undenominational, to list but a few; all come under the heading of Christendom. No matter where or with whom God fearing Christian believers meet in any of the forgoing, or in Chapels, Meeting Rooms and simple Gospel Halls, all are within the system of Christendom today. Christendom therefore embraces all that acknowledges the God of creation and own Jesus Christ as the Son of God. However, within the system of Christendom is the true Church of God (Matthew 16:16-18). Such a Church (not a building or man approved body) is comprised of all individuals that have repented of their sins before God, and put their faith and trust in a living Saviour, the Lord Jesus Christ (Acts 17:30). Yes, every one who believes the Lord Jesus Christ died for their sins and the sin of the world, that He was buried and rose again the third day, is a Christian believer (Romans 10:9-10). This then is the definition of the mustard plant the Lord Jesus referred to, that grew in size and character out of all proportion to its natural form. The Lord went on to say that 'the birds of the air nested in the branches of the mustard tree'. The birds of the air represent evil, unregenerate individuals within Christendom who take advantage of every facility afforded by the tree to promulgate and exercise their ungodly, unclean, polluting and lawless activities unabated. We would do well to heed the warning given in the Scriptures concerning such individuals. A few of the many references are: 2 Timothy 3:12-14; 2 Peter 3:3-4 & Jude 4.

In Matthew 17:20 the Lord Jesus censured His disciples about their lack of faith, and referred to the enormous potential in a grain of mustard (seed). If only the disciples had such quality of faith, equal in strength to the latent, natural energies and resources present in a small mustard seed, they too would have been able to perform miracles. However, the Lord said that such quality of faith comes only with prayer and fasting. Furthermore, He said that the power and might of the world as seen in the mountains, disappear through the exercise of faith, no matter how small that faith may be. The Lord had previously sent His disciples out by two's in the power of His Spirit, to preach the gospel of the Kingdom (Matthew 10:1-42). He also gave them, through the exercise of their faith, power to heal the sick, raise the dead, cleanse the unclean and cast out devils. Alas, their mission ended prematurely and coincident with their loss of dependent faith. Accordingly, when the occasion arose for them to exercise their faith in healing the lunatic son, they were impotent; the quality of their faith was poor and deficient. The disciples would learn, as we should, that nothing short of total commitment and unswerving faith in God, is necessary in the service of the Lord (1 Thessalonians 1:3).

> *In the midst of opposition, let Thy servants trust in Thee;*
> *When success attends their mission, let them ever, humble be.*
> *Never leave them, pray we for them, that Thy glory all may see.*
>
> T Kelly (Arr.)

Myrrh

Commiphora abyssinica

Hebrew: Mor = As distilling in drops; bitter. Greek: Smurna = A fragrant perfumed oil.
Greek: Smurnizo = To tincture with Myrrh; a narcotic.
Exodus 30:23 + thirteen other references.

Myrrh is an aromatic resin obtained from the small, commiphora abyssinica bush. The plant grows in wild desert places and survives harsh environmental conditions. It is a deciduous shrub with thorns, growing to about 2 m high with heavily knotted branches. The leaves are units of three ovate leaflets; the flowers are small and white, followed by olive-like fruits. The plant has the general appearance of having survived extremely hostile growing conditions; yet, notwithstanding such adverse circumstances, it continues to yield precious, aromatic resin. The reddish-brown, translucent, teardrop size nodules of solidified resin are painstakingly gathered by hand two or three times a week.

Without exception, myrrh in Scripture speaks of the fragrance that arises to God from the righteous sufferings of His people. Myrrh resin exudes spontaneously from the branches of the shrub, very much like our Lord in His pathway here; for no matter how much He suffered at the hand of man, He continued to yield sweet fragrance to God. Hence, the quantity of liquid myrrh for use in the Holy Anointing oil was 500 shekels. This was twice as much as two of the other constituents, giving us, in measure, an impression about God's estimate of His beloved Son in manhood. The world's opposition to the testimony of the Lord Jesus was in no way concealed. The deep wounds inflicted upon Him and the consequent sufferings He endured, were plain for all to see (Lamentations1:12).

For well over three years, the Lord experienced hostile reactions against His Person, His Words and His Work; yet He faithfully continued to minister pleasure and glory to His Father (John 8:29). He was truly the lonely, solitary stranger of Galilee; the despised Nazarene who found no place to lay His head in the world His hands had made (Luke 9:58). He was rejected by His own nation, misunderstood by His followers, hated by His foes, harassed by Satan, persecuted, mocked, abused and finally crucified on Calvary's cross. On that cross, He was subjected to the rude gaze and unholy utterances of a frenzied mob; and while beset by bulls of Bashan, and encompassed with dogs; He lovingly said, "Father, forgive them, for they know not what they do" (Luke 23:34). Who could possibly comprehend the profundity of such suffering love, save God alone? Yet it is on sinful man that such love is unsparingly poured (1 John 4:9-10). The 500 shekels of 'liquid myrrh' that had to be taken as a constituent of the Holy anointing oil (Exodus 30:23), would have been obtained by incising the small trunk and branches of the shrub. In figure, the liquid myrrh also flowed freely from the Lord Jesus during the three hours of darkness on the cross, when He exhausted God's judgment for sin, culminating with His words, "It is finished" (John 19:30). On that occasion, the incising was by the hand of Almighty God; for never before had such enduring suffering occasioned so great an outpouring of incense, redolently unique and solely for the delight of God, His Father. Our blessed Lord had glorified His Father, and completed the work given Him to do (John 17:4).

We have seen that the primary reason for the inclusion of myrrh in the Holy anointing oil was that it spoke of what would arise to God from the sufferings of Christ for righteousness sake. However, the effect of myrrh is typical also of what should mark all Christian believers indwelt with the Holy Spirit of God. As we have seen, myrrh speaks of the sweet fragrance that ascends to God when His children endure suffering as a good soldier of Jesus Christ (2 Timothy 2:3). The apostle Paul spoke often of his experiences consequent on his testimony; how he was troubled, but not distressed; perplexed, but not in despair, persecuted, but not forsaken, cast down, but not destroyed, always bearing about in his body the dying of the Lord Jesus (2 Corinthians 4:8-10). The reason for the death of the Lord Jesus Christ should ever be in our thoughts and hearts, and reflected in our path of testimony, just as it was with the apostle Paul.

It is clear that the only place on earth where the Lord Jesus is wanted is in the hearts of His loved ones. It is the bride who is speaking in Song of Solomon 1:13, when she said, "a bundle of myrrh is my well-beloved unto me; He shall lie all night betwixt my breasts". While this verse has reference to the remnant of Israel in a coming day of trial, it nevertheless has a lovely application for Christian believers today. If we enclose Him in the affections of our hearts, we shall have the ongoing experience in our souls of the worth, preciousness and fragrance of His Holy Person. The Scripture tells us that during the long, dark night of our Lord's shameful rejection by the world, He was valued and treasured in the personal and innermost affections of His own. We would do well to challenge our hearts and ask; why did our Lord become a man to experience suffering, hunger and thirst; to be 'made a little lower than the angels for the suffering of death'? Why did He allow Himself to be mocked, spit upon, assaulted and crowned with a cruel crown of thorns, and then not resist when He knew He would be 'stricken, smitten and afflicted'? Why did He take the position where He knew He would be despised and rejected by men; where He would be a 'man of sorrows and acquainted with grief', why did He give Himself a ransom for all? The answer, "Christ loved the Church and gave Himself for it" (Ephesians 5:25). From such unique sufferings, there is a precious, rich and eternal fragrance filling the courts of heaven.

Mark 15:23 records that when the Lord Jesus arrived at the place called Calvary, "they gave Him to drink, wine mingled with myrrh; but He received it not". Matthew's record of the event says, "they gave Him vinegar to drink mingled with gall", while Luke simple says, "soldiers also mocked Him, coming to Him and offering Him vinegar". By all accounts, it was the custom to offer an opiate drink to those to be crucified and so render numb all sense of pain. However, whatever the draught offered; it was clear the Lord would take nothing to alleviate His physical sufferings. *Do please refer to my thoughts on this subject under 'Gall'.*

While Smyrna is the Greek noun for myrrh, it is also the name of a city in Western Turkey, referred to in the second letter to the seven Churches (Revelation 2:8-11). The Smyrnean era of the Church's history covered the period from A.D. 54 (some think a little later) to A.D. 313. In any event, the Church at Smyrna survived the cruel reign of 10 tyrannical emperors, from Nero to Diocletian; it was a time of the severest trial Christian believers have ever experienced in this day of God's grace. Furthermore, never since the Smyrnean period has there ascended to God a comparable richness of fragrance, occasioned by the patient and faithful endurance by Christian believers of such cruel persecutions. The incising of the myrrh shrub (the Smyrnean church in this instance) allowed the precious and fragrant 'liquid myrrh' to flow out freely for the pleasure of God. In contrast with the Laodicean Church, the Church at Smyrna was materially very poor, but very much alive and abounded with spiritual wealth. It should be a great comfort to our souls to know that Satan cannot eliminate the Church (Matthew 16:18), for she is a habitation of God through the Spirit (Ephesians 2:22). We pray the Lord will help us, to not only hear what the Spirit says to the Churches, but also daily seek the Lord's mind for our individual paths of service for Him. We too can be a source of sweet fragrance of Christ to God if we have the same yearning in our hearts as the apostle Paul. Paul's great desire was, "that I may know Him, and the power of His resurrection, and the fellowship of His sufferings, being made conformable unto His death." (Philippians 3:10).

> *We praise Thee Lord, for all that precious myrrh,*
> *That from Thy sufferings did so freely flow;*
> *Its fragrance pure, unique, still will endure,*
> *To tell of love Thou hast on us bestowed.*
>
> T H Ratcliffe

Myrrh - Lot

Cistus incanus, C. laurifolius, C. ladaniferus

Hebrew: Lot = From its sticky nature, a gum. Ladanum.
Genesis 37:25 & 43:11.

According to the late Michael Zohary, Professor of Botany at the Hebrew University, Jerusalem, 'lot' is the resinous substance (ladanum) obtained from cistus incanus. Other biblical botanists believe that 'lot' came from cistus laurifolius, while some say the source of the resin was cistus ladaniferus. However, all three species produce the resin. The substance oozes from the base of the leaves and from the stem, but unlike commifera abyssinica, incising the stems does not increase the flow of resin. The shrubs grow wild in Middle Eastern desert regions, which is their natural habitat. The resin was collected by dragging leather-thong rakes over the bushes; it was then scraped off the thongs and moulded into rolls ready for sale. A wooden comb is sometimes used to gather the gum from the beards of goats that graze amongst the bushes. Ladanum is fired like incense to allow the fragrant, disinfecting cloud to sweeten and cleanse the atmosphere of rooms and houses.

Under the guidance of the Spirit of God, Jacob included Lot (myrrh) in his gift to the

Rock rose (Lot)
Cistus incanus

151

'man of all Egypt' (Genesis 43:11). Unbeknown to Jacob, the Lord was going to effect a miraculous cleansing in the hearts of his sons who had corrupted their consciences by concealing from their father the heinous crime they committed 22 years earlier. Another thought arising from the inclusion of lot (myrrh) in the gift, is that the presence of Joseph in Pharaoh's palace would have had a unique cleansing effect on the entire establishment both in administration and on the moral environment. Once the brothers had confessed to the nefarious crime committed against their brother Joseph, they were conscious that his disposition toward them had a cleansing influence on their hearts and in their minds. Furthermore, having filled his brothers with such a glorious hope, Joseph made them feel perfectly at ease in his presence. The brothers could now relax in a peaceful, pure and fragrant environment created by their younger brother whom they once rejected, but now happily acknowledge as the one God had prepared to save them alive.

As the Lord Jesus moved among the people, He left in His wake a fragrant, cleansing influence that changed the lives of many who were genuinely exercised by His presence (Luke 6:17-19). In the early part of His ministry, He was in Capernaum preaching, when suddenly an unclean spirit that had taken possession of a man, cried out in mockery. Jesus responded by silencing the demon and commanded it to leave the man (Mark 1:23-28). Here was an example of what would mark the service of the Lord Jesus, confirming to the people that God was among them for blessing (John 3:34-36). The active residence of the spirit of Satan in man renders him unclean; only the Spirit of the Lord Jesus can free him of its defiling influence. Today, the Gospel reaches out to mankind, announcing that repentance

Rock rose (Lot)
Cistus laurifolius

152

toward God and faith in the finished work of the Lord Jesus Christ on the cross, is the only way to get right with God and secure everlasting life in heaven (John 3:16).

Rock rose (Lot)
Cistus ladaniferus

The narrative in Luke 7:36-38 carries a powerful message. The Lord Jesus enters Simon's house to eat meat. While Simon was busying himself trying to make a good impression on his guest, a sinner woman, broken in spirit with tears of repentance, prostrates herself at the feet of the Saviour. Whatever her past life, the woman recognised in her heart and conscience that the Lord Jesus was the only One who could cleanse her morally. The woman first refreshes the Lord by washing His feet with her tears of repentance; she next seals the token of her affection for Him by kissing His feet. Next, she displays the spirit of worship by anointing His feet with fragrant ointment. The woman's silent action spoke volumes to the heart of the Lord Jesus, way above the hubbub in Simon's house. What the woman saw in the Lord Jesus melted her heart to produce a lovely response to the divine love that had reached out to her. The Lord cleansed her heart and took possession of it to shut out corrupting influences. Although Simon had prepared a lavish table to set before the Lord Jesus, we may safely say that the divinely furnished table at which the Lord Jesus sat, was in the heart of the penitent woman (Rev. 3:20).

Two more miracles of cleansing are recorded in Luke 5:12-15 & 17:11-19. Leprosy in

Scripture is a physical illustration of the horrible, disfiguring nature of sin and its defiling impact on the individual. In all the miracles relating to lepers, we always find they are 'cleansed' rather than 'cured'; this is because leprosy is a gross, defiling disease. This truth is confirmed by the ordinances recorded in Leviticus 13 & 14. If the priest had previously identified the leprosy, his judgment would be that the individual, thing or place was either clean or unclean. In Luke 5, the leper makes no claim of right or entitlement to cleansing, but in falling at the feet of the Lord Jesus; humbly implores Him, saying, "Lord, if Thou wilt, Thou canst make me clean". The leper's words implied acceptance of the sovereignty of the Lord Jesus to do what He would. His appeal was a statement of faith which the Lord Jesus instantly recognised and responded to by saying, "I will, be thou clean, and immediately the leprosy departed from him" (Luke 5:13).

The lone leper in Luke 5 made a direct appeal to the Lord Jesus based on his faith in the Messiah. Whereas the cry from the ten, while recognising the One who had performed many miracles, was more for relief from the cruel, defiling disease. On that occasion, instead of putting forth His hand and saying, "I will have mercy, be thou clean"; He commands them to, "go show yourselves unto the priests" (Luke 17:14). It was while they were on their way to the priests – who were completely impotent and could only discern and pronounce the men clean – that they experienced the miracle of cleansing. Nine of the ten, although cleansed by the power of the Lord Jesus, still needed the assurance of the priests that they were clean. They would continue in the lifeless, Jewish tradition; while the tenth recognised in his heart that praise was due to God. For him, the Lord Jesus was greater than the Temple, greater than the priests and greater than Judaism. As another has said, it was the Samaritan, who on that occasion represented God's portion, the tithe. May the Lord touch our hearts more deeply in the recognition that having been cleansed by His precious blood, He is worthy of our highest praise. God has said, "whoso offereth praise, glorifieth Me" (Psalm 50:23).

Finally, Paul writing to the Christian believers at Colosse, said, "let your speech be always with grace, seasoned with salt, that ye may know how ye ought to answer every man" (Col. 4:6). Our conversation with, and responses to the world, should always be holy and pregnant with the Grace of our Lord Jesus Christ, to occasion a cleansing influence on everything of a corrupting nature. We should ever be like burning 'ladanum', a fragrant and disinfecting influence on all around.

Lord Jesus, our hearts do most gladly respond,
To love that now cleanses, to Lot that now burns,
To sweeten the air and to purify thought;
For soon Blessed Lord, to Thy home we'll be brought!

T H Ratcliffe

Myrtle

Myrtus communis

Hebrew: Hadas = the Myrtle bush.
Nehemiah 8:15 + five other references.

Myrtle is a bushy, evergreen shrub, reaching a height of about 2 m, with dark green, 5 cm long lanceolate leaves. The shrub flowers in the summer months, producing single stemmed blossoms from the axil of the leaves. Each of the white, fragrant and delicate five-petal flowers has superimposed on it a prominent boss of wide-spreading stamens,

giving the impression of a very elegant and well-ordered structure. Myrtle is a delightful and accommodating shrub that flourishes in a wide range of environmental conditions; its form, character and fragrance convey a feeling of rest and peace, which is exactly what will exist during the Millennial reign of Christ.

In Leviticus 23:33-43 we have details for the celebration of the Feast of Tabernacles, which was the seventh and last feast in the Jewish year. The Feast of Tabernacles looked on to the time when Israel would be at rest in the Promised Land. When in the land, the people were to continue to celebrate the Feast as a memorial of the time Jehovah made the nation dwell in booths throughout their wilderness journeys. Sadly, after Joshua had led the people across Jordan and into the land, they quickly forgot to celebrate the Feast of Tabernacles in full. They may well have observed the Feast at the set time of the year, but they did not construct booths, as the ordinance required, until after the captivity in the days of Ezra and Nehemiah (Nehemiah 8:17). The Feast of Tabernacles was also a figure of the Millennial age, when all will be peaceful and glorious, with everyone resting under his own fig and vine. During the time of Solomon's reign, Israel had a foretaste (albeit a transient and imperfect taste) of the Millennial glory. It was a time when, "Judah and Israel dwelt safely, every man under his vine and under his fig tree, from Dan even to Beer-sheba" (1 Kings 4:25). Alas, through idolatry, the peace and prosperity of Solomon's reign came to an end, never to return until the coming in of a day still future. A day when the King of Kings and Lord of Lords will reign in righteousness (Revelation 20:4 & 6).

Zechariah, a post-captivity prophet received many visions from the Lord, one of which related specifically to a time of peace and rest for Israel. "In that day, saith the Lord of host, shall ye call every man his neighbour under the vine and under the fig tree" (Zechariah 3:10). According to the institution of the Feast of Tabernacles, the children of Israel were to take, "boughs of goodly trees, branches of palm trees, and boughs of thick trees, and willows of the brook" (Leviticus 23:40). With the branches, they were to make their booths and live in them for seven days. The Hebrew word for 'goodly' is 'hadar', very similar to the Hebrew word 'hadas' translated, myrtle in six Old Testament references. Among the many definitions of 'hadar' are adjectives such as, beauty, comely, excellent, glorious, honourable, and ornamental, any one of which, in a specific way, could apply to the myrtle shrub. It is most likely therefore, that myrtle was one of the plants referred to in the institution of the Feast of Tabernacles.

The references to the myrtle in Nehemiah (Feast of Tabernacles) and Isaiah relate to the time when Israel will rest peacefully in the Promised Land. The nation has never taken possession of its inheritance, due entirely to its idolatry and disobedience to the Lord. One day soon, the Promised Land that has never yet yielded its potential in terms of abundance of everything rich, fruitful and beautiful, will be transformed by the hand of God. Included among His plantings, will be the lovely myrtle bush (Isaiah 41:19). The little myrtle bush has a message for us today. It speaks: of eternal life, for it is evergreen; it is of a gentle nature, being without thorns and of a humble and unassuming character, as a non-invasive bush. Furthermore, the bush speaks of purity, from its white flowers; of the fragrance of Christ, from the leaves that are charged with a redolent oil, and finally, of unique and lively beauty in the form of its flowers. All these characteristics should be seen in the saints of God. Oh, that our lives were even a feeble reflection of the lovely features seen in the lowly myrtle bush!

When we come to Isaiah 55, the prophet contrasts the current situation in the land of Israel with the transformation that will occur under the hand of Almighty God for the bringing in of the Millennial age. Everything in the land at present is an offence to God, for there is nothing reflective of His goodness and gracious provision. When the remnant repents of its heinous sin, as it surely will, and be saved (Romans 11:26), the Lord will remove from the land everything that is offensive to Himself and painful to man. Instead of the thorn, shall come up the fir tree, and instead of the brier shall come up the myrtle (Isaiah 55:13).

In the opening chapter of Zechariah's prophecy, we have, in figure, the Lord's assessment of the behaviour of the heathen nations toward His people who had been in captivity for seventy years. In the first of Zechariah's visions, he beheld a man riding upon a red horse and standing among the myrtle trees in the valley. Following Zechariah's enquiry about the other three horsemen, it soon became clear to him that the angel of the Lord on the first red horse was none other than the Lord Himself. The three other horsemen were figures of divine representatives recording their findings on the attitude of the heathen nations toward the Lord's people. The myrtle trees, among which the angel of the Lord stood, represented the remnant of the Jews who had come out of captivity; small, non-threatening and defenceless. Through the vision, the Lord was assuring Zechariah that although the remnant was surrounded and over-shadowed by the might of the nations, it was the Lord Almighty – in the figure of man on the red horse – Who enveloped and over-shadowed them; this was their sure protection.

The Gentile nations were quite unmoved and cruelly indifferent to the plight of the remnant in its struggle to rebuild the Temple and survive by their own endeavours. Accordingly, the Lord was deeply aggrieved by such cruelty toward His people (Zechariah 1:15). He revealed to His prophet in a second vision, how His measured judgment would be executed on the heathen. The Gentile powers that had oppressed and scattered the Jews were represented by the four horns Zechariah saw in the vision. The Lord then revealed to Zechariah how, in His time, four craftsmen (instruments of God) would be used to cast out and nullify the power of the heathen oppressors. The Scriptures teach us that the completion of God's judgment on the Gentile nations is still future (Luke 21:24, & Romans 11:25). Meanwhile, we should seek the Lord's help through prayer, to mirror in our lives some of the lovely features seen in the myrtle bush (Colossian 3:12-14).

Saviour, Thy lovely nature tells, in pure and holy strains;
How grace and perfect Godliness, met all God's holy claims.

T H Ratcliffe

Nut / Pistachio
Pistacia vera

Hebrew: Boten = The Pistachio nut.
Genesis 43:11.

The only reference in the Scriptures to the 'pistachio nut' is Genesis 43:11. Pistacia vera is a small deciduous, bushy tree, 4 – 6 m high, producing an abundance of reddish, ovoid fruits about 2 cm long. The edible nut develops within a brittle two-valve shell that is cracked open after harvesting to release the kernel. Biblical scholars believe the name of the nut derived from the name of the city Botonim, East of Jordan, which exists to this day and where pistachio nut trees are grown commercially. The nuts are a delicacy in Middle Eastern countries, and quite often offered to important dignitaries. As far as Jacob was concerned, the 'Ruler of all Egypt' was a very important person and only the very best of the choice fruits at his disposal would be suitable as a gift. In due course, the nation will learn that only the things they most treasure are suitable as an offering for Jehovah. The pistachio nut (kernel) would speak of fruit in our hearts occasioned by the working of the Holy Spirit of God (Galatians 5:22-23).

Joseph was, in figure, very much like the kernel of the pistachio nut. The brothers had only looked on the outside of the whole fruit and not

taken account of the inside of Joseph; i.e. his heart. While still living with the family in the land of Canaan, Joseph's brothers knew he held a unique place in the affections of their father (Gen. 37:3-4). His life was committed to doing his father's will; being wholly one with him in thought, word and deed, just as it was prophetically said of the Lord Jesus in Psalm 40:8. The best gift Joseph could and did give to his father was his life and heart's affection – the very kernel of one's being (John 8:29). Joseph would have been acutely aware of the envy and bitterness in the hearts of his brothers toward him, yet he took no evasive action, but remained steadfast, faithfully fulfilling the missions on which his father sent him. Joseph's imploring appeal to his brothers, when they had cast him into the pit (Gen. 42:21) should have convicted them as to the gravity of their crime, but it did not. It was 22 years later, in Joseph's presence that the brothers were finally broken down with repentance and grief, confessing to what they had done (Gen. 45:3). Confession and repentance had rendered the brothers morally suitable to benefit from the very best gift Joseph had ready for them, i.e. the deep and sincere affections of his heart.

The Lord Jesus said, "a good man out of the good treasure of his heart bringeth forth good things" (Matthew 12:35). Throughout the life of the Lord Jesus, there was from His heart, the continuous outpouring of His good treasure, expressed through His words, miracles, signs and wonders, together with the enduring affection for His people and the world (John 3:16). The powerful testimony of the Lord's divine attributes overwhelmed many with lasting blessing, and produced outbursts of praise from grateful hearts. "Thou art the Christ, the Son of the living God" (Matt. 16:16). "Is not this the Christ" (John 4:29). "This is indeed the Christ, the Saviour of the world" (John 4:42). "This is the Christ" (John 7:41). "Lord I believe" (John 9:38). "Lord, I believe that thou art the Christ, the Son of God" (John 11:27) *et al*. The Pharisees experienced no such movements in their hard, unregenerate hearts. They were more concerned about external appearances, no matter how corrupt within; they sought the praise of men, and the Lord condemned them for their hypocrisy (Matt. 23:27-28).

May the Holy Spirit move in our hearts to occasion fresh and more frequent outbursts of praise, worship and thanksgiving to God our Father (Psalm 100:4). Such praise would be a suited response from the redeemed that recognise the might, power and dignity residing in the One who is Lord and Saviour of the world. Surely, that is the best gift God desires from grateful hearts (Hebrews 13:15).

Lord, the things we dearly treasure; we would render unto Thee;
Thou hast giv'n Thine all to have us, with Thee and Thy glory see.

T H Ratcliffe

Nut - Walnut

Juglans regia

Hebrew: 'Egoz = Walnut.
Song of Solomon 6:11.

The walnut fruit is referred to just once in the Scriptures, under the noun 'nut'. Josephus Flavious, A.D. 58 – 101 a Jewish scholar and historian, records that the walnut was a common tree around lake Gennesaret; and much cultivated along with other economic trees and fruits. In eastern Jerusalem today, there is a place called 'the valley of walnuts'.

Biblical scholars and botanists confirm that the nut referred to in the Song of Solomon 6:11, is the walnut. A noble, deciduous, spreading tree, reaching 10 to 12 m in height and affording ample shade from the mid-day sun. The leaves are pinnately compound (like the ash) and fragrant. The flowers, which are wind pollinated and appear before the foliage fully opens up, are borne separately as long, male catkins and female clusters of small, white flowers. The fruits are globular with an outer case that splits open while still on the tree to reveal the walnut. Eventually, the walnut, with which we are familiar, falls to the ground. The economic values of the walnut tree are in the nut as a food, and the excellent vegetable oil, extracted from the nuts. In addition, walnut wood is a timber much sought after by the furniture industry for use as a veneer for facing the surface of cheaper woods.

We have seven references to garden or gardens in the Song of Solomon. In our thoughts on Henna, we referred to an Oasis at Engedi that probably abounded with fruit orchards of every kind. Solomon, in his song, appears to highlight all the rich and beautiful qualities of the place to which he frequently retired in order to rest and muse upon the delights that overwhelmed his soul. Christian believers today experience the preciousness of such delights, each time they resort to God's sanctuary and Throne of Grace. It is in the sanctuary where we recline in His love and absorb fresh impressions about His worth. It is there we drink from the well of everlasting goodness, feast at the table spread with divine excellencies, then prostrate our souls in worship, praise and adoration (Hebrews 10:19 – 22; & 13:15). What a garden of delights!

The walnut tree provides ample shade for all that care to shelter beneath its over-spreading boughs. It is most likely, that in the garden frequented by Solomon, he would have reclined in the cool shade of the noble, fragrant walnut tree, as he also did under the apple trees (Song of Solomon 2:3). The painful effect of the blistering heat from the sun is a figure of the trials God's children experience when exposed and vulnerable. The shepherds of the flock of God should be like a walnut tree. Not only do they bear nutritious fruit, but have a responsibility to afford shelter under the umbrella of cooling, protective and fragrant love (Acts 20:28). Let us not be found wanting in this service.

The fruit of the walnut is nutritious and satisfying, and although freely available, does require personal effort to access; just as a single minded endeavour is necessary if we

Nuts (Walnut fruits)
Juglans regia

are going to benefit from the Truth of God's Word. As lambs of the flock, we depend on the shepherds to lead us into the Truth of Holy Scripture under the guidance of the Holy Spirit. However, there must be a yearning on our part for the sustaining food (1 Peter 2:2). As we grow in grace and in the knowledge of our Lord Jesus Christ, we require the meat of God's Word to build us up on our most holy faith (Jude 20). The noble Bereans searched the Scriptures daily (Acts 17:11); which was tantamount to cracking open the walnut to access and benefit from the nutritious food. Let us study the Word in depth to show ourselves approved unto God, workman that needeth not to be ashamed, rightly dividing the Word of Truth (2 Timothy 2:15).

Furniture manufacturers today use walnut wood as a veneer over cheaper, inferior woods. The grain of walnut wood is uniquely beautiful, and furniture made entirely of the wood is much sought after and very expensive. A careful study of the Old Testament Scriptures will show that typically, wood speaks of the humanity of man, and in the case of the walnut wood, that of our Lord Jesus Christ. Just as the grain in the walnut wood is unique, so too the intrinsic humanity of our Lord Jesus Christ reflected an unparalleled moral excellence.

The apostle Paul in writing to the Colossian Christians was anxious they should reflect the Person of Christ. Accordingly, he reminded them that they, "have put on the new man, which is renewed in knowledge after the image of Him that created him". Next, Paul exhorts them to, "put on therefore, as the elect of God, holy and beloved, bowels of mercies, kindness, humbleness of mind, meekness, longsuffering, forbearing one another and forgiving one another". Finally, "above all these things, put on charity, which is the bond of perfectness" (Colossians 3:10 & 12-14). What a rich tapestry of the divine, moral attributes of the Lord Jesus! Surely, the umbrella of shade, the fragrant leaves, the fruits and wood of the walnut tree carry a powerful message for our hearts. "For as many of us as have been baptised into Christ, have put on Christ" (Galatians 3:27). May all these things be borne out in our lives to His praise and glory.

Lord Jesus, we shelter 'neath Thy fragrant bower;
O'er spread to protect us, secure in Thy love;
The food of Thy Word, Lord, it gives us the power,
On earth, here to serve Thee, 'til with Thee above.

T H Ratcliffe

Oak (1)
Quercus coccifera / Quercus ilex

Hebrew : 'Elon = A strong tree; mighty, supporting post.
Genesis 12:6 + eight other references.

The KJAV, translates the Hebrew noun 'elon in the above references, as 'plain' or 'plains'; instead of 'oak' or 'oaks', the latter being the correct translation. The tree is an evergreen oak, also known as the 'holm oak' and should not be confused with the deciduous oak referred to by the Hebrew noun 'allon. The KJAV has also translated the Hebrew plant nouns allah, 'ayil and 'elah as 'oak' or 'oaks', yet the trees referred to are in fact terebinths. The type of oak referred to in Joshua 24:26 is uncertain, however, as the tree was linked to a memorial, it was in all probability an evergreen.

The biblical evergreen oak is a large, spreading tree found growing throughout Israel today. The strength, stability and evergreen protective canopy of the oak would speak to us of the enduring constancy and care of the Lord for His own. The tree, which can often be seen standing alone in all its robust, resolute, steadfast strength and imposing power; has a canopy that offers ample shade to the weary traveller. In the desert way, the shelter of such trees affords opportunity for quiet meditation and contemplation. In Hebron (Mamre), there is a famous evergreen oak, known as the

'Abraham oak'; the common name is 'holm oak'. The noun holm comes from an obsolete word 'holin' meaning holly; the holm oak has holly-like leaves. Tradition has it that the tree is the one under which Abraham was sitting when the Lord appeared to him as recorded in Genesis 18:1, but this is most unlikely. It is approximately 3900 years since the Lord appeared to Abraham by the oaks of Mamre, and according to eminent plant scientists and botanists, any species of oak would not survive more than 500 years.

When the Lord first appeared to Abraham, it was to direct him to leave the country of his nativity (the world), his family (the flesh) and his father's house (inheritance). He was to go out by faith to possess a land that God would show him. Abraham went out in faith relying on the strength of the Lord, confident about the stability of His word and assured of the Lord's protective care. That is much like the calling of the redeemed in this day of God's grace, we are on a heavenly journey and, "waiting for the adoption, to wit, the redemption of our body" (Romans 8:23). Today, Christian believers are called upon by the Lord to leave (separate from) the world, have no confidence in the flesh, surrender all their expectations in the world, and to walk by faith (2 Corinthians 5:7). The apostle Paul said, "I press toward the mark for the prize of the high calling of God in Christ Jesus" (Philippians 3:14).

The next time the Lord appeared to Abraham was when he had arrived in Shechem in the land of Canaan and was resting under the isolated, evergreen oak of Morah. The Lord said to Abraham, "unto thy seed will I give this land" (Genesis 12:7). That was the second time Abraham experienced the stability, strength and power of the Word of the Lord; it moved him to build an altar to worship the One Who had called him out of the realm of idolatry. What a lovely thought for our souls to cherish when consciously enjoying by faith our inheritance with Christ in God. We too have an altar, not of stone, but a living Person at the right hand of the greatness on high (Hebrews 1:3). Through Him, we should continually offer to the Father, the sacrifice of praise, worship and thanksgiving in the acknowledgement of all the Lord Jesus accomplished for the glory of God.

In Genesis 18:1, the Lord, with two angelic beings, appeared before Abraham as he sat in his tent door under the oaks of Mamre. Abraham had already been made aware of the strength, force and power of Almighty God – El Shaddai (Genesis 17:1). 'El' means 'the strong One', so it was not by accident that Abraham was again sitting in the shade of sturdy oaks when the Lord came to confirm His promise to him that Sarah would have a son. But more than that, the Lord by His mighty, resolute hand determined to deliver Lot and his family from Sodom and then destroy both Sodom and Gomorrah by fire.

The stand of evergreen oaks mentioned in Deuteronomy 11:30, was a landmark from which to locate the Canaanites who, by the power of Jehovah, were to be driven out from before the Israelites. In Judges 4:11, Heber the Kenite moved to a secure place under an oak while conspiring against Sisera. In Judges 9:6, the wicked citizens of Shechem made the murderer Abimelech king, and celebrated the event by the memorial oak that was in Shechem, thereby preserving a testimony of his evil deeds. Judges 9:37 (JND) reveals that another of the beautiful evergreen oaks had been renamed the 'magician's oak' and was recognised as the place for the covert activities of soothsayers, sorcerers and wizards. Finally, the oak referred to in 1 Samuel 10:3 was an important landmark for Saul. It would have been disastrous for Saul if he had missed the oak of Tabor while on his first mission as king of Israel. He would not have met the three men going up to God to Bethel, nor partaken of the provisions God led them to share with him. Furthermore, Saul would have missed the company of prophets and the opportunity, by the power of the Spirit of God, to prophesy, thereby confirming that his

anointing as king, was of God. What a lesson for us; if we continue in the way God leads, He will, by His Spirit give opportunity to witness about His saving grace and thereby testify, "that we are the children of God" (Romans 8:16).

All references to the evergreen oak have to do with landmarks for worship, communication, and shelter, and for taking one's bearings. Although the oaks referred to in Judges 9 were landmarks, evil men had defiled their locations. Whenever the Lord communicated something to His servant, that servant would build an altar near to an individual or stand of oaks, as in the case of Abram (Genesis 12:6-8). The evergreen oaks say something to us about the unchanging steadfastness, strength, power and viability of God's promises. When king Darius discovered that the power of Almighty God had shut the lion's mouths and thereby saved Daniel, he issued the following decree. "That in every dominion of my kingdom men tremble and fear before the God of Daniel, for He is a living God and steadfast for ever" (Daniel 6:26).

The apostle Paul exhorted the Christian believers at Corinth to remain strong in their faith, saying, "therefore, my beloved brethren, be ye steadfast, unmoveable, always abounding in the work of the Lord" (1 Corinthians 15:58). Like the sturdy, resilient and robust evergreen oak standing firm as an ancient landmark, we should look to our gracious Lord for help to stand firm against all attempts to diminish the authority, strength, power and truth of Holy Scripture. The incidents linked with the oaks in Judges 9:6 & 37 (JND), reflect a serious abuse of facilities provided by Jehovah for His people. Abimelech desecrated an important memorial site, instead of a place for worship, evil men used the site for the practise of the occult, etc. We would do well to heed the warnings God gives in His Word about behaviour after the like of Abimelech and his followers. Do please read 2 Peter 2. The apostle Paul said, "watch ye, stand fast in the faith, quit you like men, be strong" (1 Corinthians 16:13). "Be strong in the Lord, and in the power of His might" (Ephesians 6:10). Finally, "be strong in the grace that is in Christ Jesus" (2 Timothy 2:1).

Stand then, in His great might, with all His strength endure;
And take, to arm you for the fight, the panoply of God.

C Wesley

Oak (2)

Quercus aegilops or Q. ithaburensis

Hebrew: 'Allon = A strong tree.
Genesis 35:8 + seven other references.

The Hebrew noun 'allon refers to a deciduous oak tree. A tree that is sturdy, strong, rugged, and in the case of mature trees, will always have dead, twisted boughs among the living branches. The 'stag oak' is so called because it has dead and twisted branches that protrude above the crown of the tree, such as one may see on open farmland. This

particular oak speaks of the arrogant, unregenerate man who naturally is void of eternal life (deciduous) and inextricably connected with death (the dead branches). Apart from the main trunk, there is little value in the head of the tree because the branches are always so twisted. The hard, twisted wood is much like the natural man, whose heart is hard and unresponsive to God's love and grace. Indeed, so twisted are the natural thoughts of man about God, that nothing can be done to straighten them out (Isaiah 55:8-9). The answer to man's plight lies in death to all that is natural, and being born again by the power of the Holy Spirit of God – creating an entirely new person (John 3:3-8). We see this principle worked out in Jacob.

In Genesis 35:8, we read that Deborah died and was buried beneath an oak. An earlier reference to Deborah is in chapter 24 verse 59, when Rebekah left her father's house to go with Abraham's servant to become the wife of Isaac. The death and burial of Deborah would have been confirmation to Jacob that everything in his past life, associated with the name bestowed upon him at his birth, was set aside for ever. Furthermore, God confirmed that his name should no longer be Jacob, but Israel – a new person with a new identity. Clearly, Deborah was an integral part of Jacob's family; she was highly respected and much loved for her faithful service to Rebekah and Jacob. Hence, Deborah's death occasioned much lamenting, to the extent that the oak tree under which Jacob buried her, was called the 'oak of weeping'. The burying of Deborah beneath an oak tree was in no way an adverse reflection on her, but rather an acknowledgement by Jacob that everything linked to his past life had now passed. Christian believers too, love to know that the record of their unregenerate past has been blotted out for ever through the atoning work of Christ (1 Peter 1:18-19).

Reference to "the oaks of Bashan" in Isaiah 2:13, is prophecy relating to the time of "Jacob's trouble" (Jeremiah 30:7). Unregenerate persons who strengthen themselves against the Lord and elevate their standing out of all proportion to their state, are designated the 'oaks of Bashan', and will be laid low. The chapter opens with details of conditions prevailing immediately before the beginning of the glorious millennium, when those who exalt themselves will be abased, their arrogant pride dissolved, and their idolatry judged. In that day, Israel's heart will be changed, as prophesied in Ezekiel 11:19, & 36:26. However, the change in Israel's heart will only come about under the influence of God's new covenant based on the eternal efficacy of the shed blood of Christ (Matthew 26:28). Today, the biblical Bashan is part of the Republic of Syria, including the Golan Heights (Joshua 21:27), east of the sea of Galilee and stretching from the southern end of the sea northwards towards Mount Hermon.

Isaiah 6:13 speaks of the trunk of the oak tree that will remain after the tree – idolatrous Israel – is cut down, for the holy seed is in the trunk. In other words, a faithful remnant will survive the Great Tribulation. The gravity of the nation's idolatry was such that the Lord says, the heart of the people will be made fat (verse 10), implying that the nation will become listless and indifferent, unable to hear, see and understand. The Lord Jesus said that the prophecy of Isaiah was fulfilled in the people who rejected Him and His ministry (Matthew 13:14-15). Of the disciples, who represented the faithful remnant, the seed; the Lord Jesus said, "blessed are your eyes, for they see; and your ears, for they hear", verse 16. The apostle Paul's desire for the Colossian church and for Christian believers in this day of God's grace is, "that we might be filled with the knowledge of His will in all wisdom and spiritual understanding" (Colossians 1:9). "Let us not be weary in well doing: for in due season we shall reap, if we faint not" (Galatians 6:9).

The prophet Isaiah includes the oak among the trees of the forest where the wood was misused to fashion idols (Isaiah 44:14-15). We know from examples in the Scriptures, that the shameful folly of man when he is away from God knows no bounds. Under the guidance of the Spirit of God and through the divine pen, Isaiah expresses contempt for a people who, while held in Babylon, conformed to the idolatrous habits of their captors. The smithy with his metal and the carpenter with his wood, employed their skills to fashion something after the likeness of sinful man. The graven images, being the work of their hands, could not speak, see, think, talk nor act. To compound their wicked deeds, they deified and elevated the status of their images to that of gods, making themselves dependent on such for guidance, help and intercession. By so doing, they denied the only true God that brought the nation out of bondage, carried them through the wilderness and brought them into the Promised Land. The smithy made spears, tools and armour with his metal, and the carpenter made furniture and tools with his wood, yet with the residue of their materials they fashion idols with the intention of bowing down and worshipping them. In this particular, the gravity of Israel's sin cannot be over-estimated. What utter blindness to expect help from the dumb, inert idols made from the same material used for cooking, heating and household utensils. In degradation, Israel had sunk to new depths, it was the measure of the distance they were separated from God in their hearts.

The Scriptures warn Christian believers today about the dangers of having idols in their lives. Stephen, defending his faith in the Lord Jesus Christ before the council of the high priest, reminded them how Israel soon after leaving Egypt became idolaters. Stephen said, "they made a calf in those days and offered sacrifice unto the idol (calf), and rejoiced in the works of their own hands" (Acts 7:41). When the apostle John exhorted the children of God to keep themselves from idols (1 John 5:21), he had in mind anything that could come between us and the Lord Jesus Christ. It is very easy, like Israel of old, to rejoice, love and admire our own achievements, to the extent of robbing God of the affection, worship and praise due to Him from our hearts. May our gracious Lord help us, "that in all things He might have the pre-eminence" (Colossians 1:18). The Thessalonians, "turned to God from idols to serve the living and true God; and to wait for his Son from heaven" (1 Thessalonians 1:9-10).

> *Have I an object, Lord, below, which would divide my heart from Thee;*
> *Which would divert its even flow, in answer to Thy constancy?*
> *Oh, teach me quickly to return, and cause my heart afresh to burn.*
>
> G W Fraser

Oak (3) Terebinth
Pistacia terebinthus or P. atlantica

Hebrew: 'Elah or 'Ayil = A hard-wood tree.
Genesis 35:4 + fifteen other references.

The majority of biblical scholars believe the tree referred to in the 16 references listed at the back of the book, is in fact the terebinth, and not an oak as translated in the KJAV. Also in the KJAV, the Hebrew noun 'elah as it occurs in Isaiah 6:13 has been mistranslated as 'teil', rather than terebinth as given in the NIV and JND translations. It is possible, although one cannot be sure, the translators who produced the KJAV, had the terebinth tree in mind, and for want of a common name, came up with 'teil'. The terebinth is a large, deciduous tree with a short trunk and spreading, thick, ragged and twisted branches that lack symmetry. It has nasty, dead boughs, some of which hang low ready to snare the unwary who dares pass under its canopy (2 Samuel 18:9). The leaves are lance-like and pinnate (leaves longer than broad and growing opposite each other in pairs on either side of the stem). Although the timber of the tree was of little use for building, the short, twisted lengths of hard wood were ideal for carving out

idols. The tree was, and probably still is, the source of the product 'cyprus turpentine'. During the summer months, the bark of the tree would be incised in several places to yield a very sticky, transparent fluid. The fluid would go through various cleansing processes to prepare it for marketing as 'purified cyprus turpentine'.

The low-growing terebinth tree reflects the natural character of unregenerate man who is of the earth, earthy (1 Corinthians 15:47), much like Jacob in his early life. The record we have of Jacob's life up to Genesis 35, reveals that he focused his objectives on everything that would benefit him personally on earth. A feature of his character was his low-down, twisted scheming behaviour, first with his brother Esau, then with his equally artful, uncle Laban. However, by the end of his time with uncle Laban, and in the will of the Lord, Jacob succeeded in outwitting him (Genesis 30:27-43).

It was while Jacob was still in Shechem that the idols which had been kept within his house, were buried beneath a terebinth tree (Genesis 35:4). In all probability, the idols were carved from the wood of the terebinth, so it was fitting that Jacob should dispose of them at the point of origin. As we noted briefly in our consideration of the deciduous oak, Jacob was going to begin a new life with divine objectives. Shechem was the place of decision, it was there that Jacob decided his old way of life had ended, and that a new life must begin; this was confirmed at Bethel where God spoke with him (Genesis 35:15). When God, in His sovereign grace, first spoke to us by His Spirit, we repented of our sins and put our faith in a living Saviour. That was the point of decision for us to leave our old life behind and begin the new. We are now a new creation in Christ, for our old life has been crucified with Christ. As the apostle Paul said to the Galatian Christians, "I am crucified with Christ: nevertheless I live; yet not I, but Christ liveth in me. And the life which I now live in the flesh, I live by the faith of the Son of God, who loved me and gave Himself for me" (Galatians 2:20).

In the days of the Judges, Israel again turned to idolatry; and because of their wickedness, the Lord allowed the Midianites to harass them for seven years. As on previous occasions when the people failed, there was always a faithful remnant under the eye of Jehovah, persevering in the path of obedience and faithfulness. Gideon was just such a person. The Lord had first sent a prophet to speak to the people with a view to stirring their consciences about the gravity of their sin. The words of the prophet may well have led some of the people to repentance, but certainly not all (Judges 6:25-30). Before the Lord can come in with blessing, there must first come repentance. Next, the angel of the Lord came and sat under a terebinth. The significance of the Lord sitting under the terebinth was an open declaration that although the nation (the terebinth tree) had turned to idolatry, the Lord was ready to come in to deliver them because of the faithful few. Much like the occasion when the Lord appeared to Moses in the burning bush (Exodus 3:2). While the thorn bush represented Israel; the fire was, in figure, a measure of the severe suffering the people were enduring, yet could not be consumed because the Lord was with them. The voice out of the bush confirmed that the Lord

Jehovah was ready to deliver His people out of bondage and from the power of the heathen. It was a similar message from the angel of the Lord to Gideon.

The narrative recorded in 2 Samuel 18:9-15, is a salutary warning to us all. If we pursue our own selfish ambition without regard for what is right and pleasing to the Lord, the Lord will deal with us in His way and time, and probably in a way least expected. That is exactly what happened to Absalom. Notwithstanding his father David's love for him, Absalom persevered in his life's ambition to dislodge his father from being king of Israel. The slippery slope down which Absalom fatally fell, began when he arranged a successful conspiracy to kill his stepbrother Amnon (2 Samuel 13:28-29). As Absalom rode his ass at speed under a terebinth tree, his heavy, waving locks of hair caught up in the low boughs to leave him, without his ass, suspended between heaven and earth, from where he was slain. How fitting, the very tree that is typical of the hard, rebellious and twisted heart of the natural, unregenerate man, like Absalom, is used in governmental judgment by the Lord.

Soon after the death of Solomon, Jeroboam drew 10 of the twelve tribes of Israel around himself; he became their king, and quickly led the people into idolatry. He set up two idolatrous altars, one in Bethel, the other in Dan, each with a golden calf, before which, the people bowed down and worshipped (1 Kings 12:28-30). The Lord sent a prophet to Jeroboam with a message designed to convict him of his wickedness and bring him to repentance. Jeroboam was angry with the prophet and put out his hand to assault him, but as he did so, it withered, and his idolatrous altar fell apart around him. Jeroboam appealed for God's mercy through the prophet that he might have his hand restored. The prophet prayed to the Lord, and Jeroboam was healed. The prophet rightly rejected any gift from the king, and was told by the Lord to return home by a different route, accepting neither food nor drink from anybody on the way. A false prophet in Bethel chased after the prophet of the Lord, and found him resting under a terebinth. It was there, the weary and unwary prophet of the Lord let his guard slip to become the victim of a cruel hoax that led him to disobey the word of the Lord (1 Kings 13:9 & 18). The false prophet who lied in the name of the Lord, was in all probability an idolater himself. Just as the Lord spoke to Balaam through his ass (Numbers 22:28-30), so He spoke through the false prophet (1 Kings 13:20-22) to His true servant. Sadly, the message from the Lord was about the true prophet's fate because of his disobedience. He had previously acted only on the word of the Lord to himself, not through a second person. That is a vital principle for our souls to lay hold of today. In our service for the Lord, we must get our instructions direct from Him through prayer in the sanctuary (Psalm 25:4-5). The subtlety and scheming of unregenerate man is ever ready to mislead those who seek to serve the Lord.

Saul was buried under a terebinth in keeping with his character (1 Chronicles 10:12). In Isaiah 1:29-30; the shame of those in Israel who refused the word of the Lord and rebelled against Him shall, in a coming day, have their shame exposed as the terebinth without leaves (see the second sentence in the opening paragraph). With the exception of Isaiah 61:3 that speaks of the time when Israel will have a new heart and character, the remaining references to the terebinth relate to the judgment that will fall upon Israel because of their idolatry. Nevertheless, a remnant shall be saved (Isaiah 6:13).

Be Thou the object bright and fair, to fill and satisfy the heart;
My hope to meet Thee in the air, and nevermore from Thee to part;
That I may undistracted be, to follow, serve and wait for Thee.

G W Fraser

Olive

Olea europaea

Hebrew: Zayith = Berry, tree, yard. Shemen = Oil of the Olive. Greek: Elaia = Tree, fruit berries.
Deuteronomy 24:20 + two hundred & fifteen other references.

The olive is an evergreen tree rarely higher than 5 m with grey-green lanceolate (lance-like) foliage. Cultivated trees are pruned annually to keep the head compact and make it easier to harvest the olives. Biblical scholars and botanist generally, accept that the longevity of the olive tree is probably the greatest of all trees. The californian redwood (sequoia sempervirens) is reputed to live for 1500 years, while the mammoth tree (sequoia wellingtonia) is thought to live up to 4000 years. Nevertheless, we believe that the olive tree from which Noah's dove plucked the leaf, along with other olive trees in the area, survived the flood and continued to flourish to the day when our Lord was on earth, and may well be living today.

The olive tree with its fruit speaks of the promises of God; promises that are eternal, sure and steadfast. God will never set aside His promises, no matter what man's circumstances may be. While God's judgments are severe, extensive and catastrophic,

174

nothing can annul His promises. God's promise to Abram was that, "in thee shall all families of the earth be blessed" (Genesis 12:3). God's promise is being fulfilled on earth even now, and will continue to its climactic conclusion in the Millennium. Although the word 'promise' is not used in God's direct communications with Abram, there are no fewer than 36 promises from Genesis 12 – 22. All the verbs, such as shew, make, bless, give, be, multiply, establish, et al. which follow the words; I will, I shall, and will I, are incontrovertible promises. When God planted His holy promises in Abram, He determined they would remain viable to the time of their fulfilment through and by Christ.

Unlike most trees whose age can be determined by counting the 'annual rings' through the transverse section of the trunk, the age of the olive cannot be so calculated. Once the olive tree reaches 40 to 50 years of age, the centre of the trunk develops a hollow cavity that continues to enlarge year after year, thereby making it impossible to accurately age a mature tree. Accordingly, man cannot measure the longevity of God's promises, for His promises have no time limit. Unlike the promises made by man that are subject to circumstances, God's promises are made never to be broken, but are sure and steadfast. "All the promises of God in Christ are yea, and in Him, Amen" (2 Corinthians 1:20). We read in Genesis 15:8, that Abram enquired of God, as to how all His promises would be brought to fruition. Abram did not doubt God's word, but was anxious to know the means God would employ to bring fulfilment to His promises. The compound sacrifice Abram was told to offer, typically spoke of how all would be fulfilled through the death of Christ, so removing all that would hinder the nation entering into their promised rest.

Olive-tree wood has the tightest and closest grain of any tree wood found growing in those areas of the world where the olive is indigenous. Olive wood speaks of the saints of God being indissolubly fused together by His Spirit into one body in Christ (John 17:21). The vast majority of tree woods are prone to splintering, not so the olive. Notwithstanding the battering the Church is daily subjected to by Satan, it cannot be splintered. On Peter's confession of faith, "Thou are the Christ, the Son of the living God", the Lord replied, "upon this rock I will build my Church, and the gates of hell shall not prevail against it" (Matthew 16:18). Sadly, the witness of the Church has been splintered and fractured in many ways, for reasons far too numerous and sad to detail. Here, it must be said, that the testimony has been damaged by the work of the enemy who from the beginning wreaked havoc among the saints of God (Acts 20:29). Nevertheless, while such damage is to our shame, we comfort our hearts in the knowledge that the Church, with Christ as its Head, cannot be splintered (Colossians 1:18). The redeemed have been fused into one body by the unifying power of the Spirit of God (Ephesians 4:4).

There is no tree more glorious than the olive when it is in full flower. The tree, transformed to a mass of white flowers, has a splendour that outshines all other flowering trees. Such a glorious show speaks of the inscrutable and incomparable beauty of the Lord Jesus when He was here as man in the power of the Spirit. His image as dependant man was of unparalleled loveliness which God beheld with inexplicable pleasure and delight (Luke 3:22). Speaking of Israel in a coming day of glory; Hosea says, "his beauty shall be as the olive tree" (Hosea 14:6). In this particular, it is significance that Hosea is led by the Spirit of God to parallel the beauty of the olive, with Israel in the day of her restoration. During the Millennium, no nation will outshine restored Israel for beauty, glory and power. The manner in which the flowers of the olive are shed, is unique among the flowering trees of creation. On a given day from the date when the first flowers appear, and within the space of one day, the olive tree sheds all its flowers. There is nothing phased or gradual, it is a phenomenon as remarkable as it is startling. The angel Gabriel's message to Daniel was, "and after threescore and two weeks shall Messiah be cut off, but not for Himself" (Daniel 9:26). Like the olive, our blessed Lord was one day in full flower and glory, and the next day bowing His head in death. Eliphaz, the first of Job's three comforters; speaking of unregenerate man, said, "He shall cast off his flower as the olive" (Job 15:33).

The primary product of the olive fruit is oil, a type of the Holy Spirit of God. All Christian believers have been baptised with the Holy Spirit of God (1 Corinthians 12:13). 'Pure oil olive beaten' was the major constituent of the Holy anointing Oil (Exodus 30:24). Olive oil is a solvent of resins, so that when the other four constituents were mixed with the oil, a redolent, homogeneous cream was produced. Typically, the fusing of the different resins to produce the unique fragrance, spoke of the precious

Olive fruits
Olea europea

attributes of the Lord Jesus in Whom no one particular divine quality was more prominent than another. That blessed Person was full of the excellencies of the Godhead (John 1:14). When Aaron and his sons, together with the tabernacle furnishings were anointed with the Holy anointing oil, the fragrance lingered for a long time. No person or article was ever anointed a second time. Since Pentecost, no Christian believer has been anointed twice with the Holy Spirit of God and neither indeed can they. The apostle John, in his first epistle said, "little children......ye have an unction from the holy one..." (1 John 2:20). The moment we repented before God, put our faith and trust in the Lord Jesus Christ, we were anointed/baptised/indwelt with the Holy Spirit of God. (See chapter on 'Calamus')

Olives fruits are harvested by beating the trees. The oil for the service of the sanctuary was of the highest possible quality, obtained from the main harvest and designated, "pure oil olive beaten" (Exodus 27:20, et al). The harvesting of the fruit would speak of the deep exercise of soul, which was a personal, unique and daily experience of our blessed Lord, culminating in Gethsemane's garden. The oil-press, through which the olives were passed, typified the unparalleled crushing forces of God's unmitigated judgment against sin, sustained by the Lord Jesus throughout His atoning sufferings on the Cross. When the Lord, on the Cross said, "It is finished", He confirmed there could be no more judgment of sin, for He had exhausted God's judgment of sin. The result of such divine bruising was the advent of the Holy Spirit fifty days after our Lord's resurrection. The Holy Spirit of God now indwells every repentant and believing soul redeemed back to God by the blood of Christ.

When Moses came down from Mount Sinai, having spent 40 days and nights with the Lord, "he wist not that the skin of his face did shine" (Exodus 34:29-30). If such a power could manifest itself in Moses, following his time with the Lord; should there not also be "a burning and a shining light" radiating from us (John 5:35)? The Psalmist spoke of, "oil to make his face to shine" (Psalm 104:15). May the Lord help us to accept what the Psalmist says; that the world may see the lovely, holy nature of Christ in us by the power of His Spirit. When Stephen, being full of faith and of the Holy Spirit, stood before the Sanhedrim to answer false accusations against him; those comprising the Sanhedrim, "saw his face as it had been the face of an angel" (Acts 6:15).

The products of the olive tree have the greatest range of uses of all fruiting trees. The wood is used for very high quality furniture; see (1 Kings 6:23 & 31-33). The fruits are a valuable, nutritious food. The oil is used for anointing, lighting, heating fuel, healing, medicine and for cooking; also as a solvent of resins. The uses of the olive products give us an impression of the rich variety of gifts extant in the Church today in the power of the Holy Spirit. Paul said, "neglect not the gift that is in thee" (1 Timothy 4:14). The words of James are, "Every good gift and every perfect gift is from above, and cometh down from the Father of lights" (James 1:17).

We already have referred to Genesis 12. Typically, Abram became the olive tree of promise. It was the sovereign favour of God that Israel as a nation should be the natural branches of His olive tree (Deuteronomy. 7:6-9). Paul said, "unto them were committed the oracles (unique utterances) of God" (Romans 3:2). For centuries, Israel had an exclusive position of favour before God. However, because of unbelief and idolatry, the nation forfeited its privileged position, and for the time being is set aside. The allegory employed by the apostle Paul in Romans 11 confirms that Israel in no way reflected the holiness and faithfulness of Abraham. Accordingly, God broke them off as the natural branches in the 'tree of promise', i.e. faithful Abraham; and in their place grafted in branches of the wild olive (faithful, believing Gentiles) which, Paul said, is "contrary to nature" (Romans 11:24). In the normal course of vegetative propagation in fruit tree husbandry, man would take a choice scion (branch) and graft it into a strong, healthy stock. In due course, the husbandman would expect to reap the desired fruits. But if the husbandman grafted into his choice stock, the scion of a wild, unhealthy, barren tree; the result of his endeavours would be a wild, unhealthy, worthless and unproductive plant. God alone, through His sovereign husbandry, is able to reverse the natural sequence of events in order to bring into prominence that which will honour Him and His blessed Son. To this end, all the promises made to faithful Abraham are being worked out through a glorified Christ, and testified to by the saints of God on earth. God's promises are no longer reposing solely on the natural children of Abraham, but on the faithful in Christ (Galatians 3:29).

Paul's figure of the olive tree on earth with faithful Abraham as its root and stock, conveys the truth that Abraham is the father of a faithful race, blessed with the promises of God. Today, there are no national or ethnic differences (Romans 10:12.). Paul reminded the Galatian Christians, "Christ hath redeemed us from the curse of the law...that the blessing of Abraham might come on the Gentiles through Jesus Christ, that we might receive the promise of the Spirit through faith" (Galatians 3:13-14). Christian believers have been grafted into the olive tree, and are now drawing on the inestimable riches of God's grace. The ministry of Romans 9-11 is that Israel has been set-aside for the time being. But in God's time, her position will change for her good, when, as the natural branches of the olive, she will be grafted in again. However, this will not happen, "until the fullness of the Gentiles be come in" (Romans 11:25); that is, not until the completion of the sovereign purposes of God in this day of His grace. In a coming day, "all Israel shall be saved" (Romans 11:26) to be the recipients of God's promises according to His covenant with faithful Abraham.

O may Thy Holy Spirit, blest unction from on high,
With all His rich infilling, lead us to glorify;
The risen Christ our Saviour, by loyal witness true,
Constraining us to serve Him, in all we say and do.

A Cutting

178

Onycha

Hebrew: Shecheleth = Nail, claw, lid.
Exodus 30:34.

For many centuries, Bible scholars have pondered over the question: What is 'onycha'? A few Bible dictionaries give the following definitions. George Morris says, 'onycha is one of the ingredients of the holy perfume. The Hebrew word for onycha is shecheleth. Onycha is from the Greek, and means, 'nail or claw' and is supposed to refer to the operculum or claw of one or more species of the 'strombus' a shell-fish: the claw of which gave off a sweet odour when burnt'. James Strong in his exhaustive concordance said, 'onycha is a scale or shell; i.e. an aromatic mussel'; whilst Robert Young in his analytical concordance believes, 'onycha is onyx or perfumed crab'. The Illustrated Bible Dictionary, IVP, suggests that onycha is a, 'pungent component of holy incense, produced by burning claw-shaped valves; the shell apertures of certain molluscs'.

However, Dr. Patrick Fairbairn in his 6 volume Imperial Bible Dictionary, gives what I believe to be the clearest and probably the purest and most accurate explanation about the origin of 'onycha'. Fairbairn accepts, that the word onycha (onyx Greek) as a noun may rightly have reference to the marine onyx, 'unguis odoratus'. Unguis odoratus is found in the Red Sea and along the shores of Arabia; the shell of the creature does diffuse an agreeable odour when burnt. Nevertheless, Fairbairn believes onycha to be a ' resin' originating from a plant; Nigel Hepper, former Principal Scientific Officer, Kew Gardens, agrees with Fairbairn.

For many years, I had been uneasy in my conscience about accepting that the substance 'onycha' came from a sea mollusc. My exercise is confirmed by the specific instructions given to Israel on what was to be judged clean or unclean, as detailed in Leviticus 11:10-12. Jehovah declared to Israel, through Moses, that all sea and fresh-water creatures without fins and scales were to be deemed unclean and an abomination. The category of unclean creatures would have included all shellfish and crustacea such as mussels and crabs. It is inconceivable therefore, that Jehovah would have required the product of an unclean creature to be a constituent of His holy, sweet incense. What then are we to understand about the origin and significance of the resin 'onycha'?

If we accept that the Hebrew word for 'onycha' and its Greek equivalent, means; 'a lid; claw; nail'; could not its name have derived from the characteristics of the flower and fruit of a plant? If that were so, then botanists today would most probably have classified such a plant within the genus 'opercularia'. Opercularia is the name for a group of plants with an unusual botanical feature. The name derives from the way the calyx of the flower develops a claw-like lid to securely enclose and hold safe the ripening seed pod up to the moment of full maturity. Would this not then speak of our security in Christ? (John 10:28-29). Our Lord said to His Father, "those whom thou hast given me I have kept, and none of them is lost" (John 17:12).

In Australia today, there is a very small group of sub-shrubs – about 14 species – of the genus 'opercularia'. The plants grow to approximately 1 m high, are perennial and bear small, insignificant white flowers. However, none within the group produces resin, but rather a putrid, evil smelling watery sap. Such plants may well be within the same botanical family and genus, as might have been the biblical species 'onycha', however, like many species within a given genus, they are morphologically different.

God knew the substances (resins) which, when combined, tempered with salt and fired, would best express to the physical senses of man, the dignity, fragrance and sweetness of the nature and person of Jehovah. The last time we read of the Sweet Incense and the altar of Incense in relation to the Old Testament economy, is in Luke 1:10-11. So why is the plant 'onycha' not with us today? It seems patently clear, that following the rejection of the Messiah of Israel by the nation, God ensured that never again would man be able to produce that unique fragrance of the Most Holy Place. The burning of the sweet incense communicated to the physical senses of the high priest, the reality, fragrance and preciousness of Jehovah's presence. Today, the Lord's presence among His people is spiritually discerned by those indwelt by the Holy Spirit of God (Romans 8:9-11). The Lord's own words are, "where two or three are gathered unto my Name, there am I in the midst of them" (Matthew 18:20). In view of the distinctive character of the onycha plant, it must surely speak to our hearts about the Christian believer's security in Christ (Romans 8:35-39).

Much incense is ascending, before the eternal throne;
God graciously is bending to hear each feeble one;
To all our prayers and praises, Christ adds His sweet perfume,
And He the censer raises, these odours to consume.

M Bowly

Palm

Phoenix dactylifera

Hebrew: Tamar = Erect date palm tree. Timmor = Decoratively carved palm wood.
Greek: Phoinix = A date palm.
Exodus 15:27 + thirty-one other references.

The familiar date palm is a valuable food source in Middle Eastern countries. The genus Phoenix is comprised of about 30 species that survive to this day in sub-tropical conditions, but only a few bear fruit. Quite a number within the group do not develop long trunks like the date-bearing species, but remain short and shrub-like. In all probability it was from the stem-less types the people obtained the branches to wave and lay on the ground to welcome the Lord Jesus when He entered Jerusalem for the last time (John 12:13). Botanically, the date palm is dioecious, i.e. the male and female flowers are borne on separate trees. Normally, one male tree provides enough pollen to fertilise about 20 fruit-bearing trees. From the planting of juvenile trees – shoots taken from the base of a parent – it takes between 5 – 8 years before they will bear fruit. The height of the evergreen date palm will reach as much as 12 m and more, and the length of leaves (fronds), with which we are all familiar, may be anything between 4 and 6 m.

The date palm is valuable in all its parts, providing food, wine, sugar and date honey from the fruits; from the fronds, sun-hats, mats and thatching for roofs of basic, temporary housing, i.e. booths.

The date palm speaks of rest, peace, triumph and rejoicing (Leviticus 23:40), also of the righteous who shall flourish (Psalm 92:12) and of the stature of the God-fearing (Song of Solomon 7:7). When the children of Israel reached Elim – half way down the West side of the Sinai Peninsula – during the first year of their deliverance from the bondage of Egypt, they came to an oasis where were twelve wells of water and seventy mature date palms (Exodus 15:27). Elim was a place where the people could rest in peace and reflect with thanksgiving on the way Jehovah had delivered them from the cruel hand of Pharaoh. Numbers in Scripture are always significant, and no less so than here. Twelve in Scripture always speaks of perfect government, able to control and refresh those under its charge through faithful administration. Thus, the twelve wells at Elim were there to refresh the children of Israel provided they submitted themselves to the government set up by Jehovah with Moses at the head. The seventy palm trees remind us of the 'prayer of Moses, the man of God'. "The days of our years are threescore years and ten" (Psalm 90:10). As with Israel in Old Testament times, God has today assured His own about the provisions He will make to sustain them throughout their pilgrim journey. For so long as we walk in accord with His will, He will provide all that is necessary to sustain us in this life (Matthew 6:31-34). He did it for Israel; He will do it for us (Hebrews 13:5).

The last of the set feasts of Jehovah, detailed in Leviticus 23:33-43, relates to the 'Feast of Tabernacles (booths)'. It was a feast of joy, to be an annual celebration when the people were in the Promised Land. The feast would remind them that they and their fathers dwelt in booths throughout their wilderness journeys. "Ye shall rejoice before the Lord thy God seven days" (verse 40). The palm leaves (fronds) used for their booths would have reminded them of God's protective goodness and rich provision throughout their pilgrimage. Sadly, from the time of Joshua to the days of Nehemiah – approximately one thousand years – the people neglected to keep the feast (Nehemiah 8:14-16). The feast also looked on to the glorious millennial age that would commence once the harvest of all the redeemed has been gathered in and secured. That is, when all that corresponds to the mind and will of God for the blessing of His people, has been settled. Only then will the nation rest in peace and be able to rejoice in the God of their salvation. The apostle Peter reminds us Christian believers, that we are, "strangers and pilgrims" (1 Peter 2:11). It should be our daily service to render praise and worship to the One Who watches over us and holds us safely in the palm of His hand (John 10:28-29). Furthermore, our shelter in Christ gives us a sense of rest, peace and security.

Deborah, who was a judge in Israel (Judges 4:4) had a dwelling beneath a mature palm tree (verse 5). This is very interesting because she was a God-fearing prophetess who judged Israel at a time when there was no man equal to the task. Such a state in Israel was a sad reflection on the men in Israel. It was to their shame that God raised up a faithful woman through whom he would work to deliver the nation from the hand of Jabin king of Canaan (verse 24). Deborah was a righteous woman and flourished like the palm tree (Psalm 92:12); furthermore, her moral stature was way above that of the men in Israel. Deborah's heart was set on doing what accorded with the mind of Jehovah; she was therefore very much like the palm tree that soars heavenward (Song of Solomon 7:7). The rich, nourishing fruit of the upright palm, produced in figure from the exploits of Deborah's faithfulness, was forty years of rest and peace (Judges 5:31). How beautifully David summarises God's blessing for one like Deborah. "Mark the perfect man and behold the upright, for the end of that man is peace" (Psalm 37:37). James has a lovely thought for all whose hearts are set on things above; like the palm, ever soaring heavenward. "The wisdom that is from above is first pure, then peaceable, gentle and easy to be entreated, full of mercy and good fruits, without partiality and without hypocrisy. For the fruit of righteousness is sown in peace of them that make peace" (James 3:17-18). Christian believers should be ever moving forward and upward as the apostle Paul said, "Till we all come in the unity of the faith, and of the (full) knowledge of the Son of God, unto a perfect man, unto the measure of the stature of the fullness of Christ" (Ephesians 4:13).

The respective temples of Solomon (1 Kings 5 – 7) and Ezekiel (Ezekiel 40 – 43) were decorated with fashioned palm trees. Solomon's temple was functional for the worship of Jehovah by the people in the Promised Land. Ezekiel's temple on the other hand, was a vision he had from the Lord about a glorious edifice that will reflect the glory of the Lord in a coming day. Furthermore, unlike the detail given for Solomon's temple, the only tree referred to in the building of Ezekiel's temple, is the date palm, and that is significant. In Solomon's temple, the worship and service of Jehovah was led by sanctified priests, but not all priests were God-fearing and sanctified in their hearts, as we know from the sad history of both Judah and Israel. However, Ezekiel's temple has to do with a coming time of total triumph and untarnished rejoicing. A time when all Israel will have a new heart, a heart responsive to the rights and claims of the King of kings and Lord of lords – the Messiah they had rejected, cast out and crucified. They will gladly bow before Him in worship, praise and adoration. Furthermore, the palm branches will also illustrate the joy and triumphal praise of all those redeemed back to God by the precious blood of Christ, for these too, belong to the whole family of God (Ephesians 3:15). Both temples looked on to a day of glory when the Lord Jesus will reign in righteousness over the whole earth for a thousand years. In that day of glory, the God-fearing down through the centuries, together with those that are upright in heart and spirit today, will reflect the glory of the Lord Jesus. The Psalmist has confirmed this wonderful truth, "surely the righteous shall give thanks unto Thy name, the upright shall dwell in Thy presence" (Psalm 140:13). 'Upright' in this context means, uprightness, just, well-pleasing and righteous as before God (Romans 5:19). The palm tree decorations in both temples are a figure of those whom God has designated upright, "the Lord knoweth the days of the upright, and their inheritance shall be for ever" (Psalm 37:18).

Finally, the reference to palm branches in Revelation 7:9 relates to an event yet future when a vast company comprising all nations of the earth, stand before the Throne and before the Lamb. The occasion will be one of victory, triumph and rejoicing because of complete deliverance, as signified by the palm branches they hold in their hands. They are clothed in white robes because, "they have come out of great tribulation and have washed their robes and made them white in the blood of the Lamb" (Revelation 7:14). The white robes of this redeemed company have reference to the moral adjustments they made to their lives once they had accepted the 'Gospel of the Kingdom' preached by the Lord's faithful witnesses throughout the 'Great Tribulation' period. May the Lord help us to be like the palm trees, upright in all our ways and rejoicing in God our Saviour and being fruitful in every good work (Colossians 1:10).

> *We celebrate Thy victory Lord, and rest complacent in Thy love.*
> *We worship, serve Thee here below; yet yearn to be with Thee above.*
> *Our longing hearts rehearse the call; Come, come Lord Jesus, take us all.*
>
> T H Ratcliffe

Pine

Pinus halepensis

Hebrew: Tidhar = An enduring, lasting tree.
Isaiah 41:19 & 60:13.

Pinus halepensis is known as the aleppo or Jerusalem pine. The mention of pine branches in KJAV for Nehemiah 8:15 is an unfortunate translation of 'ets shemen', which simply means 'wood oil' or 'oily wood'. Several biblical scholars believe *ets shemen* refers to the wild olive 'olea europaea oleaster'. However, as the scriptural

reference to a specific plant is imprecise on this occasion, it is probably best to adhere to the simplicity of the text and accept that what is implied are branches of a particular tree.

The aleppo pine is an evergreen that grows to a height of approximately 20 m. It is a fast growing tree, and flourishes on most types of soil found in the mountainous regions of Israel and Lebanon. Traces of ancient pine forests exist in different parts of Israel today, particularly in the Mount Carmel area. This seems to suggest that many centuries ago, a great deal of the Palestine and Lebanon mountainous regions may have been shrouded with pine forests. What is very interesting today is that the Israeli Government has an ongoing programme for planting millions of broad-leaf and conifer trees in general, but the aleppo pine in particular because it is faster growing than most other species. Seeds of the aleppo pine readily germinate, and the seedlings quickly colonise previously barren areas. The objective of the Israeli government is reforestation on a grand scale to remove man-made scars in the ancient landscape and to prevent further surface erosion of the thin layer of fertile soil. The government is also anxious to control the flow of precious water during the rainy season and to nurture the revival of a green and pleasant land (see Jeremiah 3:18-19).

The only two references to pine trees, relate to the time when Israel will be fully restored in the Land of her inheritance (Exodus 15:17). Isaiah 41:19 lists seven trees that will fill the land. A perfect number to ensure that the capital land of the world in that coming day, will at long last have the divine environment of peace and rest suited to the Prince of Peace (Isaiah 9:6-7). Such a One, shall reign for a thousand years (Revelation 20:6). Furthermore, the nation will, "see and know and consider, and understand together, that the hand of the Lord hath done this, and the Holy One of Israel hath created it" (Isaiah 41:20). The second reference to the pine tree is in Isaiah 60:13; the verse names only three evergreen conifers that will beautify the land to make glorious the place for His feet to stand (Isaiah 60:13). The number 'three' in scripture speaks of the triune Godhead; i.e. Father, Son and Holy Spirit, three in One. The scripture therefore confirms that the restored land will be the work of God alone; indeed, the whole Godhead will be involved in a glorious administration throughout the millennial age.

Christian believers are very much like the aleppo pine. Our salvation is the work of God alone (Ephesian 2:8-10). The landscape of our hearts was once a barren, rocky desert, unable to yield anything suitable for God. The seed of the Word of God alighted on our hearts; the Holy Spirit changed the ground from a sterile to a fertile state. The seed germinated to produce a testimony of our faith in the Lord Jesus Christ. May the Holy Spirit work unhindered in our lives, that, like the aleppo pine flourishing in once desolate, desert conditions; we too will freely grow up in Christ to the glory of God.

> *In the wilderness before thee, desert lands where drought abides;*
> *Heavenly springs shall there restore thee, fresh from God's exhaustless tides.*

J N Darby

Pomegranate
Punica granatum

Hebrew: Rimmon = A tree with its fruits.
Exodus 28:33 + twenty-four other references.

The pomegranate plant is a medium size, deciduous, many-branched bush-like tree reaching a height of about 6 m. The rich green foliage sets off the beautiful waxy-red flowers to startling effect. The red to bright orange fruit is as large as a medium-size apple. A feature of the fruit is that the reddish-yellow coloured calyx of the original flower has the form of an ancient, kingly crown surmounting the actual fruit. This is in contrast to the apple where the calyx is recessed. A red, juicy gel covers each of the pearly seeds within the pomegranate fruit. A cordial drink, sold as 'grenadine' is made from the juice of freshly harvested pomegranates. The pomegranate was one of the three fruits the spies found and brought back from their exploration of the Promised Land (Numbers 13:23). According to Deuteronomy 8:8, the pomegranate was among the seven indigenous fruits of Canaan.

The first mention of pomegranates is in Exodus 28:33-34. Decorative pomegranate fruits in blue, purple and scarlet, were set around the hem of Aaron's robe of the

ephod. Functional, golden bells were set between each embroidered pomegranate, to sound whenever Aaron went into the Holiest of all. Why pomegranates, we may ask? Well, unlike any other fruit, every seed within a mature pomegranate is contained within a separate sac of red fluid. God would have all Israel to remember that their redemption from Egypt was not through any merit of their own, but as a whole, due to the sprinkled blood of an innocent victim. Likewise, Christian believers are safe and secure, having been redeemed by the precious blood of Christ, shed on Calvary's tree (1 Peter 1:18-19). Accepting, that in the figure the seeds in the pomegranate represent the redeemed covered by the blood of Christ; then all such are contained within the fruit that speaks of Christ Himself (Colossians 3:3). The most unusual crown-like calyx of the fruit would tell us that our Redeemer is now crowned with glory and honour (Hebrews 2:7 & 9), and that we are with Him in spirit (Ephesians 2:6). What a lovely thought to generate grateful praise.

The three colours used to embroider the pomegranates were blue, purple and scarlet. Blue is the heavenly colour, speaking of the Lord Jesus Who was the One out of heaven, and as the Son of Man who is now in heaven (Hebrews 2:9). Throughout His pilgrimage on earth, the Lord Jesus reflected the mind of heaven, and heaven itself was of one mind concerning Him (Hebrews 1:6). In manhood, He was heavenly in thought, word and deed. The Lord Jesus has left us an example that we should follow His steps (1 Peter 2:21). Let us daily mind the things of heaven so that we take on heavenly features to confirm our testimony that we are pilgrims and strangers here. If we keep our eye on the Lord Jesus, we shall see the things of earth growing strangely dim, in the light of His glory and grace.

The colour purple would convey to our hearts and minds, the imperial character of the Lord Jesus Christ. When He came unto His own as the long promised Messiah and King, they refused to accept Him. Rather, they cast Him out, mocked Him by putting a purple robe upon Him, smote Him with their hands, then persuaded Pilate to have Him crucified (John 19:2-3 & 16). Throughout His life, the Lord Jesus conducted Himself with imperial dignity; for no matter what the people thought or did to Him, they could not take away His supreme, royal title; King of kings and Lord of lords (Revelation 19:16). The apostle Paul could not refrain from bursting forth into praise when he wrote to Timothy about the gospel of the glory of the blessed God. He wrote of his acceptance that the Lord Jesus Christ had come into the world to save sinners, of whom he was the chief. He then launches himself into a glorious doxology. "Now unto the King eternal, immortal, invisible, the only wise God, be honour and glory for ever and ever. Amen" (1 Timothy 1:17). Oh, that our hearts might rise more frequently to utter suited praise that acknowledges the greatness, worth and honour of His Imperial Majesty!

The last of the listed colours worked into the embroidered pomegranate design was scarlet. Scarlet refers to wool or plant fibres dipped in a scarlet dye. The dye came from the larva of the beetle 'coccus ilicis'. In our consideration of hyssop, we noticed that scarlet speaks of the glory of man in general, but that the type in particular reflects the peerless dignity and perfect manhood of Christ. All the references to scarlet from Exodus 25:4 – 39:29; Leviticus 14:4 – 52 & Numbers 4:8 relate, in type, to the manhood glory of Christ. In the Lord Jesus, there was a shining forth of the unparalleled glory of a perfect man. He was the man of God's counsels, the man after God's heart, doing always those things that pleased His Father (John 8:29). The uniqueness of the Lord's death as Son of Man, brought glory to God in a way no other man could ever achieve. Lowly obedience marked the Lord Jesus in every step of His pathway here, in contrast to the first man Adam, who took the line of least resistance, and with no exercise of conscience, disobeyed the God Who created him. The reference to scarlet in the ordinance given in Numbers 19:6, is the exception. Along with cedar wood and hyssop, scarlet is included in the figure of the transient glory of sinful man. Man's lofty pride (cedar wood), his arrogant vanity (scarlet) and false humility (hyssop), all had to disappear in the death of Christ – the burning of the red heifer. Christian believers have a responsibility today to let their heavenly light shine before men (Matthew 5:16); to be marked by divine moral qualities (Titus 3:8) and to be adorned with the meekness of Christ (Colossians 3:12-14).

Pomegranate tree
(Punica granatum)

In 1 Samuel 14:2 we read that Saul sat under a pomegranate tree, probably pondering his fate for not having kept the commandment of the Lord. The pomegranate fruit with all its seeds surrounded with red gel, and the whole covered with a thick protective rind, was a figure of Israel as God would have them. The crown-like calyx would convey the thought that Jehovah was their King. Although God gave the nation an earthly king, it would no longer be Saul. The new king would be David, a man after the Lord's own heart (1 Samuel 16:13-14). Today, Christian believers are likened unto the pomegranate seeds, covered by the blood of Christ, and being with Christ as the apostle Paul spoke of the church in Colosse (Colossians 3:3).

Solomon put very large chapiters upon the tops of the two pillars he set up in the porch of the House of the Lord. He then covered the chapiters with fashioned pomegranates; two hundred to each chapiter (1 Kings 7:16-21). The Spirit of the Lord guided Solomon in the choice and number of fruit to decorate the tops of the columns. Why not one of the other six fruits that flourished in the land? The answer is that any other fruit would not have carried the correct message in relation to the glorious anti-type that will become evident at the beginning of the glorious millennial age. We have seen that the pomegranate fruit is a figure of the redeemed in Christ, with Christ as Head, crowned with glory and honour.

Throughout the millennium, the saints will be set in the highest place, over and above all the kingdoms and activities on earth. They will not only sound forth the praises of Him Who redeemed them, but will display to all creation that they are one with Him and in Him (John 17:21-24). The two hundred pomegranates at the top of each chapiter would signify adequate and complete testimony of God's love, mercy and grace. Four hundred pomegranates in total would typify the redeemed gathered from the four quarters of the earth (Revelation 5:9-10). The chorus that will echo throughout the courts of heaven will be, "Worthy is the Lamb that was slain, to receive power and riches, and wisdom and strength, and honour and glory and blessing" (Revelation 5:12).

> *Immortal honours crown Thy name, Thou blessed Priest and King;*
> *May heaven and earth resound Thy fame, each day fresh praises bring.*
>
> I Watts

$\mathcal{P}oplar$

Populus alba

Hebrew: Libneh = Whiteness, a white tree, the white poplar.
Genesis 30:37 & Hosea 4:13.

Populus alba is a deciduous tree, reaching a height of 30 m with smooth, grey bark and white woolly shoots. The 4-5 cm broadly ovate leaves are dark green above, white and woolly beneath. Poplars in general are fast growing and short-lived, producing softwood suitable only for the manufacture of paper pulp, matches and fruit crates. The white poplars are readily identifiable from among groups of mixed trees; and from a distance are easily picked out by the flashing white and grey leaves that move in the slightest breeze. The characteristics of the white poplar tree are much like the unregenerate natural man, fickle and capricious as seen in the leaves, short lived, of little value as a wood, and degradable.

Jacob used the wood sap of populus alba in the same way he used the peeled rods of the plane tree (Genesis 30:37-39). His objective was to make himself rich at the expense of his uncle Laban by taking advantage of his shepherding skills and knowledge of plant products. Jacob subsequently justified his action as fair recompense for the cruel way his uncle had treated him during the previous twenty years (Genesis 31:38-42). Sadly, Jacob had not yet learnt that judgment and recompense were in the hand of the Lord. "To Me belongeth vengeance and recompense; their foot shall slide in due time, for the day of their calamity is at hand...for the Lord shall judge His people" (Deuteronomy 32:35-36). Alas, all too often, we are little different to Jacob. Sadly, when we sustain an act of wrongdoing to our hurt, we become anxious to secure immediate redress, rather than committing ourselves into the hand of the Lord. The apostle Paul suffered much at the hand of those who opposed his preaching the gospel of God's grace. Yet Paul could say, "recompense no man evil for evil...dearly beloved, avenge not yourselves, but rather give place unto wrath: for it is written, vengeance is mine, I will repay, saith the Lord" (Romans 12:17-21). Of that blessed One, who left us a perfect example, it is said, "Who, when He was reviled, reviled not again; when He suffered, He threatened not, but committed Himself to Him that judgeth righteously" (1 Peter 2:23). Skills that we acquire naturally should never be employed to settle personal scores against those who may have occasioned our hurt. However, when such skill are exercised under the influence of the Holy Spirit of God, they are deemed gifts in the service of God and for His glory (Romans 12:6-8).

Hosea, who was contemporary with Isaiah, faithfully prophesied in the service of Jehovah for more than fifty years. The faithful prophet was grieved deeply in his heart and mourned long about the failure of the princes in Judah who had left the people without truth, mercy, and a knowledge of God (Hosea 4:1). He wrote about the people to whom Jehovah had vouchsafed the oracles of God (Romans 3:2). A people with much light, in contrast to the nations in heathen darkness (Luke 2:32). Jehovah had called the people to worship Him, yet long before Hosea's time, "they forsook the Lord God of their fathers...and followed other gods" (Judges 2:12). The nation's sin of idolatry was the more heinous because of the light they had from God. The people were also guilty of indifference to the love Jehovah had poured upon them; and their idolatry violated the covenant of love God made with the nation (Deuteronomy 7:8-9).

The reference to populus alba in Hosea 4:13 confirmed that the hearts and minds of the people were far removed from the thoughts of God. God had established the place where He had set His Name, the place where the people should regularly worship Jehovah. It was Jerusalem, "God...chose...to put His Name there" (Deuteronomy 12:5-7). The place was also confirmed by the Psalmist, "...the city of our God, in the mountain of His holiness. Beautiful for situation, the joy of the whole earth, is mount Zion, on the sides of the north, the city of the great King" (Psalm 48:1-2). Yet, in defiance to the Word of Jehovah, the unregenerate princes took to the tops of the mountains to profane the Name of the Lord. Indifferent to the gravity of their sin, they rested complacent under the shadow of the trees, perhaps believing that the eye of God could not see them. However, like the deciduous oak, terebinth and poplar, the time will come when all their leaves will fall, exposing the apostates as naked before God and ready for judgment (Revelation 3:16-17).

Today, a great responsibility rests on those Christian believers who act as princes in the assembly of God's people, exercising their gifts of ministry and pastoral care. The formative ministry for the Church is as important now as in the time of the apostle Paul (Ephesians 4:11-13). The diminishing factors in Christendom, are truth, mercy and knowledge of God, the very elements of godliness that were absent among the people in Hosea's time, leading Jehovah to say that He had a controversy with them (Hosea 4:1). The absorption of God's word into our heart and soul has a purifying effect upon us (1 John 3:2-3). However, the absence of such precious truth will render us vulnerable to the corrupting influences in the world around, just as the people in Hosea's day were corrupted by the idolatry of the princes. That is why the Lord Jesus prayed that we might be, "sanctified through the truth" (John 17:17 & 19).

When Israel rebelled against God, through Moses and Aaron; Moses appealed to the Lord on behalf of the people for mercy, recalling that, "the Lord is longsuffering and of great mercy, forgiving iniquity and transgression..." (Numbers 14:18). The exercise of mercy is the cancelling of punishment due to the guilty. The apostle Paul reminded the Ephesian Christians, "God, who is rich in mercy, for His great love wherewith He loved us, even when we were dead in sins, hath quickened us together with Christ, (by grace are ye saved)" (Ephesians 2:4-5). God's mercy is also known by His tender and compassionate regard toward the weak and suffering on earth; meeting the needs of those in trouble, trial, weakness and difficulty (Exodus 33:19). As the Psalmist says; an awareness of God's sovereign mercy toward us should daily occasion fresh outbursts of praise in the sanctuary (Psalm 100:4-5).

Knowledge of God was the third element of godliness the princes denied to the people in the land. We can only know God through our Lord Jesus Christ, the One who, as Son of Man on earth was the perfect expression and revelation of the nature, mind and will of God (John 1:18). The more we learn and know about the Person, work and worth of the Lord Jesus, the deeper will be our knowledge of the Saviour God. Paul yearned to know more about the Lord Jesus (Philippians 3:10), accepting that an increasing apprehension of the life and work of that blessed Person would enrich his understanding of the ways of God in grace. The more Paul learnt about the One who gave Himself a sacrifice for sin on Calvary's Cross, the more ready he was to burst out in praise and worship to the God and Father of our Lord Jesus Christ (Philippians 4:20).

The vital work of evangelism, spiritual teaching and the shepherding of the flock of God, must always have as its objective, the worship of the Father (John 4:23). No occasion is more precious to the heart of the Father than when His children are before Him in the spirit of worship, making much of the glorious attributes and worth of His beloved Son (Revelation 5:9-10). May our gracious Lord keep us standing firm and steadfast in the truth of God's Word (Ephesians 4:14-15).

> *Brought to know Thy Well-beloved, drawn to Him in boundless grace,*
> *Thine effulgence, love and glory, shining in His blessed face;*
> *We adore Thee, God and Father, may Thy Name exalted be;*
> *Praise and worship we would render, now as in eternity.*
>
> T Willey

Pulse

Cicer arietinum; Lens culinaris; Vicia faba

Chick pea; Lentils & Beans
Hebrew: Zeroa = Seeds as vegetable food; pulse.
Daniel 1:12 & 16.

The Hebrew, plural noun 'zeroa' refers to cooked edible seeds, seethed rather than roasted (Genesis 25:29; & 2 Kings 4:38). The great majority of biblical botanists believe the above seeds comprised the pulse food given to Daniel and his three companions. While the noun 'pulse' is found in 2 Samuel 17:28 of both KJAV and JND translations of the bible, it does not appear in the original Hebrew text.

Daniel and his three friends were healthy, young men of the tribe of Judah, therefore of the royal seed. Their Hebrew names, which were given to them of God, had reference to the dignity, wisdom, grace, strength and mercy of the God in Whom they trusted and to Whom they remained faithful throughout the time of their captivity. Daniel = God is my judge. Hananiah = the grace of the Lord. Mishael = He that is the strong God. Azariah = the Lord is a help. Although the prince of the eunuchs gave Daniel and his three friends Chaldean names after the idol gods of Babylon, he could not change their

God-fearing nature. The Chaldean prince did not want to have individuals in the King's court with Hebrew names. The prince was in fear of constantly being reminded of Jehovah, Israel's God and His mighty triumphs on behalf of the children who were now his captives. The world at large is reluctant to use the title 'Christian believer' for the simple reason that such a title pricks the consciences of the unsaved. People of the world do not want to hear about the Lord Jesus, still less do they want to be reminded of the One who died for their sins on Calvary's Cross.

The first chapter of Daniel covers the proving time for Daniel and his friends who, in a hostile and idolatrous environment, were anxious to be vessels, "unto honour, sanctified and meet for the Master's use" (2 Timothy 2:21). They represented in figure, the faithful remnant of Israel that will come through Great Tribulation (Revelation 7:14), i.e. the fiery furnace and the lion's den. Daniel and his friends were fervent in prayer, zealous to ensure they did not defile themselves by eating the King's meat. They were aware of the fact that in heathen countries, meats are usually first offered to idols. Neither would they drink the King's wine, for they wished to preserve themselves clear, sound and receptive in heart and mind to the Word of the Lord (Ephesians 5:18).

Daniel's actions confirmed his exercise in matters relating to the uniqueness of a nation that remained the, "apple of His (God's) eye" (Deuteronomy 32:10). The faithful four might have lost the honour of being princes in Babylon, but they could not lose the God-given distinction of being Israelites, the chosen people of God (Deuteronomy 7:6). How often are we tempted to set aside the esteem and dignity God has placed upon us through His Son (Ephesians 1:4-6), in order to enjoy for a moment the adulation and pleasures of the world? May we, like Daniel of old, also be ready to identify with those who suffer for righteousness and His Name's sake.

In the pursuit of righteousness and at the risk endangering their lives before the King, Daniel had asked, on behalf of his friends, that their fare be pulse and water, the very basic of food sustenance. The four were far more concerned about preserving the integrity of their faith in the God of their fathers, than their physical appearance. They would not fall into the trap of the Pharisees who were all clean and white on the outside, but whose hearts were corrupt, dark and full of the symbols of death (Matthew 23:27-28).

Although God had brought Daniel into favour with the prince of the eunuchs, it was a test of his faith in God to proffer such a request. From the outset of Daniel's presence in the King's palace, his priority was to stand in defence of his God (Deuteronomy 4:39-40). He never attempted to ingratiate himself with the princes in the palace, nor did he conceal his honour, love and faith in the God of Abraham, Isaac and Jacob. Like Joseph long before him, Daniel was a bright, shining light in a dark and heathen country. He was respected in the palace for his integrity, industry and faithfulness to duty. What a challenging example are Daniel and his three friends for us today!

Daniel asked if he and his friends might have the basic fare, pulse and water for ten days. He would prove that the physical appearance of a man has more to do with one's state of heart before God, than with the intake of delicately prepared food. Nevertheless, Daniel knew that the eating of food that had first been offered to idols would have a corrupting influence in the hearts of those indifferent to the evil of idolatry. The spiritual food of the Christian believer is the Word of God which we should daily enjoy eating and digesting to produce the features of that perfect Man, our Lord Jesus Christ (Ephesians 4:13).

To ensure Daniel and his friends could both eat and enjoy the food, the pulse seeds were seethed (boiled). It would have been impossible to eat and enjoy such seeds if they were roasted. Likewise, the ram of consecration (Exodus 29:31) had to be seethed to ensure Aaron and his sons would enjoy eating it in celebration of their consecration to the priestly office. Clearly, if we indulge in the food of the world – its pleasures, objectives and associations – we shall take on the characteristics of the unregenerate man. In that event, we would grieve and quench the presence and work of the Holy Spirit of God within us (Ephesians 4:30; & 1 Thessalonians 5:19).

The figure 10 in Scripture speaks of responsibility Godward. Ten days was the span of time in which Daniel and his friends would prove themselves faithfully responsible before God. They were totally committed to God's service in heart, mind and soul. There is a sense in which we may view the ten-day period as paralleling the entire time of the Christian believer's testimony on earth. From the moment of our conversion to the time of our home-call, we are responsible to walk by faith, being sustained only by the Word of God (2 Corinthians 5:7). At the end of the ten days, Daniel and his friends appeared fairer, fatter and healthier than the children who had eaten the King's meat. Moreover, for so long as they remained in the service of the King, they would continue to be nourished with pulse and water (Daniel 1:16). At no time did they relax their commitment to putting God first in their lives. Daniel and his friends gladly applied to themselves the divine principle encapsulated in the exhortation given to the Jews by the Lord Jesus in His manifesto (sermon on the mount) 630 + years later (Matthew 6:31-34). Furthermore, they were blessed with ten times more wisdom, knowledge and understanding than any of the magicians and astrologers in the King's realm. Daniel was also a prophet of the Lord, for God gave him understanding in all visions and dreams. Are we employing to the full, the gift God has given us for use in His service?

Because of his faithfulness to God, together with his friends, Daniel was raised to be ruler over the whole province of Babylon (Daniel 2:48). We today, are challenged to present our bodies a living sacrifice, holy, acceptable unto God, which is your reasonable (intelligent) service (Romans 12:1). If we do this in the way Daniel and his friends committed their lives to God; we too, will be blessed of God with the apprehension and enjoyment of all spiritual blessings in the heavenlies in Christ (Ephesians 1:3). Many Christian believers simply claim this verse as promises, and never realise the reality of present enjoyment from our standing in Christ. The Christian believer's position in Christ is the highest God can bestow on once lost sinners who were dead in trespasses and sins. The more we eschew the delicacies of the world, and feed on the Word of God, the more Christ-like we shall become (2 Corinthians 3:18); it happened to Daniel and his three friends, it should happen to us.

Lord, Thy Word abideth and our footsteps guideth,
Who its truth believeth, light and joy receiveth.
When our foes are near us, then Thy word doth cheer us,
Word of consolation, message of salvation.

H W Baker

Reed

Phragmites australis

Hebrew: Qaneh; Greek: Kalamos = An erect reed, a measuring rod, cane, shaft, tube, stem.
Genesis 41:5 + 32 other references.

The Hebrew word qaneh, means, to be erect, a reed stalk, a rod especially for measuring, shaft, tube and stem. The botanical name, 'phragmites' means: a fence, stockade, screen; defining the way in which reeds develop. Reeds grow and flourish on

the banks of rivers and streams, and in swamps and marshes. The plant develops a long, running rootstock for anchorage, and produces 3 – 4 m long cane-like stems heading up to a conspicuous, cream to white plume or tassel of flowers. In the every day life of biblical times, people relied heavily on the annual harvest of reeds for use in thatching, fencing, hedging, mat making, musical flutes and measuring rods. In a spiritual sense, reeds represent the vulnerability and weakness of the natural man, God's measure of man.

In 1 Kings 14:15, Israel is likened to reeds growing in water and not having a firm anchorage. Instead of being established firm on the Word (Rock) of Jehovah, they resorted to the unstable footings of idolatry and disobedience. The wicked king Jeroboam appointed base men to the priesthood; and unashamedly desecrated the House of the Lord. The Lord responded to the evil of Jeroboam with a message through His blind prophet, Ahijah. Israel will be shaken, said the Lord, as a reed in water, uprooted and scattered throughout the heathen nations; and that is exactly what happened. Here is a salutary warning for Christian believers. The moment we find anchorage in anything other than Christ through the Word of God; we too will become unstable, void of strength and exposed to ungodly influences tossing us to-and-fro with every wind of doctrine (Ephesians 4:14). May our gracious Lord help us, "to be strengthened with might by His Spirit in the inner man" and to remain, "rooted and grounded in love" (Ephesians 3:16-17).

In the days of Hezekiah, king of Judah, the Assyrian king, Sennacherib, invaded the fenced cities of Judah, but stopped short of Jerusalem. Nevertheless, through his ambassador Rabshakeh, Sennacherib threatened to overtake the city, claiming greater strength than that of Egypt on whom Hezekiah would rather depend for the peace and security of his kingdom. Together with his threatening gestures, Sennacherib parallels the reliability and strength of Egypt to a "bruised (damaged) reed". To lean on such a bruised reed, said Sennacherib, is to inflict serious injury on oneself (2 Kings 18:21 & Isaiah 36:6). The fracture point of a broken bamboo-like reed produces a series of sharp small spears; to fall on such, would inflict painful wounds on the victim. In the judgment of the Lord, Sennacherib died and his army defeated (2 Kings 19:35-37).

A similar thought is recorded in Ezekiel 29:6-7, where the Lord declares that His judgment will surely fall on Egypt because of its cruelty to Israel (Deuteronomy 26:6). Egypt had pretended to be a strengthening staff to Israel, but was only a broken reed (Isaiah 36:6). When the nation took hold of Egypt's outstretched hand, they grasped a splintered reed that ripped their hands, tore open their shoulders and injured their backs. By cruel deception, the king of Egypt had ensured that Israel, for a time as least, would not be able to serve Jehovah, nor put their shoulders to the work of the Lord. Furthermore, because of the injuries inflicted on the people, they were not able to stand upright in their own strength. Rather than relying on Egypt for protection, the nation should have put their trust in the Lord, as did Hezekiah when he enquired to know the mind of the Lord through the prophet Isaiah (2 Kings 19:1-2). The Psalmist said, "it is better to trust in the Lord, than to put confidence in man. It is better to trust in the Lord than to put confidence in princes" (Psalm 118:8-9). Sadly, we all too often find that those who claim to provide spiritual support and strength for the saints, are a cause of great pain and suffering. In other words, they are nothing more than a broken and damaging reed. The Lord Jesus warns us against hurting His people (Matthew 18:6). The apostle Paul suffered greatly at the hands of those opposed to the Gospel of God. Although he sometimes despaired even of living, he nevertheless could say, "that we should not trust in ourselves, but in God which raiseth the dead....in Whom we trust that He will yet deliver us" (2 Corinthians 1:9-10). All who trust in the flesh (bruised reed), will find it unreliable, unstable and useless. Those who love and rejoice in the Lord Jesus, have no confidence in the flesh (Philippians 3:3).

God spoke to Job about the reeds that hide behemoth – thought to be the hippopotamus – in (Job 40:21). Job had previously considered himself above other men in respect of his personal righteousness and reverence of God his creator. Furthermore, like the hippopotamus hiding among the weak reeds in the water, Job was content to hide behind the moral standards (frail reeds) of his own estimate of godliness, appearing quite indifferent to his vulnerability before the eye of God. In the narrative, the amphibious creature represents all that are self complacent and indifferent to the divine reckoning of themselves by God, their creator. The hippopotamus is yet another figure of the natural man. The creature cannot be tamed nor controlled; is proud of its strength, fears and wants for nothing, lives solely for itself, conceals itself among weakened reeds, provides nothing for man and is totally indifferent to its creator. In considering the disposition of the hippopotamus, we see that everything about the creature is an outward expression of the inner disposition of man's unregenerate heart before God.

God challenged Job to abhor himself rather than emulate the brute beast. In time, Job did humble himself; he came out from behind the reeds that had been his unreliable shield and security, and confessed to a true and accurate assessment of himself before God. Job said, "I am vile, what shall I answer Thee? I will lay mine hand upon my mouth. Wherefore I abhor myself and repent in dust and ashes" (Job 40:4 & 42:6). The apostle Paul, as Saul of Tarsus, arrived at a similar conclusion about himself, when he said, "I know that in me, (that is, in my flesh,) dwelleth no good thing" (Romans 7:18). Let us come out morally into the open and readily own we are weak and wanting. Let us confess our sins and repent before God, believing in the Lord Jesus Christ and His work of redemption on Calvary's Cross. We then, shall no longer be a bruised reed, but one healed and ready to be used in the Lord's service for the glory of God (1 Thessalonians 1:9-10).

The prophet Isaiah, is led by the Spirit of God to speak of the Lord Jesus Christ in terms that encapsulate the divine estimate of One who was God's perfect servant on earth (Isaiah 42:1). Isaiah's declaration was a unique accolade that exalted the worth, honour and delight God found in a man after His own heart (Matthew 3:17). When Isaiah wrote his prophecy, about 700 + years before Christ; Israel already was a bruised reed, and would remain bruised until the coming of the promised Messiah. The nation's acceptance of Christ and their repentance before God would have brought about a healing of the bruised reed, but they refused and rejected Him. The ungodly response from the people, whom the Lord Jesus had come to save, merited divine, summary judgment (a complete breaking of the reed). However, in line with Isaiah's prophecy, the Lord did not intend to break irreparably the bruised reed during His time as God's servant on earth. He daily prayed for the healing of the nation through its repentance before God (Mark 1:35). In this dispensation of God's grace, the nation of Israel is still a bruised reed by choice, and a symbol of unregenerate man. Nevertheless, along with all mankind, it has the opportunity to repent, as the apostle Paul declares in Act 17:30,

"God...now commandeth all men everywhere to repent". Very soon, God is going to send forth judgment unto victory, annulling every force opposed to His divine plan. The penitent remnant of Israel will be healed of the injurious bruising it has long sustained.

Twenty five years on from when Nebuchadnezzar took the remnant of Israel into captivity in Babylon, Ezekiel had a vision from the Lord. In the vision, the Lord carried Ezekiel back to the land of Israel and set him on a very high mountain, where he received details for the building of a new Temple (Ezekiel 40:2). Such a Temple, known, as 'Ezekiel's Temple' will, in God's time, be constructed for use during the glorious millennial reign of Christ. The building of Ezekiel's Temple will be at the beginning of the millennial reign of Christ, at which time all Israel will be saved. The nation will no longer be a bruised, despised and useless reed, but a people healed of all its weaknesses, failures and backsliding (Hosea 14:4), going forward in the strength of the Lord.

The world will be witness to the miraculous recovery of a nation that for centuries had suffered at the hands of oppressors, notwithstanding that in large measure most was due to its own malfeasance. The world will also see that the external building work of the Temple is carried out by a remnant of the people that had so very recently suffered unspeakable tribulation, almost to the point of extinction (Mark 13:20). The industrious and faithful remnant represents the once bruised reed, now healed and strengthened, engaged initially in building the outward defences of the new Temple. More than this, in that coming day, it will be Israel that will exercise guardianship and protection of all the holy interests touching the King of kings and Lord of lords (1 Timothy 6:15).

We have mention of the same reed in Matthew 27 and Mark 15. Here, according to Mark 15:19, the people used the reed to mock and buffet our blessed Saviour. Those who themselves were morally bruised and wasted reeds, took the article itself to ridicule and batter the One of Whom it was said, "a bruised reed (Israel) He would not break (judge and sentence)" (Isaiah 42:3). Having already thrust a cruel crown of thorns upon His head, they placed of a reed in His right hand to maximise the mockery and pain they happily inflicted on Him. They demeaned the dignity of His holy person, and assaulted His divine title and right as, King of kings and Lord of lords (Psalm 24:10). In spite of the dreadful things the people said and did to Him, His profound love and mercy toward them, constrained Him to say, "Father, forgive them for they know not what they do" (Luke 23:34). In a coming day, all the souls of Godless men and women, down through the centuries from the time of Adam, will stand before the Great White Throne for judgment. It will be the Lord, the judge of all the earth, Who will then hold the true sceptre (rod) of power in His hand to judge the world in righteousness (Acts 17:31).

The last mention of the 'reed' is in Matthew 27:48 & Mark 15:36. The occasion was after the three hours of darkness, during which the Lord Jesus exhausted God's judgment of sin. The spiritual trauma of those three hours left the Lord Jesus with His strength dried up like a potsherd and His tongue cleaving to His jaws (Psalm 22:15). When the Saviour cried out, "I thirst"; a sympathetic onlooker quickly bound a sponge with hyssop branches to a reed, soaked it in vinegar and put it to His lips. On that occasion, the Lord Jesus did take a drink, then boldly cried out, "It is finished". Could it be that the undamaged reed used here, was a figure of the faithful in Israel at that time; certainly, there were very many true disciples of the Lord Jesus. It may well have been a secret disciple of the Lord who rushed forward to offer his Saviour a drink, hoping it would slake His thirst and soothe His tongue, (see last paragraph on Hyssop). As we said at the beginning of this short dissertation, reeds speak of the weakness and vulnerability of the natural man. However, when God's Spirit moves in a newborn, converted person, they are no longer bruised and weakened reeds like the ungodly, but sound and strong, ready to be used in the service of the Lord. We would remind ourselves that the Hebrew word for Qaneh means; to be erect; accordingly, God calls upon Christian believers to walk uprightly before Him unto all pleasing (Colossians 1:10-11).

The measure of Thy mighty love; draws me to where Thou art;
Lord, may my walk be close to Thee, with pure and upright heart.

T H Ratcliffe

Rie

Triticum dicoccoides

Hebrew: Kussemeth = Bristly, from its broken off awns, shorn.
Exodus 9:32. Isaiah 28:25. Ezekiel 4:9.

The reference to the Hebrew noun kussemeth, in Ezekiel 4:9, has been incorrectly translated in the KJAV as 'fitches' instead of 'rie' as given in Exodus and Isaiah. However, the rie of scripture is not, as some have supposed (see Isaiah 28:25 JND translation), the rye cereal we know today. Rye, which is 'secale cereale', is not a native plant of Middle-Eastern countries, for it requires cooler climatic conditions; whereas, triticum dicoccoides, a variety of emmer wheat, is an indigenous cereal plant of Palestine. It is a two-row wheat with double-seeded spikelets – as the Latin name implies – and must be harvested in the 'green-ear' stage when the ears are fully developed and fat. Harvesting the crop as mature, green ears is very important; for if left to ripen as a conventional wheat crop, the ears will readily shatter and scatter the seed to waste on the ground.

The wheat harvest has always been an important and influential factor in the economy of Middle Eastern countries. At the time of the seventh plague on Egypt, the Lord was

generous in His mercy toward the Egyptian nation, especially to Pharaoh. Pharaoh had the opportunity to repent of his evil ways and thereby save his nation from the prospect of a grievous famine, but he continued to rebel against the Lord. Of all the plagues, only in the seventh do we get mention of specific subjects in Egypt not affected by the judgment; in this case, the wheat and rie crops (Exodus 9:32). Typically, Egypt represents the world that, in a coming day is going to suffer severe judgments from God; but through such judgments, a faithful remnant is preserved.

Throughout scripture, wheat and fine wheaten flour speak of the Lord Jesus Christ. In John 12:24, the Lord Jesus speaks of Himself as, 'a corn of wheat falling into the ground and dying in order to bring forth much fruit for God', and that is exactly what has and is happening. God has established a new order of things through the death, resurrection and glorification on high of His beloved Son. The millions of people comprising earth's population today spring from Adam and Eve; but they are of the earth, earthy. Under the new, heavenly order, the final total of spiritual fruit springing from the 'corn of wheat' (Christ) that fell into the ground, died and rose again, will be incalculable. The saving of the wheat and rie from damage by the hail in the seventh plague is significant in relation to the three plagues that followed, all of which typify judgments yet to fall upon the world. The Church of God has suffered greatly since its inception at Pentecost; yet through its darkest hour, a faithful remnant – the wheat and rie – is preserved. Following the rapture of the Church (1 Thessalonians 4:16-17), the severity of the judgments to come upon the earth during the 'week of Jacob's trouble' (Jeremiah 30:7); will be horrendous. Nevertheless, those who acknowledge the Lord Jesus as Sovereign and Lord during that time will live to enjoy the millennial glory.

It was from the cereal plant triticum dicoccoides that the green ears of corn, roasted by fire and beaten out of full ears, were to be given to Jehovah as an 'offering of firstfruits' (Leviticus 2:14-16). The 'green ears' spoke of the Lord Jesus, His manhood in full maturity, perfect before God. 'Roasted with fire' carries the thought that the fire of God's wrath consumed the sin our Lord had made Himself answerable for during the three hours of darkness on the Cross. The 'corn, beaten out of full ears' would relate to the sufferings our Lord endured that God might secure for His eternal delight, the Man of His counsels who fulfilled His will and glorified His Law (John 8:29). We have in Leviticus 23, the 'set feasts of Jehovah'. The 'feast of firstfruits', verses 9 – 14, makes clear that nothing was to be eaten of the new harvest, including 'green ears of corn', before offering the firstfruits to Jehovah. Typically speaking, the celebration of the 'feast of firstfruits' is the acknowledgement of Christ risen from the dead and that He is the firstfruits of them that sleep. It was ever God's purpose to ensure that in all things, His Son should have the pre-eminence (Colossians 1:18). The 'feast of firstfruits' was obligatory on the nation throughout the year, whereas the 'offering of firstfruits' in Leviticus 2 was a free will offering.

The reference to rie in Isaiah 28:25 is in the context of a professional farmer labouring under the guidance of the Spirit of God (verse 26). Isaiah's lovely parable details, the way the ground should be prepared; where to sow the seed, and the methods to employ when harvesting the different crops. The portion is full of instruction for the Lord's servants today. We should daily challenge our hearts by asking; do we adequately prepare ourselves for His service? Through lack of prayer, the disciples were impotent when it came to the casting out an evil spirit (Mark 9:28-29). Where the seed should be sown, relates to where the Lord would have us serve Him. The range of seeds sown would suggest that our ministry should be specific to spiritual needs; and the method employed to harvest the crop would have reference to our shepherd care for the flock. The Hebrew word for the noun 'place' at the end of verse 25 in Isaiah 28, is Gebulah, and means, boundary region, border, outer bound, coast. Rie sown in the border region of a field, possibly surrounding a barley or wheat crop, would ensure easy access when it was ready to harvest, without risk of damaging other, unripe crops. The figure here is of the Lord Jesus, as Son of Man on earth – the full green ear – surrounding His own to ensure "none of them is lost" (John 17:12).

> *Firstfruits of Thy new creation; faithful, holy, may we be;*
> *Joyful in Thy full Salvation, more and more conformed to Thee.*
>
> C Wesley

205

Rose of Sharon
Narcissus tazetta

Hebrew: for Rose – Chabatstseleth = uncertain origin. Sharon from Yashar = straight, upright, pleasant, prosperous, esteemed.
Song of Solomon 2:1 and Isaiah 35:1.

Narcissus tazetta is a bulbous, perennial plant, native throughout Israel, flowering in the autumn through to November. Although referred to in Scripture as the Rose of Sharon, in Middle Eastern countries it is 'the wild daffodil'. The flower spathe (stem) is rarely more than 30 cm high, and heads up with 6 – 8 beautiful, fragrant flowers, each having two rays of three pure white petals called the perigonium, together with a prominent, golden, central cup. When there is little else around after the summer months, the narcissus gives a most welcome splash of colour on an otherwise barren landscape.

The significance of the reference to the rose in the two scriptures becomes clear when we understand the context in which the subject occurs. In Song of Solomon 2:1, the typical teaching is this; it is the bride – not the bridegroom – who acknowledges God's mercy bestowed on her. Comparing herself with the narcissus was not an expression of pride or vanity, but a recognition that whatever she may appear to be in the eye of her beholder; all is of sovereign grace. The bride would boast in nothing of her own natural character. The narcissus flower has six pure white petals, a number that in scripture speaks of the weakness of man, falling just short of seven, the perfect number. That the petals are pure white would remind us that the Blood of Jesus Christ has cleansed us from every sin (John 13:10). However, in the case of the narcissus, we have the seventh element, the all-important central, gold-coloured crown that dominates the flower. It is a feature to which one's eye is automatically drawn, being the focal point. In the figure, we accept that the golden crown speaks of Christ whose glory bestows divine dignity on Christian believers – the white petals.

We readily accept that without Christ, we are nothing and would ever remain nothing, just as the narcissus flower would be nothing without the central, golden crown. The bride in the Song of Solomon 2:1 felt the same, that without her bridegroom, she would be nothing. The apostle Paul said, "At one time we were without Christ...having no hope, and without God in the world. But now in Christ Jesus, we who sometimes were far off, are made nigh by the blood of Christ" (Ephesians 2:12-13). The individual narcissus flower also is a figure of all the redeemed in Christ before the eye of God. John Nelson Darby wrote of the time when all the redeemed will be in heaven, 'There Christ the centre of the throng, shall in His glory shine, but not an eye those hosts among, but sees His glory Thine'. The bride rests complacent in the knowledge that her standing and acceptance is of pure grace alone (Ephesians 2:8-9). 'Of grace then let us sing, a joyful, wondrous theme; Who grace has brought, shall glory bring, and we shall reign with Him' (T Kelly).

The reference to the rose in Isaiah 35:1 presents something entirely different to the scene we have in the Song of Solomon 2:1. Chapter 34 of Isaiah, details the severity of God's judgment to befall all the people and nations of the world that have fought against the Lord and His anointed. Such judgments will be at the end of the age when the hosts of heaven shall be dissolved and the heavens themselves rolled together as a scroll, and their hosts fall as a leaf falleth off the vine (Isaiah 34:3-4). During the millennial age, righteousness will reign on the earth; and although conditions will be immeasurably better and without parallel since Eden's Garden, – for Satan will be imprisoned (Revelation 20:2-3) – it will not be a perfect state. The fact that scripture speaks of righteousness reigning, implies that restraint will be necessary during the millennium; such a time cannot therefore be termed perfect. The perfect state comes when righteousness dwells in the new earth. That is the time Isaiah speaks of in chapter 35 of his prophecy; the apostle Peter refers to the same time in his second epistle. "Nevertheless, we, according to His (God's) promise, look for new heavens and a new earth, wherein dwelleth righteousness" (2 Peter 3:13). It will be the consummation of God's objective, as set out in the third and fourth chapters of the epistle to the Hebrews; God's eternal rest. What a precious thing to know, that God will rest complacent in His own throughout the endless ages of eternity.

From a state of desolation, following God's judgments against His enemies, there will arise a scene of peace, prosperity, beauty and rejoicing to gladden the heart of God and man (Psalm 46:4-5). The desert shall rejoice and blossom as the rose (narcissus). Let us stop for a moment and ask, 'what are the first flower colours to appear on the earth after a long, cold, barren winter'? Answer: white and yellow; the white almond and the snowdrop; the yellow crocus and the primrose to mention but a few. So when there is a new earth, all who fill that realm will be likened unto the narcissus flower, the snow-white petals representing man, and the centre golden crown, God Himself with them, in their midst (Revelation 21:2-3). The inhabitants of the new earth will be those who, having lived through the millennium, were not deceived and did not rebel against the Lord when Satan was loosed for a short time at the end (Revelation 20:7-8). The new heaven, on the other hand, will be the destiny of all the saints up to the end of the present day of God's grace. The realm of the saved in the new earth will resound with eternal praise to God their Saviour, and the praise of the redeemed will echo throughout the courts of heaven for ever and ever, Amen (Psalm 149 & 150).

This is our redeeming God, ransomed host will shout aloud;
Praise, eternal praise be given, to the Lord of earth and heaven.

J Swain

Saffron

Crocus sativus

Hebrew: Karkom = Crocus – deep golden yellow.
Song of Solomon 4:14.

Crocus sativus belongs to the iridaceae family of plants. It has a subterranean corm, which in the autumn produces long, narrow leaves and one or two large blue to reddish lilac, six-petal flowers, veined with a deeper red and displaying large red stigmas and golden-yellow anthers. The name saffron is an anglicised form of 'zafran', an Arabic

word meaning 'golden yellow'. The fragrant colouring substance marketed as saffron comes from the prominent, golden yellow stigmas and style of the flower. Pure saffron has been much sought after as a delightful, yet expensive perfume since biblical times. As many as 200 flowers are required to produce just 1 g of the pure product. This may account for the use of a cheap substitute obtained from the flowers of the thistle-like, safflower, Carthamus tinctorius, a plant of the daisy family (compositae). The fragrant saffron product was so highly prized in biblical days, that it was cultivated to meet the requirements of the rich in society. Solomon fully appreciated the value and use of the saffron product. What is most interesting is that the specific botanical name given for saffron is 'sativus', meaning 'cultivated as a crop'.

The primary colours making up the saffron flower are red, blue and golden-yellow. The red reminds us of the blood of Jesus Christ, shed at Calvary to atone for our sins and the sin of the world. Blue would tell us that Christian believers are a heavenly people by new birth, "for our conversation (citizenship JND translation) is in heaven, from whence also we look for the Saviour, the Lord Jesus Christ" (Philippians 3:20). Gold, on the other hand, speaks of the glory of God, to remind us that the redeemed have been spiritually and eternally fused with God through Christ (Colossians 3:3). Our lives should reflect that we are in the good of all we have been brought into through Christ, based on God's sovereign grace (1 Corinthians 6:19-20). Then there is the fragrance of the flower, distinct, pleasing and lasting. The consecration of Aaron and his sons as priests for the service of Jehovah was with a holy anointing oil that was unique in both composition and enduring fragrance (Exodus 30:30).

God has also anointed every Christian believer with His Holy Spirit, sealing them for His possession, and consecrating them ready for divine service (1 John 2:20). Finally, the saffron comes into flower in the autumn when there is little else to brighten the landscape. There is no doubt we are in the autumn of God's 'day of grace' to this world. Jeremiah knew about the gloom of autumn days, when he cried out on behalf of the children of Judah. "The harvest is past, the summer is ended, and we are not saved" (Jeremiah 8:20). Millions of souls today are in the same predicament as were the children of Judah in Jeremiah's day. Are we letting our lights (saffron flower) shine brightly and consistently enough to convict men of their need to repent before God, and to put their faith and trust in the Lord Jesus Christ?

In Song of Solomon 4, the bridegroom is speaking of the delight He finds in His bride. He uses every appropriate adjective to define her inestimable worth to His heart. Already we have seen that the primary subject in the Song of Solomon, is Israel. The book sets forth Israel in a position of dominance and glory in a coming day, a day when the nation will freely own the Lord Jesus Christ as Sovereign Lord. Israel's recovery is compared to a garden enclosed; shut in and sealed against everything outside. Whilst within, the Lord is relishing all that fills His heart with delight from a people presenting features that are the product of His love, mercy and grace. To get the gain of the verses before us in Song of Solomon 4:12-16, we must apply the scenario to our own lives. As individuals, our hearts should be a closed garden unto the Lord, one in which he is pleased to reside exclusively, with running water as evidence of the Holy Spirit active in our lives. There should also be a harvest of pleasant fruit, being the product of His work in the power of the Holy Spirit. Finally, the garden must yield fragrant products that minister delight to His Soul, i.e. the precious and redolent attributes of the Lord Jesus, left in our wake wherever we go. Whatever our experiences and circumstances in this life, if we daily remain in the will of the Lord, we shall be unto God, a sweet savour of Christ (2 Corinthians 2:15).

There will however, be times of trial, sorrow and disappointment blowing into our lives

– our gardens – to generate deep soul exercise. These are the cold north winds, designed to ensure production of the highest quality fruit and richest fragrances possible for our Lord to enjoy (Hebrews 12:11). The blowing of the warm south winds relate to the occasions when we experience great joy and blessedness, generating an uninhibited outflow of fragrant praise and worship (John 12:3). The local company of Christian believers should also be a living, productive and fragrant garden in which our Lord delights to move. As with the garden, so are the children of God; they are enclosed with their Lord, He would not have it otherwise. Every plant in the garden presents a unique, fresh and delightful attribute of the grace of God found in the hearts and lives of the redeemed. "The fruit of the Spirit is love, joy, peace, longsuffering, gentleness, goodness, faith, meekness, temperance; against such, there is no law" (Galatians 5:22-23).

Lord, the beauty of Thy Person and the sweetness of Thy love;
From Thy garden, spread their fragrance, o'er our path that leads to God.

T H Ratcliffe

Shittim Wood

Acacia seyal

Hebrew: Shittah = Scourging, piercing thorns.
Exodus 25:5 + 27 other references.

The biblical Acacia seyal is a tree of the desert wadis of Sinai, and belongs to the leguminosae (pea) family of plants, sometimes called, 'white whistling wood'. The tree is of the same family as the familiar Australian mimosa, acacia dealbata. There seems little doubt that when the Israelites reached the Sinai desert, following their deliverance from Egypt, the shittim-wood trees would have been far more substantial in height and girth than anything found growing there today. If we consider the specifications for the building of the Tabernacle, as given in Exodus 26:16; the trees would need to have been at least 8 m tall, with 1 m diameter trunks. Down through the centuries, charcoal producers have decimated the Sinai peninsular of mature shittim-wood trees. Today, such trees in the wadi regions of the Sinai are little more than 4 m high (including the head of the tree), have relatively narrow trunks and conspicuous flaking red bark.

The head of the shittim-wood tree is a mass of intricate branches with pinnatified foliage, similar to the mimosa, but with 10 cm long, sharp, piercing thorns coming from the base of each stem. Globular heads of fragrant, yellow flowers are borne on stiff stalks, followed by 10 cm long, seed pods. Shittim-wood is the hardest of any tree native to the Sinai peninsular, and not only is it incorruptible, but also resistant to attack by damaging insects. Unlike the majority of trees in the world flora that grow towards the heavens, the head form of acacia seyal is somewhat flattened or dome-shaped, a characteristic we shall consider later.

Mature shittim-wood trees, while retaining a full head of foliage and beautifying the desert plain with fragrant, yellow flowers, bear the appearance of having survived adverse and hostile growing conditions. Was that not exactly the experience of the Lord Jesus when here on earth as dependant man? He found the world a wilderness desert, a place of testing, void of spiritual comforts (Luke 9:58); a place where one daily depended upon another for sustaining provisions (Luke 4:4). When He was manifested to the people at the age of 30 years, it soon became evident that he was, "a root out of a dry ground" (Isaiah 53:2). All the potential of eternal life, power and blessing resided in that root, for God His Father was with Him (John 16:32). The dry ground, on the other hand, was and still is a figure of Israel, barren, and lacking any resource to sustain life. The Psalmist spoke prophetically of the Lord Jesus, when he said, the people compassed Him about with words of hatred, and fought against Him without a cause. In response to His love, they became His adversaries; they rewarded Him evil for good and hatred for His love (Psalm 109:3-5). In such a hostile environment, our Lord was daily sustained through communion with God, His Father (Luke 6:12); an example for our souls to hold, cherish and follow without demur!

The penetrating thorns on the shittim-wood tree tell us about the power of our Lord's testimony, as man on earth. His words and the moral light of His way, convicted men of their sinful state before God; and this is why the people frequently sought occasion to kill Him (John 7:1). Unlike the visible thorns on the plant zizyphus spina christi from which the 'crown of thorns' was made; the thorns on the shittim-wood tree are concealed by the mass of foliage. The Lord had not come to harm mankind, but to be a light in the world, to heal, to cure and to deliver man from moral darkness (Luke 4:18-19). The thorns are therefore typical of the effect the Word of God had and continues to have in the hearts and upon the consciences of men. The writer of the Hebrew epistle said, "the Word of God is quick and powerful, and sharper than any two-edged sword; piercing even to the dividing asunder of soul and spirit, and of the joints and marrow, and is a discerner of the thoughts and intents of the heart" (Hebrews 4:12). Whenever the Pharisees and people, together with the priest verbally attacked the Lord Jesus; they experienced in their hearts the extreme pain of His Word as it summarily demolished their argument, pricked their consciences and injured their pride. Provided you do not meddle or attack the shittim (acacia) tree, its lethal thorns remain harmless. However, the moment you question the Word of God, its Truth will pierce your conscience to effect a painful conviction of sin.

Shittim wood speaks of the incorruptibility of our Lord Jesus Christ as man. The wood is naturally resistant to disease and attack by pests. The degenerative, moral diseases in this world of darkness could never infect that Holy Person; neither could the persistent attacks of Satan penetrate the soul of the One that was pure and holy (Matthew 4:1-11). The following statements in the New Testament epistles confirm the divine, unparalleled perfection of the Lord Jesus Christ as Son of Man. Speaking of the Lord Jesus, the apostle Paul said, "for He (God) hath made Him to be sin for us, Who knew no sin" (2 Corinthians 5:21). The apostle Peter said of Him, "Who did no sin" (1 Peter 2:22); and the beloved apostle John said, "in Him is no sin" (1 John 3:5).

The form of the shittim-wood tree is indicative of the One who on earth aspired to nothing more than to do the Will of God (Psalm 40:8). The majority of trees grow up toward the heavens, but the shittim-wood tree develops a rounded head as though recognising that its place, for the time being at least, is on earth. Our Lord was here at the behest of His Father, to complete a work given Him to do (John 4:34). The Lord demonstrated on many occasions His total commitment to His Father's Will. A week or so before He was crucified, He took Peter, James and John up into a high mountain to pray (Luke 9:28). It was while praying that the fashion of His countenance changed to reflect the Shekinah (dwelling) glory of His Holy Person; the glory that in a coming day will envelop the redeemed in heaven. This is what the Lord was referring to in Luke 9:27. From the mount of transfiguration, the Lord Jesus had every right and title to ascend directly into heaven and thereby end His pilgrimage on earth. But no, our Lord knew He had to complete the work of redemption that no other could do; He was the Lamb God provided to take away the sin of the world (John 1:29). Six days later in the garden of Gethsemane; having surveyed with unspeakable anguish the contents of the 'cup of God's wrath and judgment of sin', He said, "not My will, but Thine be done" (Luke 22:42).

In Exodus 25, the 'ark of the testimony' was made of shittim wood and then overlaid with pure gold. The ark contained the two tablets of stone on which the finger of God had written the law (decalogue). The law embraced the complete mind and will of God for man on earth. Failure on man's part to keep any one part of the law, condemned him to death (James 2:10). The Scriptures declare, "all have sinned and come short of the glory of God" (Romans 3:23). The ark of shittim wood symbolised the perfect manhood of Christ in whom exclusively resided the complete Will of God and in whom the full mind of God will dwell throughout the eternal ages (2 Chronicles 5:10). The gold that covered the ark within and without, spoke of the glory of God that radiated from that blessed Person in every area of His life on earth. The ark with its Mercy seat, was the most important article of all the Tabernacle and Temple furnishings. While the ark remained with the people either journeying or at rest, it was the evidence that Jehovah was with them in times of blessing, victory and governmental judgments. Along our pilgrim pathway, our 'ark' is the Lord Jesus. The Lord would have us give Him the first and rightful place in our lives (Colossians 1:18). While a comprehensive study of the ark and its titles is outside the subject range of this book, may the Spirit of

God touch our hearts to learn more about the significance of 'the ark' today. For the Christian believer, the Lord Jesus Christ is concurrently the, 'ark of the Testimony', the 'ark of the new Covenant', the 'ark of the Lord' and the 'ark of God'!

The brazen altar on which 'burnt-offering' sacrifices were consumed by fire, was made of shittim wood, five cubits square and three cubits high, covered with bronze (Exodus 27:1-2). The number five in scripture speaks of the completeness of man as God made him, 'in His own likeness' (Genesis 1:26). God gave to man five senses; the ability to feel, hear, see, smell and taste; all to be exercised for the glory of God. God also gave man five digits on each hand for doing His will, and five toes on each foot to walk in His ways. The only Man who used all his faculties perfectly for the glory of God, was the Lord Jesus Christ. The number three in relation to the height of the brazen altar, has reference to the unity of the Godhead that rested complacently on the One consecrated to do the Will of God. The Lord Jesus never sought to live outside the bounds of His perfect manhood; He was ever dependent on His God. On the other hand, the natural man after Adam's race has ever wanted to be independent of God; seeking a 'sixth' sense, and striving to do and go beyond the limits set by his Creator (Genesis 3:6-7).

The altar covered with bronze has reference to the fact that the Lord Jesus alone could sustain and allow to burn out in His holy soul, the fiery judgment of Almighty God against sin. All that the Lord Jesus suffered at the hand of God on the Cross confirms there can be no further judgment of sin; the work of redemption is complete (John 19:30). The four horns, also made of shittim wood, were typical of the moral strength with which the Lord Jesus daily faced up to the assaults of Satan from all quarters, first in the wilderness, and then throughout His pathway. The Lord Himself said, "the prince of this world cometh and hath nothing in Me (John 14:30). The number four in scripture is the 'universal' number. In John 3:16 we read, "God so loved the world that He gave His only begotten Son, that whosoever believeth in Him, should not perish, but have everlasting life". Thus, the Lord Jesus died for the sin of all mankind, that all might be saved. "The Lord is…longsuffering to us-ward, not willing that any should perish, but that all should come to repentance" (2 Peter 3:9). May the Lord Jesus help us daily to live by faith. Through the in-dwelling of the Holy Spirit of God, each of us can display the characteristics of shittim-wood. Our testimony should be free of injury from the spiritual attacks of Satan, and unpolluted by the moral diseases in the world around.

To walk with Thee below, and learn Thy holy ways;
Each day more to Thy stature grow, to Thine eternal praise.

G W Fraser

Spikenard

Nardostachys jatamansi

Hebrew: Nerd. Greek: Nardos = A fragrant, therapeutic & cosmetic oil.
Song of Solomon 1:12 + 4 other references.

Spikenard is a perennial herb belonging to the plant order, valerianaceae. Nardostachys is a genus of just two species, the other being, gracilis. The plant is native to the mountainous regions of Napal and India, growing at altitudes of 3500 – 4000 m. Its leaves are entire, i.e. without leaf-stems, and arise from short, thick hairy stems. The foliage, stem and root of the plant contain the highly aromatic oil, used as nard. Rose-pink flowers appear in clusters at the top of 10 – 20 cm stems. A few authorities believe the Old Testament 'spikenard' came from the plant cymbopogon schoenanthus, a North African camel-grass. However, the great majority of biblical botanists accept that the spikenard referred to in both the Old and New Testament is the product of nardostachys jatamansi.

The spiritual significance of the fragrant spikenard oil relates to what Christian believers have stored in their hearts, through daily communion with the Lord. The centuries old method of extracting the oil from each part of the spikenard plant speaks

of the way our lives are daily touched by the Spirit of God to secure a full reservoir of praise, worship and thanksgiving. All spiritual development in the soul is the work of Christ; even to the storing of precious spikenard oil ready to be used for His glory and honour. Christian believers meeting together for worship and the remembrance of the Lord Jesus Christ in the celebration of the supper, gladly acknowledge Him as the host. Their filled alabaster boxes are broken in the Lord's presence to let the precious odours of Christ flow out to fill the house redolent of praise (John 12:2-3).

The setting in Song of Solomon 1:12 is one of precious communion in the spirit of worship. The King sits at His table and delights to welcome His beautiful bride. She has brought along some precious nard, the fragrance of which expresses her deep affections for and toward Him. He stirs those affections to lead her heart out in the spirit of adoring praise and worship. She makes much of His glorious attributes, for He is the sole treasure of her heart (Song of Solomon 1:13-17). Being in His presence produces uninhibited out-bursts of praise. The only desire of her enraptured heart is to minister pleasure to the One whom she delights to honour.

In Song of Solomon 4:12-15 we have the thought of a walled-in garden where every pleasant fruit has reached the stage of maturity. Among the fruits is the spikenard that adds its sweet fragrance to the other products of the garden. A walled-in garden carries the thought of the assembly of God's people, shut in with the Lord Jesus, separated from the affairs of the world and yielding the first-fruits of their hearts in a continuous sacrifice of praise (Hebrews 13:15). There is a fountain of living water in the garden, a type of the Holy Spirit of God, who ensures the on-going production of pleasant fruits. Such fruits are for the pleasure of God; they are the testimonies of the saints as they daily make much of the Lord Jesus and acknowledge the delight He ministers to the heart of God. In a local assembly of God's people, each one contributes some fresh impression of the all-various attributes of the Lord Jesus, and is therefore essential for the spiritual fruitfulness of the whole company.

Sad to say, there is much spiritual poverty among the children of God today. Many have taken their eye off the Lord Jesus and fixed it on man with consequent loss of fruit for God. We note also in the Song of Solomon, chapter 4, that the Bridegroom highlights all the divine qualities of the bride, defining such qualities as the pleasant fruits of His garden. The bride was wholly taken up with the excellencies of the Bridegroom; she was transfixed by His beauty; accordingly, all that welled forth from her heart was likened to precious fruit. May the Lord touch our hearts afresh so that the words of C.A Bernstein may be true of us, 'O fix our earnest gaze so wholly, Lord, on Thee; that, with Thy beauty occupied, we elsewhere none may see'.

The narrative recorded in John 12:1-8, is of an incident that was very precious to the heart of the Lord Jesus. So much so that the Lord Himself declared that wherever the Gospel is preached throughout the world, the record of what Mary had done would be spoken of for a memorial of her. Lazarus also was there at the table as a monument of the miracle that testified to the fact that the Lord Jesus was, "the resurrection and the life" (John 11:25). While Martha and Lazarus were equally important in the above narrative, we must focus our attention on Mary. First, we note the recurring disposition of Mary. In Luke 10:39 when all was well with her, we find her sitting at the feet of Jesus, contented simply to listen and take in what the Lord Jesus was saying. She had chosen the good part, which would not to be taken from her (verse 42). In John 11:32, Mary's brother Lazarus was dead and buried, the darkness and pain of death was fresh around her, yet when Jesus comes on the scene, she immediately falls at His feet and claims Him, Lord.

In John 12:3, Mary is again at the feet of Jesus. Did she have a premonition of what was going to happen to the One she loved so dearly? Did she have an inkling of the approaching day of deep, unfathomable sorrow, spoken of by Jeremiah the prophet (Lamentations 1:12)? There seems little doubt that the Spirit of God moved in her heart to reveal the divine plan. Very soon, five days in fact – although Mary may not have known exactly how soon – her Saviour and Lord would suffer at the hand of His enemies. Meanwhile, Mary would continue to take the lowly position at the feet of the One, she recognised as her Lord, whom she honoured and loved. What an example for us today! In the 18th century, Marie de Fleury wrote,

> *Lord Jesus, we worship and bow at Thy feet,*
> *And give Thee the glory, the honour that's meet.*
> *While through Thee, O Saviour, our praises ascend,*
> *To God and the Father through worlds without end.*

The setting in John 12:1-3; conveys the spirit of harmony among all whose hearts were transfixed by the presence of the Lord Jesus as they sat with Him around the table. J N Darby wrote, 'O Lord, Thy love's unbounded, so sweet, so full, so free; my soul is all transported whene'er I think of Thee'. Mary's soul was transported on that unique occasion in the house of Bethany. She was oblivious of all around as she focused her heart and mind on the Lord Jesus Christ. Mary placed herself at the feet of the Lord Jesus, the place where every worshipping soul should be. The pouring of the precious nard over the feet of the Lord Jesus was tantamount to emptying her full reservoir of responsive affections on Him. Mary's act demonstrated she was cognisant of who He was, where He was from, and what was due to Him from her heart. Furthermore, she knew that His path on earth, with all its glory and perfection, would lead Him to the death He had referred to on many occasions. Wiping His feet with her hair confirmed there was no pride in her act of selfless devotion; it was an act motivated by love. That was and still is the true spirit of worship that should mark every Christian believer. Like the precious oil extracted from every part of the spikenard plant, so Mary's life had been deeply touched by the Lord Jesus Christ. The outpouring of Mary's affections filled the house with divine fragrance. As with Mary, the Lord Jesus would touch our lives from day to day by the power of His Spirit. May such divine touches occasion the storing in our hearts of incorruptible, responsive affections (spikenard) ready to be poured out, at the right time and in the right place in the spirit of true worship.

> *Much incense is ascending before the eternal throne;*
> *God graciously is bending to hear each feeble one.*
> *To all our prayers and praises, Christ adds His sweet perfume;*
> *And He the censer raises, these odours to consume.*
>
> M Bowly

Stacte

Styrax officinalis

Hebrew: Nataph = To fall in drops; distil gradually; to ooze. An aromatic gum. Exodus 30:34.

Stacte resin is one of the few plant products of the Bible about which doubt remains regarding its source. However, the general feeling is that the resin came from styrax officinalis, commonly known as the storax plant, of the family styracaceae. The storax bush is a hardy, deciduous, free flowering shrub, 1-2 m high, with single, drooping white flowers in simple clusters. The highly fragrant resin with the scent of 'camphor', issues naturally from the bark in tear-like drops. For the commercial production of resin, incisions are made in the bark, causing it to flow more freely. The resin hardens on exposure to the air. Arab tradesmen have used storax for centuries, and continue to do so to enhance the perfumes to which they are so addicted.

2·5 cm

The Hebrew for stacte is 'nataph' which means: to ooze, to distil gradually, to fall in drops. Lush growing storax plants in the fertile plains of Galilee do not spontaneously ooze out resin from the stem and trunk, whereas similar plants growing under harsher environmental conditions do yield the fragrant stacte resin. Stacte was the first mentioned constituent of the 'holy incense' as detailed in

Exodus 30:34-38. The burning of the sweet incense on the golden altar every morning and evening, spoke typically of the continuous fragrance that ascended to God from the life of our Lord Jesus Christ as Son of Man on earth. Every inner feeling He experienced as He pursued the fulfilment of the will of Him who sent Him; every action, step and word, generated a sweet savour that God alone could fully evaluate. A part of the sweet incense mixture was to be beaten very small. Such a requirement by God conveys to us that the minute details in the life and death of the Lord Jesus were in perfect harmony with divine thought. The finer the constituents are ground the richer is the incomparable and delicate bouquet generated from the burning. Moreover, the fusion of such divine attributes occasioned the eternal pleasure and delight God was securing in the man after His heart (Luke 3:22 & 9:35). The exceptional fragrance of the glorified man in heaven will never diminish.

Of the constituents for the sweet incense, it says, "of each shall there be a like weight". Here we have in type, confirmation that no one of all the glorious virtues that shone out in the personal life of our blessed Lord eclipsed another. In that lovely person was perfect symmetry and congruence of all the divine, moral graces that shone brighter than the mid-day sun. As He moved from place to place, He left in His wake the unique fragrance of His Holy Person. Furthermore, there was no measured quantity laid down for each of the constituents; such a divine ordering confirmed that the moral and sweet excellencies of the person of Christ, were and are without limit; but let us consider 'stacte'.

Was it because of the way storax naturally produces its resin, that God chose the product as a constituent of the sweet incense? When we think of 'tear-drops', do not our thoughts immediately repair to the occasion when the Lord Jesus stood at the grave of Lazarus and wept? The Greek word for 'wept' as used in John 11:35, occurs nowhere else in Scripture; it means, 'to cry silently'. That divine crying outside the tomb of Lazarus was the evidence of holy emotions emanating from our Lord's innermost being. As He came face to face with the consequence of what sin had brought in by the first man, Adam, He was deeply moved in soul and spirit. Our Lord could not restrain the teardrops that trickled down His lovely face. No mortal man could have wept with such profound depths of holy feeling. When did we last weep because of the consequences of sin around us? Surely, it is wrong to remain indifferent to the deepening moral darkness in the world, to say nothing of the splintering and failure of the Testimony among Christian believers. These saddening conditions should more frequently move us to tears; if they did, would not the light of the Gospel of the Glory of Christ in us shine the brighter?

Perhaps the most poignant story about the Lord Jesus is in Luke 22, when He was in Gethsemene's garden. We shall never be able to measure the depths to which His love took Him. Neither shall we ever comprehend the very deep agony of soul He experienced as He contemplated the cross. What are our current thoughts about this lovely person? "Who in the days of His flesh, when He had offered up prayers and supplications with strong crying and tears unto Him that was able to save Him from death, and was heard in that He feared. Though He were a Son, yet learned He obedience by the things which He suffered" (Hebrews 5:7). The Lord Jesus yearned with tears, for the scattered in Israel; He said, "how often would I have gathered your children together, even as a hen gathereth her chickens under her wings, and ye would not" (Matthew 23:37). Have we a yearning for those of the household of faith who are turning aside and being caught up in the affairs of this world; or are we happy to let them drift away? Do we have a tearful exercise about the gospel outreach, which the Holy Spirit of God might work upon the souls of men to effect conviction of sin and conversion to the Saviour of the world?

When Paul was about to leave the Christian church at Ephesus, he warned them that, following his departure; grievous wolves would enter in among them, not sparing the flock. Paul went on to say that he, "ceased not to warn every one of them night and day with tears" (Acts 20:29-31). Then again, when Paul wrote his first letter to the Corinthian assembly because of the prevailing disorder, he was subsequently happy to write a second epistle and to share with the saints his innermost soul exercise. "Out of much affliction and anguish of heart I wrote unto you with many tears; not that ye should be grieved, but that ye might know the love which I have more abundantly unto you" (2 Corinthians 2:4). There was no vanity, pride, arrogance or vindictiveness in the heart of the apostle when he wrote his first letter; his single objective was their recovery to the holiness that becometh saints (2 Corinthians 7:1).

In Ecclesiastes 3:4 we read, "there is a time to weep (cry tears), and a time to laugh (rejoice)". The deeper our exercise and awareness of how far short we fall of the holy standard God requires of us, the more readily will flow the tears (stacte) that issue from a contrite heart (Ps. 51:17). Then, and only then shall we know and experience the joy and peace the Lord's presence gives us (John 20:19-20).

O Saviour, we read of Thy path, full of pain;
Thy heart moved to tears, with affections divine;
Thou gavest Thy life, that by faith we might gain,
Life with Thee in Glory, eternal, sublime.

T H Ratcliffe

Sycamine - Mulberry

Morus nigra

Hebrew: Sukaminos = Imitation of a mulberry fig tree.
Luke 17:6.

Although there is only one reference to sycamine in the Scriptures, all authorities, biblical and botanical agree that the Sycamine plant is the black mulberry tree, morus nigra. The mulberry tree to which the Lord referred should not be confused with the

white mulberry, morus alba. According to botanical records, the white mulberry, which is native to China and grown for silk production, did not arrive in Middle Eastern countries until the 16th century A.D. The black mulberry is a slow-growing, deciduous tree that in time attains substantial dimensions. The stout trunk and hemispherical comus that outspreads from just one metre above ground level, renders the tree highly resistant to the strongest of winds. The red fruits are like small loganberries, and although not highly nutritious, are nevertheless popular in Palestine, where they are known as the 'damascus mulberry'.

We may ask, why did the Lord Jesus on this one occasion refer to the sycamine tree as a natural force of resistance that the smallest element of faith could overcome? The answer is that the sycamine tree is a figure of the spirit of unregenerate man standing against the will of Almighty God. When it comes to dealing with man's intransigence and self-importance, the Lord employs the simile of the mustard seed to illustrate the power of faith to remove all obstacles, even resistance that parallels the powerful defences of the sycamine tree. The coming in of 'grace and truth by Jesus Christ' (John 1:17) introduced a new order for man, and went way beyond the requirements of the law. Whenever an offender repented of their wrongdoing, forgiveness by the offended had instantly to follow, even up to seventy times seven; in other words, times without number. In view of their upbringing under a law that demanded justice and retribution, this was a particularly difficult order for the disciples to follow without the spirit of God's grace being active in their souls. The disciples quickly realised their faith would be severely tested whenever they attempted to carry out the Lord's injunction.

Accordingly, they un-wisely ask for more faith, ignorant of the fact that what was lacking in them was 'quality' of faith and not 'quantity' of faith. Their objective was good, but the means of achieving it, wrong. The Lord Jesus refers to the inherent power in a tiny mustard seed, and implies that all they required was real, living and powerful faith equal in energy to the potential of a viable mustard seed. The Lord then assures them that with such faith they would be able to say unto the sycamine tree, "be thou plucked up by the root, and be thou planted in the sea", and it would happen.

Many Christian believers have difficulty exercising forgiveness, no matter how often the one who is the offender, repents;

they are reluctant to forgive because their pride has been hurt and their personal esteem damaged. Our Lord likens this disposition of heart and soul, to the resolute, unmoveable sycamine tree with its bold head and deeply anchored roots. It is a characteristic of the old nature within each of us, and unless we daily reckon it dead and buried, will manifest and exert itself to the detriment of our faith (see Galatians 2:20). There remains in each of us an element of self-importance; we want to stand firm on our rights, although Christian believers should confess to having no rights in this world, having surrendered all to Christ (Luke 21:1-4). The apostle Paul said to those of the assembly at Corinth: "What? Know ye not that your body is the temple of the Holy Ghost which is in you, which ye have of God; and ye are not your own? For ye are bought with a price, therefore glorify God in your body, and in your spirit. Which are God's" (1 Corinthians 6:19-20). In Matthew 17:20, it was a question of lack of faith for service, and a want of faith that could move mountains. Here in Luke 17, it is lack of faith in the exercise of God's love and grace to forgive the repentant offender and a want of faith to dispose of the deeply rooted spirit of self-importance.

Writing to the Christian believers in Ephesus, the apostle Paul said, "be ye kind one to another, tenderhearted, forgiving one another, even as God for Christ's sake hath forgiven you" (Ephesians 4:32). Paul was taking up the words of the Lord Jesus who on the Cross, cried, "Father, forgive them, for they know not what they do" (Luke 23:34). Again, to the church at Colosse, Paul wrote, "forbearing one another, and forgiving one another; if any man have a quarrel against any; even as Christ forgave you, so also do ye (Colossian 3:13).

> *O Lord, we ask of Thee, touch Thou, our hearts afresh,*
> *To live by simple faith, be ready to forgive;*
> *Depend on Thy great strength, lean wholly Lord on Thee,*
> *To walk in lowly guise, more like Thyself to be.*
>
> T H Ratcliffe

Sycomore

Ficus sycomorus

Hebrew: Shaqam. Greek: Sukomoraia = Fig tree.
1 Kings 10:27 + eight other references.

The sycomore tree and the figs it produces differ significantly from the ordinary fig (ficus carica) in both leaf and the way it fruits. The leaf of the sycomore tree is similar to the mulberry (morus nigra), which may account for the more commonly known name, mulberry fig. The ordinary fig develops from the axis of the leaf, whereas the sycomore fruit develops in small clusters direct from the stems and trunk of the tree. Furthermore, left to grow naturally, the sycomore fruit is inferior in both size and quality. To help make the fruit more palatable, the figs have to be dressed. Amos the prophet, speaking of himself said, "I was a herdsman, and a gatherer (dresser) of sycomore fruit" (Amos 7:14). The

dressing of sycomore fruits occurs when they are almost at full maturity, but still hard and unripe. The labour is intensive, requiring total commitment and patience. The dresser climbs the tree, and with a sharp knife or fine spike, makes a small incision or puncture in each fruit. Within a matter of days, the fruits mature and ripen ready for harvesting.

It would be fair to say that growers at the time of Amos, and down to the beginning of the 20th century, did not know what it was that brought about such dramatic results. Maybe, long before Amos's day, an observant grower had noted that damaged fruits developed and ripened much faster, and were sweeter than undamaged fruits. So, without knowing exactly why; an additional task in the husbandry of sycamore fruits was adopted and passed down to successive generations. In the early part of the 20th century, scientists found that Ethylene gas hastened the ripening of stored, green fruits such as oranges and bananas. Furthermore, it was also proved that the practice of incising and puncturing sycomore fruits released a small quantity of Ethylene gas that lingered around the trees. A centuries old mystery satisfactorily solved.

The first historic reference to the sycomore fruit is in 1 Chronicles 27:28 when David appointed supervisors (rulers) to control, store and disperse the produce of his kingdom. If we take careful account of the eight references to the sycomore tree in the Old Testament, it is clear that its fruit was the food of the ordinary people, but particularly the poor in Israel. The more nutritious ordinary figs were the fare of the rich and privileged. Furthermore, the poor used the wood of the sycomore tree for their building requirements, being inferior and therefore cheaper than most other woods. Accordingly, the sycomore tree is a figure of Israel as a whole. The fruits on the tree are typical of individuals who seek to minister pleasure for Jehovah, but are inhibited by the strictures of the law from which, by their own endeavours they cannot escape. Today, "Christ is the end of the law for righteousness to every one that believeth" (Romans 10:4). All the fruits must be touched (dressed) by the Spirit of God if they are to minister pleasure to God's heart. In the narrative, Amos is a type of the Spirit of God touching individuals to bring them to maturity and available for the pleasure of God (John 8:36).

When Solomon was at the height of his power and dominance in the world, he wanted the cedar trees to grow in equal abundance to the sycomore trees that flourished in the plains (2 Chronicles 1:15 & 9:27). The great yearning of Solomon to have the majestic form and growth of cedar trees in his kingdom reflecting his dominion and power, was at the time his heart had turned away from the Lord (1 Kings 11:4). Solomon had chosen to forget the many proverbs he had earlier written on the gravity of pride; one of which was, "when pride cometh, then cometh shame; but with the lowly is wisdom. The integrity of the upright shall guide them, but the perverseness of transgressors shall destroy them" (Proverbs 11:2-3). Another, "pride goeth before destruction, and a haughty spirit before a fall" (Proverbs 16:18). These, and many other scriptures referring to the sinfulness of pride, apply equally to us today as when penned by the Holy Spirit of God (see Romans 15:4).

The narrative about Amos is full of instruction. Amos lived at the time of Jeroboam 2nd a king of Israel who did evil in the sight of the Lord (2 Kings 14:24). Jeroboam 2nd followed the evil ways of his ancestor and name-sake Jeroboam the son of Nebat, who was the first king of Israel following the death of Solomon (1 Kings 12:20). Amos was a faithful child of Abraham, he feared Jehovah and lived his life dependent on the God of Abraham, Isaac and Jacob. Amos had determined he would not go along with the majority in Israel who had turned to idolatry; but was prepared to suffer hardship, threats, abuse and rejection as he followed in the way God led him (Amos 7:15).

Down through the centuries of this dispensation of God's grace, many faithful servants of the Lord have lived simple lives like Amos. They have not made the headlines of the national press, nor sought popularity among the saints, but quietly and unobtrusively pursued a path of faith (Colossians 1:10-11). The walk and testimony of such individuals has resulted in much enduring blessing for needy souls. Amos had not been educated in the school of prophets; neither was he the son of a prophet, but Jehovah used him as a worthy vessel to carry His message to king and people. The apostles, like Amos of old, did not have academic degrees, great wealth, social standing, or the honours of the world, but the Lord used them mightily. In the days following Pentecost, the people, "saw the boldness of Peter and John, and perceived that they were unlearned and ignorant men...and they took knowledge of them, that they had been with Jesus" (Acts 4:13). The divine secret of discipleship is simple faithfulness to God. May our gracious Lord help us to follow the example of Amos; to quietly, unobtrusively and faithfully walk in the current of God's will.

Unlike the conventional fig tree, the sycomore tree develops a thick head of horizontal branches, making it eminently suitable for climbing, positioning and concealing oneself, while able to observe passers-by. Zacchaeus did exactly that when he heard that the Lord Jesus was due to pass by on His way out of Jericho (Luke 19:4). Zacchaeus concealed himself in the sycomore tree (Israel as a nation), yet he was one of the sycomore fruits that would be touched (dressed) by the Spirit of God. Zaccheaus quickly learnt that the all-seeing eye of the Lord Jesus could pierce through the thickest camouflage. So, on being spotted, he made haste to descend the tree and welcome the Lord to his home. A work of God had been going on in Zaccheaus to the extent that the Lord found pleasure in sitting at his table. Through the movement of the Spirit of God in Zaccheaus, he confessed to all that had been offensive and injurious to others in his old life; whereupon, the One who is the judge of all men forgave him all. Zaccheaus's fourfold restitution to those he may have unjustly over-taxed, and the dispersal of half his goods to the poor, was surely a fruit that was pleasant to the palate of the Lord Jesus. Initially, Zaccheaus had sought the Lord Jesus simply to ascertain who He was (Luke 19:3); but in the house, he really found Him; and then the Lord Jesus saved him. Before the radical changes had occurred in the heart of Zaccheaus, he lived his life by securing and retaining everything that came within his grasp. When Salvation and new life was a reality to his soul, he was overwhelmed with a compassion that wanted to give liberally and irrevocably. May the Lord, by His gracious Spirit, daily touch our hearts to ensure our lives yield Him a continuous outflow of pleasure, delight and praise for the glory of God (Philippians 1:11).

How blest are we, who with Thee have a part.
In God's great plan to bring us where Thou art;
Lord, touch our hearts to render fervent praise,
Through Thee unto the Father, all our days.

T H Ratcliffe

Tamarisk

Tamarix aphylla

Hebrew: 'Eshel = A tamarisk tree; an isolated tree.
Genesis 21:33; 1 Samuel 22:6 & 31:13.

In Genesis 21:33, the Hebrew noun 'eshel has been translated 'grove' in the KJAV, which is unfortunate because the 40 other references to 'grove' or 'groves' in the Old Testament imply, without exception, the practice of idolatry. Furthermore, the Hebrew noun for grove and groves is 'asherah from which we get Ashtaroth, the Phoenician goddess of love, and Astarte, the Grecian equivalent. Our word 'grovel' comes from the same root and means, to bow down; so in the context of scripture, to grovel is a form of idolatry. When Joshua died, the people "forsook the Lord and served Baal and Ashtaroth" (Judges 2:13). Solomon also, when he turned away from the Lord, "went after Ashtoreth the goddess of the Zidonians" (1 Kings 11:5). The KJAV and Septuagint give 'tree' as the translation for 'Eshel in 1 Samuel 22 & 31. However, in the above references, the NIV and JND versions correctly translate 'Eshel, as 'tamarisk', a tree far removed from the thought of idolatry, but significant within the context of its occurrence.

Tamarix aphylla is a small tree that reaches a height of between 5 and 7 m. The tree develops a head of erect and weeping clustered branches, bearing extremely short sheath-like, pointed leaves. The small, pale pink flowers are borne on long, slender, thickly packed spikes. Tamarisks are essentially maritime shrubs, but frequently found growing inland wherever the soil is suitable. Tamarisk roots grow down to considerable depths through the sandy dunes, as much as 10 m or more, to reach less saline or fresh water. The plant has the ability, through osmosis – the transference of solutes of different strengths from one cell to another – to obtain the necessary nutrients for survival in barren and sometimes hostile conditions. When Abraham planted a tamarisk tree near to the well he had dug, he would have known from past experience that the tree would survive the arid desert conditions. Herein lies the significance of the tamarisk in Scripture.

According to Genesis 20, Abraham recovered from the deception he inflicted on Abimelech; and in the fear of the Lord he reclaimed from Abimelech the well he had earlier dug (Genesis 21:30). Having sworn an oath with Abimelech, Abraham called the area where he had dug the well, Beersheba. The noun 'Beer' means 'the well' and the noun 'sheba' means 7, a perfect oath. Abraham ratified the oath with Abimelech in the gift of seven ewe lambs. Such a gift was a figure of the perfect sacrifice of God's Lamb, the Lord Jesus Christ that took away the sin of the world (John 1:29). The area of Beersheba was so important to Abraham that he planted a tamarisk tree as a memorial and affirmation of the oath made between him and a Gentile. The gracious act of Abraham was further evidence of his unshakeable faith in the covenant God made with him when He called him out of the land of the Chaldees (Genesis 12:1-3).

The desert place of Beersheba is a type of the world. The well sets forth the water of life, available in this barren world to all who will repent of their sins before God, and put their faith and trust in the Lord Jesus Christ. The tamarisk tree speaks of the testimony on earth residing in all who have drunk of the Water of Life. The Lord Jesus said: "if any man thirst, let him come unto me and drink. He that believeth on me, as the scripture hath said, out of his belly shall flow rivers of living water" (John 7:37-38). A further feature of the tamarisk tree is that it is not attractive in respect of beauty, and neither has it any material use for man. However, its value lies in being the only landmark to point souls to where they will find the water of life. So it should be with Christian believers today. Our testimony of faith in the Lord Jesus Christ should be bold, visible and plain to draw souls, not to ourselves, but to the Saviour of the world – the well and source of life.

In 1 Samuel 22:6, Saul is seen sitting on a hill in Gebeah, under a tamarisk tree, a tree void of the aura of kingship and dignity. If he had not lost the throne through disobedience, he might well have been under a cedar tree to reflect the kingly government over which he should have exercised guardian care and control. He is sitting on a hill, instead of an elevated kingly throne. He has in his hand a spear, a token of his vain attempt to defend and save what he had already lost. Had he not lost the kingdom, he would have been holding the kingly sceptre, a symbol of imperial authority. Finally, a band of brigands surrounded him, rather than a group of royal and loyal courtiers. On two occasions, David had opportunity to take Saul's life; first at En-gedi (1 Samuel 24:1-20) and again at Ziph in the Negeb desert (1 Samuel 26:12). But David would not lift up his hand against the Lord's anointed. It was following the incident at En-gedi, that Saul acknowledged for the first time that David would be king (1 Samuel 24:20); yet, he inexorably pursued David with murderous intent in order to save his discredited throne for himself. Let us challenge our hearts each day regarding our spiritual state.

Are we abiding under cover of the over-spreading care of the Lord Jesus? Do our lives reflect the truth that God sees us seated in Christ in the heavenlies? Are we holding the Word of God in our hearts as sacred and inviolate so that our lives reflect its divine authority? Are we walking uprightly with all that call on the Name of the Lord out of a pure heart? The apostle Paul exhorted Timothy to: "follow righteousness, faith, charity, peace, with them that call on the Lord out of a pure heart" (2 Timothy 2:22).

The last reference to the tamarisk tree is in 1 Samuel 31:13. It was a sad end for Saul who, having already committed suicide morally, died by his own hand physically, after the Philistines had seriously wounded him. Before his final battle with the Philistines, Saul reached the lowest point morally in his life when he resorted to necromancy with the witch of En-dor (1 Samuel 28:7-19). Saul was prostrate with grief on hearing the words of Samuel, and for a time refused to eat, but persuaded by those around him, he did eat and revived in strength. Saul, with the few servants he had with him, left En-dor by night to enter a battle that would prove to be darker than his darkest night and bring his inglorious life to an ignominious end. Even in death, indignity fell upon the body of Saul when, together with his sons, they burnt his body at Jabesh, a practice of the heathen, idolatrous nations. However, the inhabitants of Jabesh-gilead gathered up the bones of Saul and his sons and buried them under a tamarisk tree. A fitting end one might say, to a person whose life had been anything but regal, noble and glorious. Eventually, David had the bones of Saul and Jonathan reburied in Zelah, in the sepulchre of Kish, Saul's father (2 Samuel 21:14). When the Lord chose Saul to be king in Israel, he was a choice young man, head and shoulders taller than any in Israel (1 Samuel 9:2). The Lord would have had Saul be like the tamarisk Abraham planted by the well in Beersheba; a landmark, standing out and indicating the way the people should follow for the water of life. Had Saul so led the people, the Lord would have morally decked him with the glory and honour befitting a king.

Today, God has clothed all Christian believers with the moral glories associated with His beloved Son (John 17:22). Accordingly, a tremendous responsibility rests upon us to, "show forth the praises (moral glories) of Him who hath called you (us) out of darkness into His marvellous light" (1 Peter 2:9).

Show me the way Lord, not to fortune and fame;
Not how to win honours or praise for my name;
But show me the way Lord, how to spread the great story,
That Thine is the kingdom, the power and the glory.

Anon

Tares - Darnel

Lolium temulentum

Greek: Zizanion = A false grain, darnel.
Matthew 13:25, 26, 27, 29, 30, 36, 38 & 40.

The majority of biblical Greek scholars believe the translation 'tares' for the Greek noun zizanion in the KJAV is incorrect. The plural noun 'tares' relates to the genus vicia of the natural order leguminosae, whereas lolium is of the order, gramineae. Darnel is the more reliable translation for the Greek noun zizanion. The plant grows to a height of approximately 70 cm, is an annual and belongs to the grass family, the same genus

as perennial ryegrass 'lolium perenne' which is a valuable herbage grass for cattle. However, lolium temulentum is not a useful grass; it is in fact a poisonous weed with seeds that contain an alkaloid harmful to man and beast, but not to fowl. Among the many adverse effects if ingested, is dizziness and sleepiness. In the early stages of growth, the darnel plant is little different to the wheat, but not to the experienced eye. The seedling strap leaves of darnel are narrower than wheat; but not sufficiently different to safely rogue out. It is not until the ear begins to break out of the sheaf that the difference between wheat and darnel is apparent. The four-row ear of the biblical wheat is bearded, i.e. has long awns; whereas the two-row ear of darnel is a series of flattish spikelets with very short awns.

Some have thought that darnel is a form of degenerative wheat; believing that wheat plants undergo a transition to darnel, particularly during wet seasons. Botanically, nothing could be further from the truth. By the natural laws of plant physiology, it is not possible for a plant of a particular genus, to switch to another genus under the influence of environmental conditions. True, darnel flourishes in exceptionally wet seasons, while wheat tends to suffer and die when the ground remains abnormally wet for long spells throughout the growing season. Happily, very few Middle Eastern farmers hold the strange belief of 'degenerative transition'; but to accept its possibility is to despise the significance of the Lord's parable.

In the parable of the darnel (Matthew 13:24-30 & 37-43), the sower of the good seed is the Lord Jesus Christ as Son of Man. The field is not the Church, but the world that belongs to the sower. The good seed are the children of the kingdom. The sleeping men represent those who were the guardians of the Truth of God's Word, but had let their vigilance slip. The enemy that came by night is the Devil, the Serpent who had no right to be in the field, just as he had no right to enter the Garden of Eden and spoil the good work of God's hand. The darnel are the children of the wicked one; they are apostates mingling with and imitating what is pure and true, sapping spiritual nutrients that rightly and exclusively belong to the children of the kingdom. The statement, 'end of the world' in verse 39 relates to the end of this dispensation of God's grace; whereas the clause, 'end of this world' in verse 40 refers to the final judgment spoken of in verse 42. The reapers are the angels of God that fly at His bidding to do His will. The fire is Gehenna, the lake of fire spoken of elsewhere as Hell, reserved for the Devil and his angels (Matthew 25:41).

It was said prophetically of the Lord Jesus, that His were the beautiful feet upon the mountain; the feet that brought good tidings, that published peace and salvation (Isaiah 52:7). Pentecost saw the establishment of the true Church growing from what the Lord had sown, and continuing to grow to the glory of God during the Smyrnean (suffering) period of the Church, A.D. 54 to A.D. 313. The young Church grew and survived the cruel reigns of 10 tyrannical emperors, from Nero to Diocletian. Augustus Constantine's reign began in A.D. 312, and in A.D. 313 he annulled the edict of his predecessor Diocletian who demanded that all Christian believers should be persecuted, even unto death. Constantine's act brought to an end the Smyrnean period in the history of the Church, and introduced the Pergamos era, a time when the unregenerate Augustus Constantine aligned himself with the Church and politicised the Christian profession. The spread of Christendom increased without restraint. It was then that the poisonous influence of darnel began to take hold.

From the beginning of the Pergamos era, the Church fell into a deep, spiritual sleep; for it ceased to live in the constant expectation of the Lord's imminent return for His own. Rather, it settled down to accommodate anything that would ensure a peaceful life on earth. Thus, for the next twelve hundred years the darnel grew and flourished alongside the wheat. While the Church was sleeping, the enemy entered the property that belonged to the Lord Jesus and sowed the scriptural darnel in the world. The Devil's work was to mingle his counterfeit with the real and so make it difficult to distinguish between the two. Jude wrote about some apostates that had even crept in unawares (Jude 1:4). Satan's second objective in sowing darnel in the field (world) was to adulterate the true crop, and rob the owner of its divine quality as born of God; but as always, he failed. The Lord Jesus had already secured for Himself those whom the Father had given to Him, and none of them can be lost (John 10:27-30).

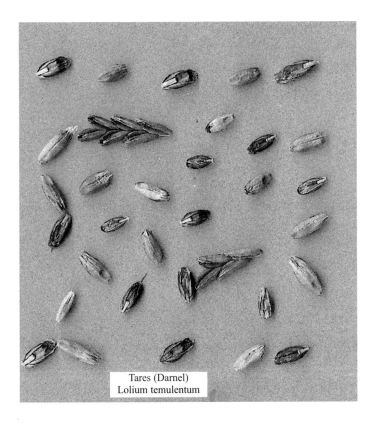

Tares (Darnel)
Lolium temulentum

It was nearly five centuries ago that the Lord's servants (Church) woke up to find darnel growing up alongside the wheat, apostates living cheek by jowl with Christian believers. There was great enthusiasm at the time to rid the testimony of apostasy. No, said the Lord, purging at this time could damage perfectly good wheat; besides, you might remove true plants and leave evil darnel behind. Better to let them grow up together to harvest, at which time the darnel will be sorted from the wheat, bundled and cast into the fire; while the wheat will be gathered into the divine repository. In a broader sense, and as the Greek noun zizanion implies, darnel represents everything in Christendom that is false. However, the acceptance of this divine fact in no way diminishes the responsibility of God's people to withdraw from any who are proved to be apostate according to God's Word (2 Corinthians 6:15-17). Like the darnel, apostates are poisonous; to accommodate and make use of them is to court disaster; for very soon their soporific influences will numb your spiritual senses and reduce you to spiritual unconsciousness. The following pertinent words are what the apostle Paul wrote to the Christian believers at Thessalonica and Rome. "Therefore, let us not sleep, as do others; but let us watch and be sober" (1 Thessalonians 5:6). "It is high time to wake out of sleep, for now is our salvation nearer that when we believed" (Romans 13:11).

It is very important to understand that the term 'apostate' should never, ever be applied to a soul that has repented of their sins before God and put their faith and trust in the Lord Jesus Christ. The words of the Lord Jesus are a warning to those who misjudge and speak cruelly about their brethren. "Whosoever shall say to his brother, Raca, shall be in danger of the council, but whosoever shall say, thou fool, shall be in danger of hell fire" (Matthew 5:22). In this text, Raca means to speak of a brother or sister with contempt and to treat them as worthless. The 'council' refers to the highest court in the land, i.e. the Sanhedrin; but the authority of the Word of God will judge the Christian believer who is guilty of such language. The expression 'fool' does not mean 'senseless one' as in Luke 24:25; but to accuse one of being heedless and stupid as a blockhead. Such a disposition toward our brethren reveals a sad, ungodly spirit, a character that is likened to wood, hay and stubble that will be discarded and burnt up at the judgment seat of Christ (Romans 14:10-12).

In the parable, the harvest of the darnel takes place some time after the end of this day of God's grace. Very soon, "the Lord Himself shall descend from heaven with a shout, with the voice of the archangel, and the trump of God. The dead in Christ shall rise first, then we which are alive and remain, will be caught up together with them in the clouds, to meet the Lord in the air. So shall we ever be with the Lord" (1 Thessalonians 4:16-17). All that will remain of Christendom on earth will be the false church comprised of apostates 'darnel', to await God's Day of Judgment. God has, "appointed a day, in the which he will judge the world in righteousness by that man whom he hath ordained" (Acts 17:31). Meanwhile, let us daily look to the Lord for His help to remain true to our heavenly calling in Christ Jesus our Lord (Hebrews 3:1); and that, "speaking the truth in love, may grow up into Him in all things which is the head, even Christ" (Ephesians 4:15).

> *This vast world is God's own field; from its furrows, made to yield;*
> *Wheat and tares together grown, unto joy and sorrow, sown.*
> *First the blade, and then the ear; next, the true corn shall appear;*
> *Lord of harvest, grant that we, to Thy praise and glory, be.*
>
> H Alford (arr.)

Thyine

Tetraclinis articulata, syn. Thuja articulatus

Hebrew: Thuinos = Blowing, in the sense of a drifting cloud of sweet, fragrant air.
Revelation 18:12.

Tetraclinis is a tender evergreen tree belonging to the cypress family of conifers, growing to a height of between 10 and 15 m. The tree can be found flourishing happily throughout the North African continent and as far east as India and China. The yellow-brown thyine timber with its fine, beautifully marked grain and citrus-like fragrance is still highly prized by cabinet-makers. Growers tap the trunks of mature trees to obtain the valuable aromatic resin, which they trade commercially as a high-grade varnish called sanderac.

The prophetic events detailed in Revelation 18, will take place during the week known as, "the time of Jacob's trouble" (Jeremiah 30:7), or Daniel's 70th week. Daniel, who was greatly beloved of the Lord, had a vision of events that would span 70 weeks of years, i.e. 490 years (Daniel 9:23-24). Sixty-nine weeks of Daniel's vision were fulfilled up to the time the Messiah, the Lord Jesus Christ was cut off – crucified (Daniel 9:26). The Old Testament does not record the current period of God's grace to this sin-stricken world. The fulfilment of Old Testament prophecies will not therefore resume until the Church, together with the Holy Spirit of God, is taken out of this world. However, "the mystery of iniquity doth already work: only he (Holy Spirit) who now letteth will let, until he be taken out of the way" (2 Thessalonians 2:7). The Lord Jesus is presently building His Church comprised of all who repent before

God of their sins, and put their faith and trust in the Lord Jesus Christ. The Lord Jesus said to Peter, that the gates of Hades will not prevail against His Church (Matthew 16:18). Before the commencement of Daniel's seventieth week, which is divided into two periods of 3.5 years (Daniel 9:27), the Church will actually be in the heavenly places in Christ, having been caught away from this earth (1 Thessalonians 4:17).

Why, we may ask, is the thyine wood only mentioned in Revelation 18:12? Bearing in mind that the scriptural reference to the wood relates to a time in the future, the most likely explanation for its occurrence lies in its suitability for fashioning idols of every kind. Planed, fashioned and polished thyine wood, whilst beautiful to the natural eye, reflects the inner spiritual deadness of man as he walks here on earth, independent of God. The beauty of an icon, if any beauty exists, is only surface deep, less than 1000th of a millimetre thick. The substance of the icon is totally inert, much like the idol worshippers who will crave the merchandise of the merchants in that coming day. The twenty-eight articles (Revelation 18:12 and 13) comprising the merchants' trade are inseparably linked to idolatry. Babylon is the figure of an apostate system that will trade in and control every commodity of life, from gold as the most valued currency of the world, to slaves and the souls of men. Just as the Bank of England controls the flow of money in the British economy, so Babylon for a while will control every area of the world's economic system.

The merchants for their part will be anxious to trade their thyine wood, together with other merchandise, to meet the demand of man for something tangible, with physical beauty to captivate their lustful and idolatrous eye. The merchants and their wares will represent the powers that control the financial, manufacturing and economic forces in the world. In the coming day of which we speak, the world's political, fiscal and industrial framework will break down, with the pillars of human society collapsing in total disarray. The kings of the earth who are referred to in verse 9 of our chapter, represent the leaders in Christendom (the Church will no longer be on earth). Such leaders, who unashamedly traded with apostate Babylon, will fear as they stand afar off and witness the catastrophic fall of the evil system by which they became materially rich. Nations that become dependent on apostate Babylon will also mourn her downfall and stand afar off for fear of being sucked into the abyss with her. Notwithstanding the fall of Babylon, which is not her final judgment, idol worship will overwhelm the world.

A careful study of Revelation 18:12-13 shows seven categories of merchandise embracing every lustful aspect of life that will be disastrously affected following the fall of Babylon (Revelation 18:2). In other words, there will be a complete breakdown of the world economy, for God is going to see to it that every material thing man idolises and worships will come under His judgments.

Let us beware, lest we unwittingly become idol worshippers of material things that show off our vanity and pride to our own condemnation. The apostle John at the end of his first epistle speaks so lovingly to the Christian believers, "children, keep yourselves from idols" (1 John 5:21).

> *Be Thou the object bright and fair, to fill and satisfy the heart;*
> *My hope to meet Thee in the air, and nevermore from Thee to part;*
> *That I may undistracted be, to follow, serve, and wait for Thee.*
>
> G W Frazer

Vine

Vitis vinifera

Hebrew: Gephen. Greek: Ampelos = coiling about a support. To bend and twine.
Genesis 40:9 + 67 other references.
Hebrew: Zemorah = vine branch, slip or cutting. Numbers 13:23; Ezekiel 15:2 &
Nahum 2:2.
Hebrew: Yayin = Fruit of the vine, wine. Genesis 9:21 + 131 other references.
Hebrew: Soreq = Choice vine producing red grapes. Genesis 49:11; Isaiah 5:2 &
Jeremiah 2:21.
Greek: Oinos = Wine, the fruit of the vine. Matthew 9:17 + eighteen other references.

The first mention in scripture of the vine and a vineyard, is in Genesis 9:20 & 21. Following the mighty flood, as detailed in Genesis 7, Noah's ark rested on the mountains of Ararat, a region that lies south west of the Caspian Sea (Genesis 8:4). Eminent botanists believe the vine plant had its origin on the mountain slopes of Ararat facing the Caspian Sea, from where it has spread throughout the continents of the world. It is worthy of note, that once Noah had left the ark to live in a new world, the vine is the first plant highlighted in scripture. It is the vine and its fruit that alone brings cheer to the heart of God and man (Judges 9:13). In the Psalm that embraces the

wonderful works of creation; the sweet Psalmist said, "wine that maketh glad (to rejoice) the heart of man" (Psalm 104:15). God desired that man should rejoice in His creation (1 Chronicles 16:33-36), and in Noah there was a new beginning. Sadly, the very product that should have brought cheer to the heart of man, brought shame upon him through misuse (Genesis 9:21).

The vast majority of trees and shrubs throughout the world have more than one pleasing and useful feature; such as decorative form, colourful flowers, fruits, foliar tints and timber for construction work or for burning to keep oneself warm. The vine on the other hand has no desirable symmetry in its form of growth; its flowers are green and insignificant; the foliage has no seasonal beauty and its timber is of no commercial value. Indeed, the wood burns so quickly when fired, that it provides very little warmth. This analysis of the vine confirms that when God chose Israel as His choice vine, He was not looking to the nation to do or be anything spectacular. God simply desired that the people should be faithful to His word, and thereby minister joy to His heart. The singular and most valued attribute of the vine is its fruit.

Why did God choose the vine and its fruit to be a picture of Israel? The answer is; He yearned for the nation on which He had set His love (Deuteronomy 7:8), to be like the vine and cling only to Him for all its needs; including wisdom, guidance, strength and nourishment. God wanted to stand as the one and only great pillar of support and strength for His choice vine. God knew the vine would never be able to support itself and be fruitful if left in Egypt. So, in due course He brought His vine up out of Egypt, He planted it, and it took deep root so that it filled the land (Ps. 80:8-9). God planted His vine in His garden with a specific objective in view. He wanted a people on earth who would love, follow and worship Him, thereby ministering joy to His heart. God looked to the vine He had planted, to yield good fruit and sweet wine.

Alas! Through disobedience and idolatry, Israel soon became, "an empty vine, he bringeth forth fruit unto himself" (Hosea 10:1). The nation departed from the divine support God had provided in Himself, and chose to climb up among the trees of the forest, i.e. the Gentile nations of the world, adhering to them for support, and worshipping their gods. Israel turned aside from its high calling, and ministered only sour grapes and undrinkable wine to the God of their salvation. The nation, "brought forth wild grapes" (Isaiah 5:2-4). The fruit of the once favoured vine was only sour grapes so that, "the children's teeth are set on edge" (Jeremiah 31:29).

Today, in the figure of the vine, Christian believers are branches in the 'true vine', the Lord Jesus Christ. The Husbandman, who cares for the vine, yearns for the branches to not only adhere, but also depend wholly upon Him for support (Philippians 4:19). Furthermore, that the branches should abide exclusively in Christ and thereby derive their spiritual nourishment and strength from the root and stem of the vine which is Christ. Only then will we bear the kind of fruit that brings joy to the heart of God.

Jacob's experience at Peniel has a valuable lesson for us today. Jacob clung to his God, saying, "I will not let Thee go, except Thou bless me" (Genesis 32:26). God touched the hollow of Jacob's thigh, putting it out of joint. Now disabled and dependent upon another, Jacob clung on more resolutely until he had received a blessing. Clinging to His God was one thing, leaning on Him for support as a dependent man, was another. That was the lesson Jacob learnt on that remarkable occasion when he prevailed by clinging to and leaning on his God (Genesis 32:28); it is the lesson for us today.

The Lord Jesus said, "I am the true vine" (John 15:1). The allegory in John's Gospel, introduces an entirely new concept when set against the teaching in the Old Testament where Israel the nation, typified the vine. When God chose Israel to be His choice vine; He purposed to nourish them with the fruits of the land, the land that flowed with milk and honey. The nation as a whole was blessed, rather than the individual. God's direct dealing in judgment was with the nation in general; the priest dealt with individuals. It was from the nation that God looked for the sweet fruit of the noble vine, and it was the overall testimony of the nation that influenced God's dealings with them. Furthermore, Israel was a corporate body with collective responsibility before God. Take for example the narrative of Achan's sin as recorded in Joshua 7. One man secretly and grievously sinned, but God allowed the whole nation to suffer at the hand of the men of Ai. The Lord said to Joshua, "Israel hath sinned, and they have also transgressed my covenant which I commanded them" (Joshua 7:11). There was also the occasion when David unwisely numbered the people of Israel (2 Samuel 24). The act of numbering the people was to recognise the nation as belonging to the Lord; a fact confirmed by the simultaneous taking up of the 'redemption money' (Exodus 30:11-16). David's action was one of bravado; not taking up the redemption money was a manoeuvre tantamount to claiming the people as his, to do with them as he wished. God's judgment for David's folly, fell on the people (2 Samuel 24:15-17).

Now in the teaching of the "true vine" in John 15, it is the individual Christian believer who is viewed as a branch in the vine, responsible to ensure their life produces fruit for the Father's delight. The Husbandman, who is the Father, deals with each branch separately (John 15:2). It is important to understand that the first eight verses of John 15 do not speak of (a) God's sovereign grace to the sinner, (b) salvation, (c) the Christian believer's security in Christ, nor (d) the testimony of the Church on earth. However, the verses do highlight a most important New Testament truth, that the Lord Jesus is the 'the true vine' and the only source of life whereby Christian believers are able to grow and bear fruit for God. The fruit refers more particularly to that in our lives which naturally flows out from our walking in communion with the Lord day by day.

When we first surrendered our souls to God in repentance, and put our faith and trust in the Lord Jesus Christ; that was fruit for God. As we progress in our Christian experience, the Husbandman prunes away the barren appendages in our lives that hinder fruit production, that we may bear 'more fruit'. The Lord Jesus said, "herein is my Father glorified, that ye bear much fruit; so shall ye be my disciples" (John 15:8), that remains the enduring test of discipleship. During the growing season of a vine, the husbandman will prune back the branches to ensure that all the goodness from the root goes into the production of fruit. So with us, our Father will constantly prune out those developments in our lives that hamper the production of fruit for God. At the end of the growing season, the branches in the vine that have borne fruit are pruned back severely to one or two buds from the stem to ensure the production of a new crop the following season. There will be many such pruning experiences during each year in the fruitful life of a Christian believer. The branch that has borne fruit must be lost sight of through pruning, while the fruit remains for the glory of God. "My son, despise not thou the chastening hand of the Lord, nor faint when thou art rebuked of Him. For whom the Lord loveth, He chasteneth" (Hebrews 12:5-6). Chastening, "yieldeth the peaceable fruits of righteousness unto them which are exercised thereby" (Hebrews 12:11).

In John 15:6, we have the case an individual who is 'not in the vine', in other words, 'not in Christ' and therefore "none of His" (Romans 8:9). The Lord would remind us of the end of all in Christendom not born of God. Like Judas Iscariot, many today make pretence of following the Lord Jesus Christ; they follow in name only. In a coming day, the Lord will say to all pretenders, "I never knew you, depart from Me" (Matthew 7:21-23). Being cast forth into the fire, will be the lot of those who are void of that life which is, "hid with Christ in God" (Colossians 3:3). For all who are 'in Christ', there is absolutely no risk of forever being lost (John 10:28-29). However, although we are eternally in Christ, if we do not bear fruit for God, we may be removed as a fruitless branch from this sphere of service and testimony. This accords with the Lord's own words, "every branch in me that beareth not fruit, he (the Husbandman) taketh away" (John 15:2). The governmental dealings of God with the saints at Corinth (1 Corinthians 11:30); confirms the action the Husbandman will take against the branch or branches in the vine not bearing fruit. The Lord has chosen us that we should bring forth fruit for the glory of God and that our fruit should remain (John 15:16). May we daily seek the Lord's help to, "walk worthy of the Lord unto all pleasing, being fruitful in every good work, and increasing in the knowledge of God" (Colossians 1:10).

Thou art the Vine, the Only and the True;
The branches, we, Thy Father's Will to do;
Much fruit to bear, to last and to remain;
To render praise and glory to His Name.

T H Ratcliffe

Willow

Salix acmophylla / Salix alba

Hebrew: 'Arab = Water willow, Osier, Osier used as wattles.
Leviticus 23:40 + Five other references.

The willow belongs to the family salicaceae comprised of two genera, salix and populus. Around 400 species make up the salix genus, but only a few are native to Palestine. Although the common Weeping willow, known as salix babylonica is a cultivated tree in Palestine today, it is generally believed that the tree was imported from China several centuries ago. Most botanists have concluded that the biblical willow is either salix acmophylla or salix alba, or that even both species may have been

referred to at different times. Willows are deciduous trees, also dioecious, that is, the male and female flowers are borne on separate trees; the flowers are very simple, having neither sepals nor petals. Unlike the catkins on the poplar that hang down against the growth of the branch, the catkins on a willow are erect – a useful identity tip. The habitat of willows is the moist plains of the Jordan valley and by the banks of rivers. The fast-growing, flexible growths of the willows, called withies, are ideal for making baskets and mats; but the children of Israel were also required to use them for something far more important.

The first mention of willows relates to the celebration of the feast of tabernacles, the last of the seven set annual feasts Israel was to keep from the first year they were in the Promised Land. On the fifteenth day of the seventh month of the Jewish year (September in the current Gregorian calendar), the children of Israel were to celebrate the feast. The ordinance would remind them of the forty years they lived in booths while journeying through the wilderness. On the fifteenth day of the seventh month they were to take boughs of trees that spoke of the richness, beauty, strength, security and heavenly character of the land into which God had brought them. With the boughs, they were to make booths in which they would live for seven days. The willow withies were used to bind the other branches together to make the booths both strong and secure. In this instance, the willow spoke of security through the unifying power of the Holy Spirit, holding everything together. Security was important because they were to live exclusively in the booths for a full seven days, typically, a complete period in time. Throughout the celebration period, all that was around them in the booths would have reminded them of the wealth of God's provision, and His faithfulness, love and grace toward them throughout their journeys. Today, Christian believers are secure in the arms of the Lord Jesus and fused together by the power of the Holy Spirit of God (John 10:28-29 & 1 Corinthians 12:13).

Where and when could we have a comparable experience to the celebration of the feast of tabernacles during our path of testimony here on earth? The answer is, each day of every week. We begin our week on the Lord's day when our thoughts are centred on the Lord Jesus in the Breaking of Bread, which we call, 'the supper'. In the glory of His presence, our worship reflects our apprehension of the greatness of His Person and Work to bring us to God. Our occupation, as we call Him to mind in the celebration of the supper, is making much of Him and of His worth to the Father. For the remainder of the week, our life testifies to the enjoyment that we have through occupation with those divine realities of which we already are partakers. The apostle Paul exhorted those of the Church at Colosse to, "give thanks unto the Father, which hath made us meet to be partakers of the inheritance of the saints in light" (Colossians 1:12). This is our day by day, and week by week service to God.

God spoke to Job about behemoth (hippopotamus) moving among the reeds of the fens, and sheltering under the shade of the trees (Job 40:21-22). Behemoth could effectively conceal himself among the reeds that grew up from the water in which he lay, but now we find him taking advantage also of the dense growth of the willows enveloping him. In this instance, the willow is a figure of the love, grace and faithfulness of God that currently surrounds mankind. Like the hippopotamus, most people are quite indifferent to the ways of God in grace toward them; no less Job, who concealed his inner pride by hiding within a dense aura of his own self-righteousness. Job had not yet heeded God's own words, "can any hide himself in secret places that I shall not see him? saith the LORD. Do not I fill heaven and earth? saith the LORD" (Jeremiah 23:24). In due course, Job surrendered his soul to God, and confessed that he had hidden counsel without knowledge, uttered things he did not understand, and things that were beyond his human comprehension (Job 42:3). Once Job opened his ear to God instead of listening to himself, and fixed his eye of faith on God rather than on himself, he was ready to say, "wherefore, I abhor myself, and repent in dust and ashes" (Job 42:6). What a mighty lesson for our souls!

Psalm 137 is a post-captivity Psalm, written by a faithful Jew who was led by the Holy Spirit of God to reminisce on his experiences as a captive in Babylon. Some authorities believe the willows referred to in verse 2 were in fact Babylonian poplar trees 'populus euphratica', a very common tree on the banks of the Euphrates river. However, what is important is the message God has for us from the passage. The willow tree is significant in the narrative because it again reminds us of God's love, grace and faithfulness to a remnant in captivity, in a strange land and with no temple in which to worship God. The remnant wept as they remembered Zion, and could not sing its triumphant songs while captive in Babylon. They hung their harps in the middle of the willow trees, out of sight to signify their belief in the words of David, "praise waiteth

for thee, O God, in Zion" (Psalm 65:1). How could the faithful Jew and those with him rejoice in song when they were in a foreign land? They determined they would not use their instruments to amuse their captors; for the songs of Zion that exalt Jehovah, belong to Zion and not to the heathen world. They knew a time would come when again they would be free to play their harps and sing the songs of Zion, in Zion (Nehemiah 12:27). Christian believers too, while strangers and pilgrims here on earth, have a song of triumph in their hearts, which they sing unto the Lord in worship and praise, but not unto the world. While our path of testimony in this world should be a witness of God's love, grace and faithfulness to us; our song of rejoicing is heard in the sanctuary. "Serve the Lord with gladness, come before His presence with singing. Enter into His gates with thanksgiving, and into His courts with praise" (Psalm 100:2 & 4). The apostle

Paul's words to the Church at Ephesus were as follows. "Sing and make melody in your heart to the Lord; Giving thanks always for all things unto God and the Father in the name of our Lord Jesus Christ" (Ephesians 5:19-20). Just as the faithful Jew knew he was not a part of Babylon, we too should live our lives in the knowledge that we are not part of this world, (John 17:14-16).

The mention of the willow in Isaiah 44:4 is by way of a simile. The chapter opens with the confirmation of the covenant relations Jehovah established with Jacob, His servant Israel whom He had chosen, and later referred to as Jesurun, the upright one. Verses 3 & 4 speak of the day when Israel as a nation will be restored according to the new covenant blessings secured through the redemptive work of Christ on Calvary's Cross. Following the Great Tribulation, during which Israel is reduced to a very small remnant; the nation will recover in number of souls at a miraculous rate, thereby fulfilling God's promise to Abraham as given in Genesis 22:17. The Lord said that the proliferation of newborn souls will be such that, "they shall spring up as among the grass, as willows by the water courses" (Isaiah 44:4). The grass is a type of the nations as we saw in the last paragraph of our dissertation on the Lily/Anemone. The 'springing up like willows' on the other hand, tells us about the instantaneous and overwhelming impact of God's love, grace and faithfulness on the people He had before claimed for a possession (Deuteronomy 7:6). The seed of the willow will germinate within 48 hours of dispersal from the tree, but become non-viable within 24 hours if it does not fall on suitable ground; an appropriate simile, signifying the speed of change that will occur when the Lord Jesus Christ sets up His millennial kingdom.

The reference to the willow tree in Ezekiel 17:5 is another simile, but this time within an allegory on how Jehovah had determined to deal with His rebellious people. The great eagle of Ezekiel 17:3, was Nebuchadnezzar, while the cedar in Lebanon was Jehoiakim who was king of Judah at the time of the captivity. The seed (vine) taken from the Land (Palestine) and planted in a fruitful field (Babylon) by great waters (river Euphrates) was Zedekiah (see Jeremiah 52). Zedekiah represented a plant cutting of the original vine, Israel, which God had brought up out of Egypt (Psalm 80:8) and planted in His land. The cutting rooted quickly by the waters of Babylon and flourished, for God would not allow His vine to die, but it did not fruit. There would be no fruit for God from the vine for another 600 years, i.e. until the advent of Christ, the Messiah. The prophet used the simile of the willow cutting, because it was probably known in biblical days that cuttings of willow shoots and stems root quicker than any tree or shrub. Everything about the willow tells us that the love, grace and faithfulness of God is immediately available to all who will surrender their lives to God through the Lord Jesus Christ.

Thy love, Thy grace, Thy faithfulness, such attributes are all divine;
They touch our hearts afresh each day, confirm that we are wholly Thine.

T H Ratcliffe

Wormwood

Artemisia herba-alba / absinthium

Hebrew: La'anah. Greek: Apsinthos = Juice that is bitter and undrinkable.
Deuteronomy 29:18 + eight other references.

Artemisia herba-alba from which we obtain the juice wormwood, belongs to a large genus of plants including shrubs, sub-shrubs, herbaceous perennials and annuals, and is a member of the daisy family, compositae. Two species of Wormwood are illustrated. The first is of a group of plants growing in Jerusalem Botanic Gardens in 2000, and labelled, Artemisia absinthium. The second illustration is from the Royal Horticultural Gardens, Wisley, England, July 2001, and labelled Artemisia herba-alba, absinthium. The biblical wormwood is a desert sub-shrub that grows to a height no more than 50 cm, with deeply cut, grey, hairy, aromatic leaves, the juice of which is extremely bitter. Notwithstanding the bitterness of the plant, goats freely eat it, and the Bedouin infuse the leaves for use as tea. According to some herbalists, wormwood juice is beneficial if used as an antispasmodic, an antiseptic or as a tonic. However, the wormwood referred to in the scriptures has always to do with what is grievously bitter, poisonous, accursed, painful and deathly. The KJAV has, for reasons difficult to tell, translated la'anah in Amos 6:12 as hemlock, whereas the context supports wormwood as the more reliable translation.

Wormwood ex Jerusalem
University Botanic Gardens

The words of Moses in Deuteronomy 29 have their counterpart for the Christian believer today in Romans 12:1-2. If Israel was to enter and enjoy their promised rest – the land of Canaan – there had to be on their part, a total commitment to do the will of God. Moses made clear that to do anything less than all the words of the covenant would result in loss of blessing in the land. Sadly, the record of Israel's history confirms that the nation was not fully committed to doing the will of God. They did not take full possession of the land by driving out the heathen (Numbers 33:52-53), rather, they accommodated their idolatrous practices with consequent loss of blessing. If Christian believers today are to enjoy all the blessings of the inheritance in which we already have a part (Ephesians 1:13-14), nothing short of full surrender to the will of God is imperative.

There were individuals in the camp of Israel determined to do anything, rather than take God's covenant into their hearts and be true to His will, such were designated 'roots that bear gall and wormwood'. The root is the primary source of all water and nourishment necessary for a plant's survival and growth. The plant takes character from what it draws up from the root, a fact that merits very serious thought concerning the simile employed by Moses. The apostates in Israel, filled with gall and wormwood, were the wilful carriers of a highly infectious and deadly malady that could rapidly spread throughout the camp of Israel. Tragically, that is exactly what happened, not once, but on many occasions with disastrous consequences. However, God determined that those responsible for leading His people into idolatry would have their names blotted out from under heaven. Such would have no inheritance either material or spiritual, but their souls would await the final and terrible Day of Judgment. While Christian believers that are baptised with the Holy Spirit of God can never be designated apostates, the writer of the Hebrew epistle warns us about the risk of bearing the root of bitterness (Hebrew 12:15). If we get away from the grace of God in our spiritual lives, we afford opportunity for Satan to sow the seed of bitterness in our hearts. As in the simile of Deuteronomy 29:18, such bitterness will have a disturbing and divisive influence on other Christian believers, a matter we should take most seriously to heart.

Solomon was well acquainted with the subtle ways of unregenerate, strange women, and therefore gives counsel to his son on how to distance himself from them (Proverbs 5:1-8). The verses highlight the poison and corruption of the lust of the flesh. Solomon expresses in graphic language how the woman – a figure of Satan – works on every area of man's weakness. The temptations of the world may appear sweet and innocent, smooth and plausible, but the soul caught in Satan's snare is made to taste the bitterness of worldly pleasure, as wormwood. Furthermore, the conscience of such a victim experiences the power of God's word, like a two-edged sword penetrating his soul (verse 4). The "word of God, quick and powerful, and sharper than any two-edged sword, piercing even to the dividing asunder of soul and spirit, and of the joints and marrow, and is a discerner of the thoughts and intents of the heart" (Hebrew 4:12). May we continue to drink in the sweetness of God's Word, and daily experience its cleansing power as we read and meditate upon the precious truth (Psalm 119:9).

The references to wormwood in Jeremiah and Lamentations have to do with the ingestion of the plant with its bitter juices. In Jeremiah 9, the prophet was so distressed about the idolatry; mockery and deceit of the people, that he feared his tears and lamentations would not be adequate to express to God his depths of sorrow. Instead of nourishing their souls with the word of God and feeding on the provisions He had made for them in the land, the people satiated their souls with deceit, lies, slander and idolatry. Furthermore, they refused to own the Lord Jehovah as their God, verse 6. Having wilfully poisoned themselves morally, God fed the people materially with the bitterest of herbs, wormwood, and made them drink the bitter juice of gall. The same thing

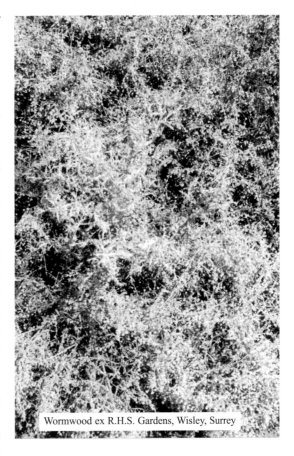

Wormwood ex R.H.S. Gardens, Wisley, Surrey

happened to the false prophets in Israel because they encouraged the people to worship Baal and sin against God (Jeremiah 23:15).

In Lamentations 3, Jeremiah identifies himself with the people and the judgments fallen upon them because of their idolatry and disobedience. The deep and intense sorrow wrought in Jeremiah's heart was such that he felt his soul sated with bitterness and made drunk with wormwood, verse 15. The lesson from Jeremiah is this; we should be more deeply moved in our hearts about the decline of the Christian testimony, and seek the Lord's help to strengthen the things that remain (Revelation 3:2).

In Amos 5:7 & 6:12, the prophet, under the guidance of the Holy Spirit, condemns the rulers in Israel for their oppression of the people. Their administration was void of justice, bitter as wormwood and nauseous as gall. In Amos 6, the condemnation is against the corrupt priests and prophets who had usurped authority and assumed a role not given them by Jehovah. They appointed themselves leaders, lived in luxury and remained indifferent to the sufferings of the people. Prophets like Amos were the horses (verse 12) sent by God to plough the ground – hearts of the people – that there might be fruit for God. Sadly, Amos, like those before him, could make no impression because of the hardness of their hearts. Amos said they had turned God's judgment into gall and the fruit of righteousness into wormwood. The Lord Jesus condemned the princes in Israel because they bound heavy burdens on men's shoulders while doing nothing to help ease the load (Matthew 23:4). We can do much to build up the Church by ministering the precious Truth of God's Word in the power of His Holy Spirit (Galatians 5:25-26). "Speaking the truth in love" (Ephesians 4:15).

The last reference to wormwood is in Revelation 8:11. The events recorded from Revelation 4 to the end of the book are still prophecy. None of the trials that are to come upon man will occur until the Church has been rapt away to glory (1 Thessalonians 4:16-17 & Revelation 3:10). In verse 10 of Revelation 8 we have the sounding of the third trumpet judgment. The great star falling out of the heavens and burning like a lamp is a figure of some great apostate dignitary, whose influence in matters of judgment had been highly respected throughout the world. Then, in a moment, his influence dissolves with devastating consequences. The name of the star is 'Wormwood' because of the impact his demise will have on a third part of the civilised and industrial world. First, on the ordinary business and domestic life of the people, typified by a third of the rivers becoming bitter; secondly, on the original thinking and inventiveness of man as seen in the fountains of water that also become bitter.

Mankind will be overwhelmed with unspeakable bitterness against God their creator. Furthermore, they will be bitter against one another, and because of the breakdown of the moral society they had known, bitter against all surviving authority. Whether the death spoken of in Revelation 8:11 is moral or physical is difficult to tell, but most likely, the former because of what we read in chapter 9. The fifth trumpet judgment is sounded to bring in horrendous plagues to afflict the souls and minds of men. The moral torment of men will devastate every element of natural dignity within them, they will yearn to die as a means of escape, but God will not let them die (Revelation 9:6).

The times referred to above are grave and serious; for very soon the events detailed in Revelation 4 – 22 will begin to unfold and overtake this world, "to try them that dwell upon the earth" (Revelation 3:10 last clause). It therefore behoves all Christian believers to witness a faithful profession of their faith in the Lord Jesus Christ. Praying, that in the closing days of this dispensation of God's grace to man, many more souls will be saved for eternal glory through repentance before God and faith in the Lord Jesus Christ. "Now unto the King eternal, immortal, invisible, the only wise God, be honour and glory for ever and ever. Amen." (1 Timothy 1:17).

O God, we acknowledge Thy greatness, Thy glory,
For of Thee are all things on earth and in heaven;
How rich is Thy mercy, how great Thy salvation!
We bless Thee, we praise Thee, Amen and Amen.

M Bowly

BIBLIOGRAPHY

EXPOSITIONS OF THE SCRIPTURES

Bellett, J G	Collected writings
Bridges, C	Proverbs
Coates, C A	Outlines of ministry
Darby, J N	Collected writings
Gaebelein, A B	The Psalms
Grant, F W	Revelation of Jesus Christ
Hole, F B	Matthew – Revelation
Henry, Matthew	Commentary on the whole Bible
Kelly, W	Ministry covering the whole Bible
Mackintosh, C H	Notes on the Pentateuch
Miller, A	Church History
Morgan, C C	Ministry on the Gospels
Scott, W	Revelation of Jesus Christ
Soltau, H W	The Tabernacle

DICTIONARIES & BOTANICAL BOOKS

Barton, L V	Seed Preservation & Longevity
Chittenden, F J	Dictionary of Gardening
Darom, D	Beautiful Plants of the Bible
Fairbairn, P	Imperial Bible Dictionary
Foggi, B	Flowers of Israel
Hastings, J	Dictionary of the Bible
Hepper, F N	Illustrated Encyclopaedia of Bible Plants
Josephus, Flavius	The Works of
Loudon, J W	Encyclopaedia of Plants
Morrish, G	Concise Bible Dictionary
Moldenkn, H N & AL	Plants of the Bible
Royle	Himalayan Mountains
Thomson, W M	The Land and the Book
Zohary, M	Plants of the Bible

Bible References of Plants, Fruits & Plant Products

BIBLE NAME	HEB / GK NAME	BOTANICAL NAME	DEFINITION	REFERENCES
ALGUM TREES	'ALGUMMIYM	Pterocarpus santalinus	Sandal – a costly wood	2 CHRON. 2:8; 9:10 & 11.
ALMUG TREES	'ALMUGGIYM	"	"	1 KINGS 10:11 & 12.
ALMONDS	SHAQED	Prunus communis	White almond tree	GEN. 43:11. NUM. 17:8. ECCL. 12:5. JER. 1:11.
"	SHAQAD	"	Like almonds	Ex. 25:33 & 34; 37:19 & 20.
ALOES	'AHALIYM	Aquillaria agallochum	Ling aloes – aloe wood (Eaglewood)	NUM. 24:6. PSALM 45:8. PROV. 7:17.
"		"		S. of S. 4:14.
ALOE			The gum of aloe wood	JOHN 19:39.
ANISE (DILL)	ANETHON	Anethum graveolens	Dill	MATT. 23:23.
APPLE	TAPPUWACH	Malus sylvestris	Apples	PROV. 25:11. S. of S. 2:3 & 5; 7:8; 8:5. JOEL 1:12.
ASH	'OREN	Fraxinus Ornus	Ash tree – strength, toughness	ISA. 44:14.
BALM	TSORIY	Commiphora gileadensis	To crack as by pressure, to leak, distillation	GEN. 37:25; 43:11. JER. 8:22; 46:11; JER. 51:8. EZEK. 27:17.
BARLEY	SE'ORAH	Hordeum sp.	Sense and touch of roughness, coarse, hairy	EX. 9:31. LEV. 27:16. NUM. 5:15. DEUT. 8:8. JUDG. 7:13. RUTH 1:22; RUTH 2:17 & 23; 3:2, 15 & 17. 2 SAM. 14:30; 17:28; 21:9. 1 KINGS 4:28. 2 KINGS 4:42; 7:1, 16 & 18. 1 CHRON. 11:13. 2 CHRON. 2:10 & 15; 2 CHRON. 27:5. JOB 31:40. ISA. 28:25. JER. 41:8. EZEK. 4:9 & 12; 13:19. EZEK. 45:13. HOSEA 3:2. JOEL 1:11.
"	KRITHINOS	Hordeum sp.	Made of barley	JOHN 6:9 & 13.
"	KRITHE	"	Pointed, piercing – seed	REV. 6:6.
BAY	EZRACH	?	Green tree – flourishing as a native of the land	PSALM 37:35.

BIBLE NAME	HEB / GK NAME	BOTANICAL NAME	DEFINITION	REFERENCES
BEANS	POL	Vicia faba / vulgaris	Bean – plump bean	2 SAM. 17:28. EZEK. 4:9.
BOX	TE'ASHSHUR	Abies cilicica	Tall & erect species of conifer	ISA. 41:19; 60:13.
BRAMBLE	'ATAD	Zizyphus spina christi	Bramble branches – to hold one fast	JUD. 9:14 & 15. PSALM 58:9.
"	BATOS	Lycium europaeum or Zizyphus sp.	Thorn bush	MARK 12:26. LUKE 6:44; 20:37. ACTS 7:30 & 35
BRAMBLE	SENEH	Rubus sp.	Bramble bush	EX. 3:2, 3 & 4. DEUT. 33:16.
BRIER	CHEDEQ		Brier – prickly plant – to sing	PROV. 15:19. MICAH 7:4.
"	SHAMIYR	Acacia sp.	Hard, diamond pointed – firm	ISA. 5:6; 7:23, 24 & 25; 9:18; 10:17; ISA. 27:4; 32:13.
BRIERS	BARQAN	Rubus sp.	Used as a threshing tool	JUD. 8:7 & 16.
"	SARAB	?	Stinging brier – thistle	EZEK. 2:6.
BULRUSH / RUSH	'AGMON	Cyperus papyrus	Rush, from a marshy pool	JOB 41:1. ISA. 9:14; 19:15 & 58:5.
"	GOME'	"	To absorb, swallow, imbibe	EX. 2:3. JOB 8:11. ISA. 18:2 & 35:7.
CALAMUS	QANEH	Cymbopogon martinii	Palmerosa oil grass – reed stalk	EX. 30:23. S. of S. 4:14. ISA. 43:24. JER. 6:20. EZEK. 27:19.
CAMPHIRE / HENNA	KOPHER	Lawsonia inermis	A cover, ransom, satisfaction, dye & fragrant flowers.	S. of S. 1:14 & 4:13.
CASSIA	QIDDAH / QETSIYAH	Cinnamomum cassia	Perfume oil from the shrivelled rolls of bark	EX. 30:24. PSALM 45:8. EZEK. 27:19.
CEDAR	'EREZ	Cedrus libani	Firmness – tenacity of its roots	LEV. 14:4, 6, 49, 51 & 52. NUM. 19:6; NUM. 24:6. JUD. 9:15. 2 SAM. 5:11 2 SAM. 7:2 & 7. 1 KINGS 4:33; 5:6, 1 KINGS 5:8 & 10; 6:9, 10, 15, 16, 18, 1 KINGS 6:20 & 36; 7:2; 3, 7, 11, & 12, 1 KINGS 9:11; 10:27. 2 KINGS 14:9; 19:23. 1 CHRON. 14:1; 17:1 & 6; 22:4. 2 CHRON. 1:15; 2:3 & 8; 9:27; 25:18. EZRA 3:7. JOB 40:17. PSALM 29:5; 80:10; PSALM 92:12; 104:16; 148:9. S. of S. 1:17; S. of S. 5:15; 8:9. ISA. 2:13; 9:10; 14:8; ISA. 37:24; 41:19; 44:14. JER. 22:7, 14, JER. 22:15 & 23.

BIBLE NAME	HEB / GK NAME	BOTANICAL NAME	DEFINITION	REFERENCES
CEDAR	EREZ	Cedrus libani	Firmness – tenacity of its roots	EZEK 17:3, 22 & 23; EZEK. 27:5; 31:3 & 8. AMOS 2:9. ZECH. 11:1 & 2.
"	'ARAZ		Made of cedar	EZEK. 27:24.
"	'ARZAH		Cedar work – used for wainscotting	ZEPH. 2:14.
CHESNUT	'ARMON	Platanus Orientalis	Plane tree	GEN. 30:37. EZEK. 31:8.
CINNAMON	QINNAMON	Cinnamomum verum	Erect rolls from inner bark of cinnamon	EX. 30:23. PROV. 7:17. S. of S. 4:14.
"	KINAMOMON	"		REV. 18:13.
COCKLE	BO'SHAH	?	Noxious, noisome, pernicious weeds	JOB 31:40
CORIANDER	GAD	Coriandrum sativum	Round, ribbed, aromatic seed, a troop	EX. 16:31. NUM. 11:7.
CORN – WHEAT	DAGAN	Triticum durum & other seeds	Cereals; grain, including vetch, beans, pulse, fitches, millet & lentils	GEN. 27:28 & 37. NUM. 18:12 & 27. DEUT. 7:13; 11:14; 12:17; 14:23; 18:4; DEUT. 28:51; 33:28. 2 KINGS 18:32. 2 CHRON. 31:5; 32:28. NEH. 5:2, 3, 10, NEH. 5:11; 10:39; 13:5 & 12. PSALM 4:7; PSALM 65:9; 78:24; ISA. 36:17; 62:8. ISA. 36:17; 62:8. JER. 31:12. LAM. 2:12. EZEK. 36:29. HOSEA 2:8, 9 & 22; 7:14; HOSEA 14:7. JOEL 1:10 & 17; 2:19. HAG. 1:11. ZECH. 9:17.
"	BELIYL	Mixed Cereals	Provender, mixed corn produce	JOB 6:5; 24:6. ISA. 30:24.
"	BAR	Triticum durum	Wheat, corn, grain	GEN. 41:35 & 49; 42:3 & 25; 45:23. JOB 39:4. PSALM 65:13; 72:16.
"	QAMAH		Standing corn	EX. 22:6. DEUT. 16:9; 23:25. JUD. 15:5. 2 KINGS 19:26. ISA. 17:5; 37:27. HOSEA 8:7.
"	SHEBER		Grain in general	GEN. 42:1, 2, 19 & 26; 43:2; 44:2; 47:14. AMOS 8:5
"	GERES	Triticum durum	Green grain – beaten out	LEV. 2:14 & 16.
"	KOKKOS	" "	A kernel – seed grain	JOHN 12:24. 1 COR. 15:37.
CORN – WHEAT	SHIBBOL	" "	An ear of grain	GEN. 41:5, 6, 7, 22, 23, 24, 26 & 27. RUTH 2:2. JOB 24:24. ISA. 17:5.

257

BIBLE NAME	HEB / GK NAME	BOTANICAL NAME	DEFINITION	REFERENCES
CORN – WHEAT	'AREM	Triticum durum	Corn sheaf; heap of grain	RUTH 3:7. 2 CHRON. 31:6, 7, 8 & 9.
,,	AREM		Corn sheaf; heap of grain	NEH. 13:15. S. of S. 7:2. JER. 50:26. HAG. 2:16.
,,	KARMEL	Triticum durum	Full green ears of corn	LEV. 2:14; 23:14. 2 KINGS 4:42.
,,	GADIYSH		Shocks, stacks and sheaves	EX. 22:6. JUDG. 15:5. JOB 5:26.
,,	ABUR		Old corn or produce	JOSH. 5:11 & 12.
,,	QALIY	Triticum durum	Parched or roasted ears	LEV. 23:14. RUTH 2:14. 1 SAM. 17:17; 1 SAM. 25:18. 2 SAM. 17:28.
,,	CHITTAH	Triticum durum	Wheat	GEN. 30:14. EX. 9:32; 29:2; 34:22. DEUT. 8:8; 32:14. JUDG. 6:11; 15:1. RUTH 2:23. 1 SAM. 6:13; 12:17. 2 SAM. 4:6; 17:28. 1 KINGS 5:11. 1 CHRON. 21:20 & 23. 2 CHRON. 2:10; 2 CHRON. 2:15; 27:5. JOB 31:40. PSALM 81:16; 147:14. S. of S. 7:2. ISA. 28:25. JER. 12:13; 41:8. EZEK. 4:9; 27:17; 45:13. JOEL 1:11.
,,	CHINTA'	Triticum durum	Wheat grain	EZRA 6:9; 7:22.
,,	RIYPHAH	,,	Ground wheat; grits	2 SAM. 17:19. PROV. 27:22.
,,	SITOS	,,	Sifted wheat or corn	MATT. 3:12; 13:25, 29 & 30. MARK 4:28. LUKE 3:17; 16:7; 22:31.
,,	SITOS	,,	Sifted wheat or grain	JOHN 12:24. ACTS 7:12; 27:38.
,,			,,	1 COR. 15:37. REV. 6:6; 18:13.
,,	STACHUS	,,	An ear of grain	MATT. 12:1. MARK 2:23; 4:28. LUKE 6:1.
,,	SITOS	,,	Grain	MARK 4:28. ACTS 7:12.
CUCUMBER	QISHSHU'	Cucumis sativus	Cucumbers – difficult to digest	NUM. 11:5.
,,	MIQSHAH	,,	Garden of cucumbers	ISA. 1:8.
CUMIN	KAMMON	Cuminum cyminum	Gives a sharp smell	ISA. 28:25 & 27.
CUMIN	KUMINON	,,	,,	MATT. 23:23.
CYPRESS	TIRZAH	Cupressus sempervirens	Tall, slender, tapering conifer	ISA. 44:14.

BIBLE NAME	HEB / GK NAME	BOTANICAL NAME	DEFINITION	REFERENCES
DESIRE	'ABIYONAH	Capparis spinosa	Caper berry, a stimulent, provocative	ECCL. 12:5.
DOVE'S DUNG	DIBYON	Ornithogalum narbonense	Ground bulb, cheap, bulbous vegetable	2 KINGS 6:25.
EBONY	HOBEN	Diospyros ebenum	Very hard, dark wood	EZEK. 27:15.
ELM (Prob. Terebinth)	'ELAH	Pistacia Terebinthus	Teil – very strong tree	HOSEA 4:13.
FIG	TE'EN	Ficus carica	Fig tree	GEN. 3:7. NUM. 13:23; 20:5. DEUT. 8:8. JUDG. 9:10 & 11. 1 KINGS 4:25. 1 KINGS 4:25. 2 KINGS 18:31; 20:7. NEH. 13:15. PSALM 105:33. PROV. 27:18 PROV. 27:18. S. of S. 2:13. ISA. 34:4; ISA. 36:16; 38:21. JER. 5:17; 8:13; 24:1; JER. 24:2, 3, 5 & 8; 29:17. HOSEA 2:12; HOSEA 9:10. JOEL 1:7 & 12; 2:22. AMOS 4:9. MICAH 4:4. NAHUM 3:12. HAB. 3:17. HAG. 2:19. ZECH. 3:10.
FIG	PAG	Ficus carica	Young, green, hard and unripe	S. of S. 2:13.
,,	OLUNTHOS	,, ,,	Out of season, untimely, unripe	REV. 6:13.
,,	SUKON	,, ,,	A fig fruit	MATT. 7:16. MARK 11:13. LUKE 6:44. JAMES 3:12.
,,	SUKE	Ficus carica	A fig tree	MATT. 21:19, 20 & 21; 24:32. MARK 11:13, 20 & 21; 13:28. LUKE 13:6 & 7; 21:29. JOHN 1:48 & 50. JAMES 3:12. REV. 6:13.
FIR	BEROSH	Juniperus excelsa	Towering, erect, pyramidal conifer; pliable wood	2 SAM. 6:5. 1 KINGS 5:8 & 10; 6:15; 1 KINGS 6:34; 9:11. 2 KINGS 19:23. 2 CHRON. 2:8; 3:5. PSALM 104:17. ISA. 14:8; 37:24; 41:19; 55:13 & 60:13 EZEK. 27:5; 31:8. HOSEA 14:8. NAHUM 2:3. ZECH. 11:2.
FIR	BEROTH	Juniperus excelsa	Towering, erect, pyramidal pliable wood	S. of S. 1:17.
FITCHES	QETSACH	Nigella sativa	Black Cumin, to incise, pungent	ISA. 28:25 & 27.
FLAG	'ACHU	Cyperus esculentus	Marsh-loving reed grass, meadow	JOB 8:11.
FLAG	SUPH	Typha latifolium	A Red-sea water reed	EX. 2:3 & 5. ISA. 19:6. JONAH 2:5.

BIBLE NAME	HEB / GK NAME	BOTANICAL NAME	DEFINITION	REFERENCES
FLAX / LINEN	PISHTAH	Linum usitatissimum	Flax, wick, tow, white linen	EX. 9:31. ISA. 42:3; 43:17.
FLAX / LINEN	PISHTEH	,,	Flax, finest thread, carded and purified	LEV. 13:47, 48, 52 & 59. DEUT. 22:11. JOSH. 2:6. JUD. 15:14.
,,	PISHTAH	,,	Flax, finest thread, carded and purified	PROV. 31:13. ISA. 19:9. JER. 13:1. . EZEK. 40:3; 44:17 & 18. HOSEA 2:5 & 9
,,	LINON	,,	Flax, white linen	MATT. 12:20. REV. 15:6.
FRANKINCENSE	LEBONAH	Boswellia sacra	Whiteness, pure white smoke; Incense	EX. 30:34. LEV. 2:1, 2, 15, 16; 5:11; LEV. 6:15; 24:7. NUM. 5:15. 1 CHRON. 9:29. NEH. 13:5 & 9. S. of S. 3:6; 4:6 & 14. ISA. 43:23. ISA. 60:6; 66:3. JER. 6:20; 17:26; 41:5.
,,	LIBANOS	Boswellia saca	Incense	MATT. 2:11. REV. 18:13.
GALBANUM	CHELBENAH	Ferula galbaniflua / gummosa	An odorous gum	Ex. 30:34.
GALL	RO'SH	Papaver somniferum	Source of Opium. Poisonous drug.	DEUT. 29:18; 32:32 & 33. JOB 20:16. PS. 69:21. JER. 8:14; 9:15; 23:15. LAM. 3:5 & 19. HOSEA 10:4.
GALL	CHOLE	Papaver somniferum	Poison. Juice from poppy sp.	MATT. 27:34. ACTS 8:23.
GARLIC	SHUM	Allium sativum	Garlic	NUM. 11:5.
GOPHER	GOPHER	Cupressus sempervirens pyramidalis	To house, live in. Building timber	GEN. 6:14.
GOURD (Ricinus sp.)	QIYQAYON	Ricinus communis	Castor Oil plant. Nauseous, to vomit, spue out	JONAH 4:6, 7, 9 & 10.
GOURD (Wild)	PAQQU'AH	Citrullus Colocynthis	Wild cucumber / gourd – splitting fruit	2 KINGS 4:39.
GRASS	DESHE'	Gramineae sp.	Tender green grass	GEN. 1:11 & 12. DEUT. 32:2. 2 SAM. 23:4. KINGS 19:26. JOB 6:5; JOB 38:27. PSALM 23:2; 37:2. PROV. 27:25. ISA. 15:6; 37:27; 66:14.
GRASS	DESHE'	Gramineae sp.	Tender green grass	JER. 50:11.
,,	DUSH	,,	Trodden down pasture	JER. 14:5.
,,	DETHE'	,,	Tender grass	DAN. 4:15 & 23.
,,	CHATSIYR	,,	Grass, hay, fodder, herb	1 KINGS 18:5. 2 KINGS 19:26.

260

BIBLE NAME	HEB / GK NAME	BOTANICAL NAME	DEFINITION	REFERENCES
GRASS	CHATSIYR	Gramineae sp.	Grass, hay, fodder, herb	JOB 8:12; 40:15. PSALM 37:2; 90:5. PSALM 103:15; 104:14; 129:6; 147:8.
"	CHATSIYR	Gramineae	Grass, hay, fodder, herb	PROV. 27:25. ISA. 15:6; 35:7. ISA. 37:27; 40:6, 7 & 8; 44:4; 51:12.
"	'ASH	Gramineae sp.	Herb grass	DAN. 4:15, 25, 32 & 33; 5:21.
"	CHORTOS	" "	Fodder grass	MATT. 6:30; 13:26; 14:19. MARK 4:28; MARK 6:39. LUKE 12:28. JOHN 6:10. 1 COR. 3:12. JAMES 1:10 & 11. 1 PETER 1:24. REV. 8:7; 9:4.
HAZEL (Almond)	LUZ	Prunus communis	White almond tree	GEN. 30:37.
HEMLOCK	RO'SH	Conium maculatum	Poisonous plant – conspicuous head	HOSEA 10:4. AMOS 6:12.
HERB-COMMON	'ORAH		Glistening, dew-covered green plant	2 KINGS 4:39. ISA. 18:4 & 26:19.
HERB	LACHANON		Probably root vegetables	MATT. 13:32. MARK 4:32. LUKE 11:42. ROM. 14:12.
HERB	BOTANE	Gramineae sp.	Herbage grass	HEB. 6:7.
"	'ESEB	"	Green, lush, glossy, edible herbage	GEN. 1:11, 12, 29 & 30; 2:5; 3:18; 9:3. EX. 9:22 & 25; 10:12 & 15. DEUT. 11:15; DEUT. 29:23; 32:2. 2 KINGS 19:26.
HERB	'ESEB	Gramineae sp.	Green, lush, glossy, edible herbage	JOB 5:25. PSALM 72:16. PSALM 92:7; 102:4 & 11; 104:14; 105:35; PSALM 106:20. PROV. 19:12; 27:25. ISA. 37:27; 42:15. JER. 12:4; 14:6. AMOS 7:2. MICAH 5:7. ZECH. 10:1.
"	YEREQ	Gramineae sp.	Mixed rich, lush, edible vegetation	EX. 10:15. NUM. 22:4. ISA. 15:6. DEUT. 11:10. 1 KINGS 21:2. 2 KINGS 19:26. PROV. 15:17. ISA. 37:27.
"			"	
HYSSOP	'EZOB	Origanum Syriacum	The Syrian hyssop, a variety of Marjorum	EX. 12:22. LEV. 14:4, 6, 49, 51 & 52. NUM. 19:6 & 18. 1 KINGS 4:33. PS. 51:7.
"	HUSSOPOS	" "	" "	JOHN 19:29. HEB. 9:19.
JUNIPER (White broom)	RETHEM	Retama Raetam, syn. Lygos Retama	White Spanish broom, pole-like stems	1 KINGS 19:4 & 5. JOB 30:4. PS 120:4.
LEEK	CHATSIYR	Allium porrum	Herb leek	NUM. 11:5.

BIBLE NAME	HEB / GK NAME	BOTANICAL NAME	DEFINITION	REFERENCES
LENTILS	'ADASH	Lens culinaris syn. L. esculenta	Lentile peas	GEN. 25:34. 2 SAM. 17:28; 23:11. EZEK. 4:9.
LILY	SHUSHAN	Lilium candidum	Trumpet like. From the whiteness of the flower	1 KINGS 7:19, 22 & 26. 2 CHRON. 4:5. S. of S. 2:1, 2 & 16; 4:5; 5:13; 6:2; S. of S. 6:3; 7:2. HOSEA 14:5.
LILY OF THE FIELD	KRINON	Anemone coronaria	Crown anemone	MATT. 6:28. LUKE 12:27.
LINEN (Flax)	SHESHIY	Linum usitatissimum	Fine, pure & white twined linen – Flax	GEN. 41:42. EX. 25:4; 26:1, 31, 36; EX. 27:9, 16, 18; 28:5, 6, 8, 15, 39; EX. 35:6, 23, 25, 35; 36:8, 35, 37; 38:9, EX. 38:16, 18, 23; 39:2, 3, 5, 8, 27, 28, EX. 39:29. Ezek. 16:10, 13; 27:7.
"	BAD	"	Linen of flaxen; divided fibres, yarn	EX. 28:42; 38:28. LEV. 6:10; 16:4, 23, LEV. 16:32. 1 SAM. 2:18; 22:18. 2 SAM. 6:14. 1 CHRON. 15:27. EZEK. 9:2, 3, 11; 10:2, 6, 7. DAN. 10:5; 12:6 & 7.
"	BUTS	"	Linen, bleached, to make white	1 CHRON. 4:21; 15:27. 2 CHRON. 2:14; 2 CHRON. 3:14; 5:12. ESTHER 1:6; 8:15 PROV. 7:16. EZEK. 27:16.
"	SADIYN	"	Linen for wrapping & enveloping	PROV. 31:24. ISA. 3:23.
"	SHAATNEZ	" + other species	Mixed materials spun together	LEV. 19:19.
LINEN	SINDON	"	Fine, bleached linen	MATT. 27:59. MARK 14:51 & 52; 15:46. LUKE 23:53.
"	OTHONION	"	Linen bandages	LUKE 24:12. JOHN 19:40; 20:5, 6, 7.
"	LENTION	"	Linen cloth, apron or towel	JOHN 13:4 & 5.
LINEN	BUSSOS	"	Fine, white linen	LUKE 16:19. REV. 18:12.
"	BUSSINOS	"	Made of linen	REV. 18:16; 19:8 & 14.
LOTUS (Shady trees)	TSE'EL	Diospyros Lotus	Shade-giving tree. Black date / Plum	JOB 40:21 & 22.
MALLOWS	MALLUACH	Atriplex halimus	Sea purslain. Shrubby orache	JOB 30:4.
MANDRAKES	DUDAY	Mandragora officinarum	Love apple – an aphrodisiac, boiler,	GEN. 30:14; 15 & 16. S. of S. 7:13.
MELONS	'ABATTIYACH	Cucumis melo	Water Melon	NUM. 11:5.

BIBLE NAME	HEB / GK NAME	BOTANICAL NAME	DEFINITION	REFERENCES
MILLET	DOCHAN	Panicum miliaceum syn. Sorghum vulgare	Millet corn	EZEK. 4:9.
MINT	HEDUOSMON	Mentha longifolia	Sweet-scented plant that gives pleasure	MATT. 23:23. LUKE 11:42.
MULBERRY	BAKA'	Populus tremuloides	Weeping	2 SAM. 5:23 & 24. 1 CHRON. 14:14 & 15.
MUSTARD	SINAPI	Sinapis arvensis syn. Brassica Sinapis	Mustard plant – to sting.	MATT. 13:31; 17:20. MARK 4:31. LUKE 13:19; 17:6.
MYRRH	MOR	Commiphora abyssinica / myrrh	Distilling fragrant, bitter-tasting drops	EX. 30:23. ESTHER 2:12. PSALM 45:8. PROV. 7:17. S. of S. 1:13; 3:6; 4:6 & 14; S. of S. 5:1, 5 & 13.
,,	LOT	Cistus incanus/ laurifolius/ ladaniferus	Ladanum gum – Cistus sp.	GEN. 37:25; 43:11.
MYRRH	SMURNA	Commiphora abyssinica / myrrh	Fragrant, analgesic gum	MATT. 2:11. JOHN 19:39.
,,	SMURNIZO	,,	To tincture with Myrrh. A narcotic	MARK 15:23
MYRTLE	HADAS	Myrtus communis	Myrtle shrub	NEH. 8:15. ISA. 41:19; 55:13. ZECH. 1:8, 10 & 11.
NETTLE	CHARUL	Urtica sp.	A Thorn – sub shrub	JOB 30:7. PROV. 24:31. ZEPH. 2:9.
,,	QIMMOSH	,,	Stinging, prickly plant	ISA. 34:13. HOSEA 9:6.
NUT	'EGOZ	Juglans regia	Walnut tree	S. of S. 6:11.
,,	BOTEN	Pistacia vera	Pistachio nut	GEN. 43:11.
OAK	'ELON	Quercus ilex	A strong tree – evergreen Holm oak	GEN. 12:6; 13:18; 14:13; 18:1. DEUT. 11:30. JUDG. 4:11; 9:6 & 37. 1 SAM. 10:3.
OAK	'ALLON	Quercus aegilops or Q. ithaburensis	A strong tree – deciduous oak – Valonia oak – Dyer's oak	GEN. 35:8. ISA. 2:13; 6:13; 44:14. EZEK. 27:6. HOSEA 4:13. AMOS 2:9. ZECH. 11:2.
OAK	ALLAH	Quercus sp.	A memorial oak, probably evergreen	JOSH. 24:26.
OAK (Terebinth)	'ELAH	Pistacia terebinthus	Source of Cyprus turpentine	GEN. 35:4. JUDG. 6:11 & 19. 2 SAM. 18:9. 2 SAM. 18:10 & 14. 1 KINGS 13:14. 1 CHRON. 10:12. ISA. 1:29 & 30; 6:13. EZEK. 6:13. HOSEA 4:13.
OAK (Terebinth)	'AYIL	Pistacia terebinthus	Hard-wood trees, used for carving Idols	ISA. 1:29; 61:3.

BIBLE NAME	HEB / GK NAME	BOTANICAL NAME	DEFINITION	REFERENCES
OLIVE	ZAYITH	Olea europaea	Berry, tree, yard	GEN. 8:11. EX. 23:11; 27:20; 30:24. LEV. 24:2. DEUT. 6:11; 8:8; 24:20; DEUT. 28:40. JOSH. 24:13. JUDG. 9:8; 2 KINGS 5:26; 18:32. 1 CHRON. 27:28. NEH. 5:11; 8:15; 9:25. JOB 15:33. PSALM 52:8; 128:3. ISA. 17:6; 24:13. JER. 11:16. HOSEA 14:6. AMOS 4:9 MICAH 6:15. HAB. 3:17. HAG. 2:19. ZECH. 4:3, 11 & 12; 14:4.
"	SHEMEN	Olea europaea	Oil tree products	GEN. 28:18 + 180 other referenes.
"	ELAIA	Olea europaea sativa / communis	Olive tree & fruits – berries	ROM. 11:17 & 24. JAMES 3:12. REV. 11:4.
"	KALLIELAIOS	" " "	A good olive	ROM. 11:24.
"	AGRIELAIOS	Olea europaea oleaster	A wild olive	ROM. 11:17 & 24.
ONION	BETSEL	Allium cepa	Onion – to peel an onion	NUM. 11:5.
ONYCHA PALM	SHECHELETH TAMAR	Probably an extinct species of Opercularia Phoenix dactylifera	A lid, claw, nail – from the plant fruit An erect, Date palm tree	EX. 30:34. EX. 15:27. LEV. 23:40. NUM. 33:9. DEUT. 34:3. JUDG. 1:16; 3:13. 2 CHRON. 28:15. NEH. 8:15. PS. 92:12. S. of S. 7:7 & 8. JOEL 1:12.
"	TOMER		A tall palm trunk	JUDG. 4:5. JER. 10:5.
"	TIMMOR	" "	Decorative, carved palm wood,	1 KINGS 6:29, 32 & 35; 7:36. 2 CHRON. 3:5. EZEK. 40:16, 22, 26, 31, 34;
"	TIMMOR	Phoenix dactylifera	To form pillars	EZEK. 40:37; 41:18, 19, 20, 25 & 26.
PALM	PHOINIX	" "	Date palm	JOHN 12:13. REV. 7:9.
PINE	TIDHAR	Pinus halepensis	Aleppo Pine, an enduring fir tree	ISA. 41:19; 60:13.
POMEGRANATE	RIMMON	Punica granatum	Tree with its fruits	EX. 28:33 & 34; 39:24, 25 & 26. NUM. 13:23; 20:5. DEUT. 8:8. 1 SAM. 14:2. 1 KINGS 7:18, 20 & 42. 2 KINGS 25:17. 2 CHRON. 3:16; 4:13. S. of S. 4:3. S. or S. 4:13; 6:7 & 11; 7:12; 8:2. JER. 52:22 & 23. JOEL 1:12. HAG. 2:19.
POPLAR	LIBNEH	Populus alba	White Poplar	GEN. 30:37. HOSEA 4:13.

BIBLE NAME	HEB / GK NAME	BOTANICAL NAME	DEFINITION	REFERENCES
PULSE	ZEROA	Cicer arietinum sp. Lens culinaris & Vicia faba	Pulse seeds	Daniel 1:12 & 16.
REED	'AGAM	Stockade of Phragmites australis	A stockade of reeds in a swamp	JER. 51:32.
REED	QANEH	Phragmites australis	Reed / stalk	GEN. 41:5 & 22. 1 KINGS 14:15. 2 KINGS 18:21. JOB 40:21. ISA. 19:6; ISA. 35:7; 36:6; 42:3; 43:24. JER. 6:20. EZEK. 29:6; 40:3, 5, 6, 7, & 8; 41:8; 42:16 EZEK. 42:17, 18 & 19.
REED	KALAMOS	Phragmites australis	Stalk, cane reed	MATT. 11:7; 12:20; 27:29; 30 & 48. MARK 15:19 & 36. LUKE 7:24. REV. 11:1; 21:15 & 16.
RIE	KUSSEMETH	Triticum dicoccoides	Bristly, from its broken-off awns	EX. 9:32. ISA. 28:25. EZEK. 4:9.
ROSE of SHARON	CHABATSTSELETH	Narcissus tazetta	Sharon = upright, pleasant, prosperous, esteemed	S. of S. 2:1. ISA. 35:1.
RUE	PEGANON	Ruta graveolens	Rue – with thick fleshy leaves	LUKE 11:42.
SAFFRON	KARKOM	Crocus sativus	Saffron crocus, deep golden yellow	S. of S. 4:14.
SHITTIM	SHITTAH	Acacia seyal	Scourging, piercing thorns	EX. 25:5, 10, 13, 23 & 28; 26:15, 26, 32, EX. 37; 27:1 & 6; 30:1 & 5; 35:7 & 24; 36:20, 31 & 36; 37:1, 4, 10, 15, 25 & 28; EX. 38:1 & 6. DEUT. 10:3. ISA. 41:19.
SPIKENARD	Hb.NERD. Gk.NARDOS	Nardostachys jatamansi	A fragrant, therapeutic & cosmetic oil	S. of S. 1:12; 4:13 & 14. Mark 14:3. John 12:3.
"				
STACTE	NATAPH	Styrax officinalis	To fall in drops, to ooze, distil gradually, sweet gum	Ex. 30:34.
SYCAMINE	SUKAMINOS	Morus nigra	Black Mulberry	LUKE 17:6.
SYCOMORE	SHAQAM	Ficus sycomorus	Sycomore fig	1 KINGS 10:27. 1 CHRON. 27:28. 2 CHRON. 1:15; 9:27. PSALM 78:47. ISA. 9:10. AMOS 7:14.
"	SUKOMORAIA	"	"	LUKE 19:4.
TAMARISK	'ESHEL	Tamarix aphylla	A Tamarisk, an isolated tree	GEN. 21:33. 1 SAM. 22:6; 31:13.
TARES	ZIZANION	Lolium temulentum	Darnel – of the rye-grass genus	MATT. 13:25, 26, 27, 29, 30, 36, 38, MATT. 13:40.

BIBLE NAME	HEB / GK NAME	BOTANICAL NAME	DEFINITION	REFERENCES
TEIL	'ELAH	Pistacia terebinthus	Terebinth	ISA. 6:13.
THISTLE	DARDAR	Centaurea iberica	Bramble – thistle	GEN. 3:18. HOSEA 10:8.
,,	CHO ACH	Calycotome villosa	Piercing thorn; bramble	2 KINGS 14:9. 2 CHRON. 25:18; 33:11. JOB 31:40; 41:2. PROV. 26:9. S. of S. 2:2. ISA. 34:13. HOSEA 9:6.
	TRIBOLOS	Tribulus sp.	Crowfoot, a triple-pointed thistle	MATT. 7:16. HEB. 6:8.
THORN	NA'ATSUTS	Probably – Acacia sp.	Thicket of thorn bushes	ISA. 7:19; 55:13.
,,	SIYR	Sarcopoterium spinosum	Rapid growing thorn – fish hook	ECCL. 7:6. ISA. 34:13. HOSEA 2:6. NAHUM 1:10
,,	TSEN	?	Thorn hedge	JOB 5:5. PROV. 22:5.
,,	TSANIYN	?	Thorns – piercing one's flesh	NUM. 33:55. JOSH. 23:13.
,,	QOTS	?	Thorny & prickly plants	GEN. 3:18. EX. 22:6. JUDG. 8:7 & 16. 2 SAM. 23:6. PSALM 118:12.
,,	QOTS	Probably – Silybum marianum	Thorny & prickly plants	ISA. 32:13; 33:12. JER. 4:3; 12:13. EZEK. 28:24. HOSEA 10:8.
,,	SILLOWN	?	Stout, pendulous thorn	EZEK. 2:6; 28:24.
,,	QIMMASHON	Urtica sp.	Prickly plant – stinging nettle	PROV. 24:31.
,,	SHAYITH	?	Thorn scrub – wild growth	ISA. 5:6; 7:23, 24 & 25; 9:18; 10:17; 27:4.
THORN	AKANTHA	Probably – Acanthus spinosus	Plant with thorned leaves	MATT. 7:16; 13:7 & 22; 27:29. MARK 4:7 & 18. LUKE 6:44; 8:7 & 14. JOHN 19:2. HEB. 6:8.
,,	AKANTHINOS	,, ,, ,,	Made of thorns	MARK 15:17. JOHN 19:5.
,,	MESUKAH	?	A thorn hedge	MICAH 7:4.
THYINE	THUINOS	Tetraclinis articulata / Thuja articulata	Fragrant – sweet citron-smelling wood	REV. 18:12.
VINE	GEPHEN	Vitis vinifera	Grape vine	GEN. 40:9, 10; & 49:11. NUM. 20:5. DEUT. 8:8; 32:32. JUDG. 9:12 & 13; JUDG. 13:14. 1 KINGS 4:25. 2 KINGS 4:39; 2 KINGS 18:31. JOB 15:33. PSALM 78:47; PSALM 80:8 & 14; 105:33; 128:3. S. of S. 2:13; 6:11; 7:8 & 12. ISA 7:23;

BIBLE NAME	HEB / GK NAME	BOTANICAL NAME	DEFINITION	REFERENCES
VINE	GEPHEN	Vitis vinifera	Grape vine	ISA. 16:8 & 9; 24:7; 32:12; 34:4; 36:16. JER. 2:21; 5:17; 6:9; 8:13; 48:32. EZEK. 15:2 & 6; 17:6, 7 & 8; 19:10 HOSEA 2:12; 10:1; 14:7. JOEL 1:7 & 12; JOEL 2:22. MICAH 4:4. HAB. 3:17. HAG. 2:19. ZECH. 3:10; 8:12. MAL. 3:11.
VINE	ZEMORAH	Vitis vinifera	Vine branch; slip – cutting	NUM. 13:23. EZEK. 15:2. NAHUM 2:2.
,,	YAYIN	,,	Product derived from the whole grape	GEN. 9:21 + 102 other references
	SOREQ	,,	Vine, producing choice, red grapes	GEN. 49:11. ISA. 5:2. JER. 2:21.
,,	AMPELOS	,,	The vine – coiling for support	MATT. 26:29. MARK 14:25. LUKE 22:18. JOHN 15:1, 4 & 5. REV. 14:18 & 19. JAMES 3:12.
,,	OINOS	,,	Grape wine	MATT. 9:17. MARK 2:22 & 15:23. . LUKE 1:15; 5:37 & 38; 7:33; 10:34. JOHN 2:3, 9 & 10; 4:46. ROM. 14:21. . EPH. 5:18. 1 TIM. 3:8 & 5:23. TITUS 2:3. REV. 6:6 & 18:13.
WHEAT see CORN WHEAT				
WILLOW	'ARAB	Salix acmophylla / S. alba	Salix tree – from: osiers used as wattles	LEV. 23:40. JOB 40:22. Ps. 137:2. ISA. 15:7; 44:4.
WILLOW	TSAPHTSAPHAH	Salix acmophylla / S. alba	Water willow – osier	EZEK. 17:5.
WORMWOOD	LA'ANAH	Artemisia herba-alba / absinthium	Artemisia – bitter, undrinkable juice	DEUT. 29:18. PROV. 5:4. JER. 9:15; 23:15. LAM. 3:15 & 19. AMOS 5:7; 6:12
	APSINTHOS	,,	,, ,, ,,	REV. 8:11.